Hypnosis, Memory, and Behavior in Criminal Investigation

THE GUILFORD CLINICAL AND EXPERIMENTAL HYPNOSIS SERIES

Editors
Michael J. Diamond and Helen M. Pettinati

Hypnosis, Memory, and Behavior in Criminal Investigation

KEVIN M. McCONKEY
PETER W. SHEEHAN

Foreword by Peter B. Bloom

THE GUILFORD PRESS
New York / London

Library of Congress Cataloging-in-Publication Data

McConkey, Kevin M.
   Hypnosis, memory, and behavior in criminal investigation /
Kevin M. McConkey and Peter W. Sheehan.
        p.   cm. (The Guilford clinical and experimental
hypnosis series)
   Includes bibliographical references and indexes.
   ISBN 1-57230-008-6
   1. Forensic hypnotism—Australia—Case studies. 2.
Criminal investigation—Australia—Case studies.   I. Sheehan,
Peter W. II. Title. III. Series.
   [DNLM: 1. Forensic Psychiatry—methods. 2. Hypnosis
—case studies. 3. Memory.   W 740 M478h 1995]
   HV8073.5.M36   1995
   363.2'54—dc20
   DNLM/DLC
   for Library of Congress   95-14251
                                                              CIP

In memory of Miranda Downes

We work in the dark—we do what we can—we give what we have. Our doubt is our passion and our passion is our task. The rest is the madness of art.

—Henry James

Foreword

I once was speaking to a graduating law student, and I playfully asked him whether it was true that the practice of law is inferior to the practice of medicine. I then told him of my own pride in having devoted my career to the biological realities of genetic disposition, physiological functioning, and psychological mechanisms—God-given elements that transcend cultural and historical boundaries and are relatively free of societal dictates. He, on the other hand, would be confined to the changing precepts of law, subject to the whims of society.

The student's response was ardent: ever since Cain slew Abel, humankind had been unable to regulate social intercourse without the guidance and enforcement of civil and criminal laws. These laws serve to restrain the primitive passions of lust and murder, creating a civilized social order that allows the biological life I cherish to flourish. In conclusion, he stated, we are each dependent on the other. He then smiled, and so did I, with the recognition that our careers were inseparably entwined.

In this book, *Hypnosis, Memory, and Behavior in Criminal Investigation,* Professors McConkey and Sheehan describe the milieu of clinicians and researchers who struggle with establishing the truth in cases of murder, rape, incest, and criminal seduction. In pursuit of elusive memories in criminal investigations, hypnotists must be able to balance the often contradictory goals of police investigators, the hypnotic subjects, and the hypnotists themselves. Subjects may fake hypnosis or lie, even in a state of trance, and their untruths can be compounded by police or courts who have their own agendas. Powerful outside forces may interfere with the hypnotist's ability to

ful to the scientific principles and clinical guidelines that hold
the subject's well-being over the demands of the investigation.
The integrity and reputation of the therapist, as well as his or
her clinical and research acumen, are often challenged, creating
ethical dilemmas in even the most well-qualified hypnotist. The
clinician must strike a balance between the search for truth and
the awareness that things are not always what they seem.
Sometimes the variable most worthy of exploration is the context in which truth is sought. For those of us who have been in
the thick of a forensic investigation, this is a risky and rewarding
enterprise.

There are many valuable features in this book, but, as a
practicing clinician, I find the case studies most interesting.
Although from Australia and New Zealand, the cases will be of
great interest to hypnotists and criminologists around the world,
for they exemplify the prevailing issues that confront all practitioners of forensic hypnosis. I am struck by the elegance of these
case presentations, and especially by the way in which they
mirror my own clinical experience in exquisite detail. The issues
are many: For instance, at what point should one shape, refine,
or even stop a hypnotic interview in the forensic setting in order
to give the clinical needs of the subject priority? Ethically, should
the therapist refuse to proceed if he or she can see that the
material being elicited from the subject is likely to harm the
subject's own case? Is it possible for the therapist to remain blind
to the needs of the police and court in his or her questioning of
a hypnotized subject? And what role should the hypnotist assume with the police when unsuspected, repressed memories are
elicited in hypnosis and corroborating evidence seems utterly
lacking? In addition to illustrating intriguing matters of ethics,
the cases in this book read like mystery novels.

Aside from the cases, the most rewarding section of the book
is the authors' superbly thoughtful and well-reasoned "Guidelines for the Forensic Use of Hypnosis," presented in Chapter 3.
Based on the authors' many years of extensive laboratory research and clinical experience, this is a major contribution. The
guidelines are presented in the context of the American, Australian, and European legal systems, and they reflect the great
uncertainties in our work in forensic settings, while responsibly
trying to limit the harmful effects of inappropriate hypnotic
induction, improperly trained hypnotists, and inadequate precautions taken during investigative hypnotic interventions. If
genius is characterized by simplicity, excellence is characterized

by the management of great complexity. These guidelines have both characteristics.

Another underlying theme in this book is the authors' concern with understanding memory. Memory defines our current sense of ourselves and forms the basis of future behavior, but how is memory originally constructed and presently retrieved? What purpose do fantasy, imagination, and even religious belief play in enriching our experience of living? In "A Laboratory View of Issues in Forensic Hypnosis" (Chapter 9), the authors explore the literature on memory, including their own probing research over the last two decades. They answer some questions and raise many more with particular relevance to the forensic setting.

In pondering the impact this book has had on me, I have become aware that, just as my young lawyer friend and I have so much in common, so do my fellow researchers and clinicians share a base of knowledge and mutual concerns. McConkey and Sheehan are consummate clinicians in their understanding and presentation of the precautions that need to be taken to avoid harming the subjects in their cases. As researchers, they pursue the questions that their forensic practices raise and thereby shed light on the problems we all share. They stress that professional judgment remains crucial and is often independent of even the best-thought-out guidelines and skillfully prepared techniques. Because such judgment may be independent of a clinician's actual hypnotic skills and adherence to proper forensic guidelines, they emphasize the need for high training qualifications in the clinician's basic discipline of psychology, psychiatry, medicine, and other related clinical specialties. In light of their belief in professional preparation it is no wonder McConkey and Sheehan question whether police officers should have any direct role in performing investigative hypnosis: Although the legal code on this varies, the authors are very clear in saying "No."

I am convinced that this scholarly work has not only broadened my understanding of hypnosis, memory, and behavior in the forensic setting, but has also given me further insights into the many other clinical issues I face in my practice. I am deeply grateful to the authors for writing this rich, rewarding, and satisfying book.

PETER B. BLOOM, MD
Clinical Professor of Psychiatry,
University of Pennsylvania School of Medicine

Preface

Over recent years we have been analyzing the use of hypnosis in criminal investigation in Australia. This book is based on that work, and in particular on selected cases with which we were involved in one way or another. In some cases we evaluated the use of hypnosis by others; in other cases we used hypnosis ourselves and then evaluated that use in the context of the criminal investigation and legal proceedings; and in others we evaluated the alleged use of hypnosis to control behavior for the purposes of sexual involvement.

This book discusses selected cases and presents an analysis of the major themes and issues that emerged for us. One thing that struck us in either conducting or evaluating these cases was that much of the complexity involved in forensic hypnosis has not been conveyed fully in the literature. The psychological and legal literature concerning forensic hypnosis focuses, understandably, on the major question of the reliability of hypnotically refreshed memory. That is an important issue, but it is not the only one. There are psychological issues of many different types that are challenging at both a theoretical and applied level, and it is those issues that we seek to articulate, evaluate, and offer comment on in this book. Although the cases are Australian, the issues that they raise are relevant to the interaction of hypnosis and the forensic system anywhere. Thus, this book is intended to allow the reader to appreciate more fully the issues that are involved when looking at hypnosis, memory, and behavior in the forensic setting. The book is written with a wide audience in mind; it illustrates the complexities of forensic work and comments evaluatively on how often the guidelines for practice and research are inadequate to provide definite answers in the judicial system.

There are 10 chapters in the book, and they seek primarily to illuminate the complexity of the issues that are involved in the reality of forensic hypnosis. Consistent with our overall experiential approach to understanding hypnosis, we essentially underline the problems encountered in forensic work. We aim to recognize the obligations, requirements, and rights of those involved in the forensic setting, and we argue strongly for detailed guidelines to be used whenever hypnosis is introduced into that setting. We seek also to offer a framework of thinking to guide the involvement of the hypnosis expert within the forensic system. While this is not a book that provides experts with clear-cut, practical answers, it does address some of the essential pragmatics of working professionally and ethically in a system that can place many different demands on professionals; such demands can be seductive in their pull away from expertise. The forensic system requires black-and-white positions, but often the professional is faced by a sea of gray. To help handle the complexity, we underscore the importance of the welfare and well-being of the subject when hypnosis is used in the forensic setting, and we argue that this must be the major influence on professional involvement.

The book initially lays out broad issues about forensic hypnosis (Chapter 1). We then examine cases that illustrate different uses of forensic hypnosis (Chapters 2, 4, 5, and 6), in particular, with witnesses of crime, victims of crime, and witnesses of crimes whose exact status is unclear at one point or another. In the cases presented in Chapters 4–6, it was clear to us that things were often not what they appeared to be, and experts in the forensic setting have to be prepared for that reality.

Chapter 3 sets out the guidelines that we developed on the basis of our research and our reading of other guidelines in the psychological and legal literature. These guidelines address issues we consider important and provide specific procedural detail. We developed and attempted to use these guidelines across the cases we present. Chapter 3 also offers specific guidelines on recovered memories, which represent an especially important issue in contemporary practice and which relate integrally to research and practice concerning emotion and memory. We recommend their use by others, but know well the limitations of any set of guidelines. No guidelines can ever accommodate all of the vagaries of human interaction in the forensic setting, or even the complexities of single interactions that can occur. Overall, we recommend the adoption of a nexus of professionalism and common sense when faced with uncertainty.

In Chapters 7–10, we draw out our concerns and recommendations about acting ethically when using or evaluating forensic hypnosis, and we present the major forensic and legal implications of the research we have conducted. The major empirical findings from the laboratory that are relevant to the concerns highlighted by our cases are then presented, and in the final chapter we offer conclusions on our research and reflect on the range of issues that our cases and involvement in them raised for us. We hope that these reflections will help others to cope better with the reality of professional involvement within the criminal investigation and legal systems. It is overall our hope that this book will contribute in some small way to providing a better standard of care in the future.

The research on which this book is based was supported by the Criminology Research Council in Australia through its funding of our project "Hypnotically Refreshed Testimony: An Applied Analysis of Forensic Hypnosis in Australia." The Australian Research Council supported the laboratory research conducted by each of us during the project. Over the period of the research Kevin M. McConkey was first at Macquarie University and is now at the University of New South Wales; Peter W. Sheehan is at the University of Queensland. These universities supported the work on this project and our preparation of this book in various ways. The National Police Research Unit and Police Services throughout Australia also provided logistical support for the project, and many individuals within those departments assisted with the conduct and evaluation of various cases. We are grateful to those individuals who understand why their names are not listed here.

We are grateful to our assistants and research students who helped in various ways. Suzanne Roche gave primary assistance during the conduct of the research, and Amanda Barnier provided major assistance with the preparation of this book; also, Bernadette Bibb, Richard Bryant, Scott Ferguson, Michelle Garnett, Vanessa Green, Sandra Hejtmanek, Graeme Jamieson, Christopher Linton, Fiona Maccallum, Rosemary Robertson, Dixie Statham, and Patricia Truesdale assisted with various aspects of the project. Our preparation of the book benefited greatly from the critical reading given by Carl Harrison-Ford and by the detailed comments made by Stephen Odgers, Campbell Perry, Alan Scheflin, and an anonymous reviewer.

Finally, Jacquelyn and Mary made many sacrifices for which we are very grateful.

KEVIN M. McCONKEY
PETER W. SHEEHAN

Contents

CHAPTER 1

Using Hypnosis in the Forensic Setting

Over the last two decades, the issues surrounding forensic hypnosis have been investigated and debated in both laboratory and applied settings. A variety of experimental and theoretical work in psychology has been used, and sometimes misused, in criminal investigations and legal proceedings dealing with the interaction of hypnosis and the forensic system. In this book, we do not try to be comprehensive in covering the issues or the literature. There are many books (e.g., Laurence & Perry, 1988; Pettinati, 1988; Scheflin & Shapiro, 1989; Udolf, 1983, 1987), chapters (e.g., Anderton, 1986; McConkey, 1992; Miller & Stava, 1988; Orne, Soskis, Dinges, & Orne, 1984; Orne, Whitehouse, Dinges, & Orne, 1988; Sheehan, 1988a; Sheehan & McConkey, 1993; D. Spiegel & H. Spiegel, 1987; Wagstaff, 1989), and other review articles (e.g., Council on Scientific Affairs, 1985; Diamond, 1980; Greene, 1986; Krass, Kinoshita, & McConkey, 1988; Mingay, 1987; Orne, 1979; Perry & Laurence, 1983; Pinizzotto, 1989; Relinger, 1984; Sheehan, 1988b; Smith, 1983; D. Spiegel & H. Spiegel, 1984; Wagstaff, 1984) that do this in very informative ways. We are selective, and choose to illustrate the complexities by addressing them through specific cases about which we have direct knowledge.

The major themes we take up concern (1) the nature and meaning of "hypnosis" in relation to forensic matters; (2) the impact on behavior and memory when hypnosis is involved forensically; (3) the motivational issues involved in forensic hypnosis; (4) the emotional issues associated with using hypnosis

1

to enhance memory or to influence sexual behavior; (5) the ethical and professional issues involved in forensic hypnosis; and (6) the implications of forensic cases and the experimental literature for understanding both hypnosis itself and how memory functions in the hypnotic setting.

In researching the cases we present in this book, we became acutely aware of how inconclusive and frustrating work in investigative hypnosis can be. What seems so obvious in fiction does not match the complexities that define real-life crime. Those same complexities reach out to affect our knowledge of how memory works in the forensic setting and ultimately should deter inexpert practitioners from working in the field. The field is not one that should involve amateurs or armchair detectives. It requires meaningful guidelines and knowledge of the issues at stake, and it is with this in mind that we have tried to select and organize the cases we discuss.

As indicated in the Preface, various cases are analyzed and discussed in this book. The first three cases (Chapter 2) establish at the outset examples of the use of hypnosis in which there is little control of its practice. Here, hypnosis is used inexpertly, and many things go wrong. These cases set the stage, as it were, for the cases that follow in which, for the most part, detailed guidelines (stated in Chapter 3) were put in place as well as the situations allowed them to be. Chapter 4 looks at two cases in which witnesses were hypnotized and focus was placed on eliciting memories that could be followed up by the police in some way. In both cases, there was little information to go on at the outset, and we evaluate the utility of hypnosis critically. Chapter 5 presents two cases, both involving alleged sexual assault, and in which victims were hypnotized and clues sought. The situation was more demanding than that considered in Chapter 4; strong emotions were involved, and almost certainly, the outcomes of the session could be expected to affect evidentiary material. In Chapter 6, cases are considered that shift the focus to hypnosis used in a situation in which there were no witnesses to the crimes and the status of the person hypnotized was unclear at times during the session. The second of the two cases considered in Chapter 6 resulted in a judgment in the High Court of Australia, where the use of hypnosis was central to the court's debate and the legal outcome. This was the only one of the cases discussed in Chapters 4–6 in which the authors were not involved in the conduct of the hypnosis session, but were involved in the case as expert witnesses. Following these cases, we extract from all of the cases the major ethical issues (Chapter 7), analyze their forensic implications (Chapter 8), review the relevant laboratory evidence (Chapter 9), and offer final conclusions and reflections (Chapter 10).

AN OVERVIEW OF THEMES

Forensic "Hypnosis"

Forensic hypnosis is essentially the label given to the use of hypnosis in the forensic setting. This setting can be defined as one that is geared especially to looking for leads, clues, or descriptions of the perpetrators of crime and in which the actions of any of the participants may have consequences that can affect the investigative and legal processes (see also Udolf, 1987). In such a setting, there appears to have been an assumption in the psychological literature concerning hypnosis that whatever happens following an induction procedure (intended to lead to the experience of "hypnosis") is indeed hypnosis. This notion is not compatible with much of what we know about the nature of hypnosis and hypnotizability. The ability to experience hypnosis varies within the population, and the experience of hypnosis is substantially dependent on that ability. Individual differences in hypnotizability and the established link between hypnotizability and hypnotic phenomena are perhaps the most basic findings in the entire field of hypnosis over the last 200 years (Hilgard, 1965). The last 20 years of forensic hypnosis seem to have overlooked some of these core findings in terms of their relevance to practice. It is curious, for example, that there has been so little discussion of the role that susceptibility to hypnosis may play in the forensic situation, even though the hints about the relevance of hypnotizability can be seen in both experimental and field-work. We emphasize this fact when we review the experimental evidence in Chapter 9 and argue (see Chapter 3) that in all forensic interrogations or interviews, testing for suggestibility and hypnotizability should always occur.

A broader problem in the area is the relative theoretical sterility of the discussion that has surrounded forensic hypnosis. Discussion in the literature to date has focused strongly on the nature of the procedures that have been used in attempts to enhance memory or to control behavior; only rarely has discussion been guided by an explicit theoretical viewpoint that encompasses hypnosis, memory, and behavior in the forensic setting. Perhaps this is because the various theoretical views about hypnosis all seem to lead to the prediction that memory is potentially distorted rather than enhanced by hypnosis. Surely, however, there is more than this to the importance of theory in guiding investigation and understanding. At the very least, theoretical positions should state their view about the role of hypnotizability, and the role of the major processes operating when hypnosis is used in attempts to enhance memory or influence behavior in the forensic setting.

The forensic importance of asking "What is hypnotic?" is thrown into bold relief when we consider in detail the use of hypnosis to control behavior, which the literature typically refers to as "antisocial" or "coercive" uses of hypnosis (e.g., Gibson, 1991; Laurence & Perry, 1988; Perry, 1979). Our evaluation of cases indicates that the field needs to think of the misuse of hypnotic procedures in this context somewhat more generally. In particular, a framework is needed to take better account of the complexities of human interaction, motivation, and emotion, and the impact that hypnosis may have on them. This point was made cogently by Perry (1979) in his analysis of the Australian "Mr. Magic" case of 20 years ago, but there has been relatively little movement since that time in our understanding of the control of behavior when hypnotic procedures are involved. The cases that we present make specific points about the interactions of memory and behavior that highlight the way in which those interactions are shaped by interpersonal context, and, in turn, how that context is shaped by the introduction of techniques that are labeled hypnosis.

Hypnosis and Memory

At the outset, it seems appropriate to state briefly what we mean by hypnosis and memory. For us, hypnosis is essentially a phenomenon that reflects genuinely experienced alterations of reality in response to suggestions administered by a hypnotist. To identify the phenomenon, one must rely heavily on the subjective testimony of the subject that he or she feels hypnotized. The person who is deeply hypnotized or highly susceptible to hypnosis can be expected to pass successfully a range of suggestions given by the hypnotist. When such suggestions are administered, the performance shown by the deeply hypnotized

subject can be expected to illustrate significant cognitive alterations. Memory is a constructive process. It changes over time
and accommodates alterations in feelings toward, or information about, events that are remembered. Hypnosis may or may
not lead to an increase in the amount of material reported as
being remembered. Frequently, however, such an increase is
manifest, and often the person in hypnosis is quite confident
about the accuracy of the material that is reported; this occurs
whether or not that material is correct.

The literature indicates that hypnosis usually increases the
amount of material that is reported as memory, some of it
correctly and some incorrectly. We review the literature on this
question in Chapter 9. We conclude there that it is difficult to
maintain a defensible view that hypnosis leads to significant
increases in memory (see also Kihlstrom, 1985). The literature
also indicates that hypnosis usually increases the confidence that
people place in their memory, although more often than not this
confidence is misplaced, as noted by Krass et al. (1988) and
Sheehan (1988a, 1988b). The consistency of memory reports
before, during, and after hypnosis; the creation of confabulated
and false memories; and the belief people develop in the memories that they report during hypnosis are matters that are illustrated clearly in our cases and link the practical work we have
conducted with major findings in the laboratory (albeit not
always simply). A framework is needed to accommodate the
bulk of the research and practical findings about the use of
hypnosis to enhance memory, and we aim to provide the essential
structure of that framework in this book. Critically, in our
opinion, such a framework needs to be one that not only captures
the niceties of the laboratory, but also the realities of the field.

The behavior of both participants (i.e., hypnotist and subject) changes when hypnotic procedures become part of a dyadic
interaction. In the laboratory, the clinic, and the forensic setting,
the administration of hypnotic procedures appears not only to
give permission for, but also to encourage a range of behaviors
that neither participant would display without the introduction
of such procedures. Moreover, this contextual shift appears to
occur independent of whether the subject experiences hypnosis
(McConkey, 1984). Thus, in a setting where hypnosis is used to
enhance memory, the hypnotist may alter his or her behavior in
ways that are not consistent with meeting the needs of the
subject. Similarly, subjects may shift their behavior in ways that
would not occur if the situation were not labeled as involving

hypnosis. If the subject testifies to hypnosis, then further changes in behavior may take place that are associated with the subject's experiences. Thus, both the use of hypnotic procedures and the experience of hypnosis may lead to significant alterations in the behavior of subjects. The nature and extent of these shifts have not been recognized fully in the literature on forensic hypnosis, and we draw special attention to these shifts and highlight their relevance to both the understanding and practice of hypnosis in the forensic setting.

An explicit appreciation of these shifts is critical when one is evaluating the alleged use of hypnotic procedures to control the behavior of another for the purposes of a criminal act, such as sexual assault. The cases that we review highlight some of the ways in which hypnotic procedures are used as either the primary or the secondary method of sexual involvement by hypnotists with other people. The parameters of the interpersonal interaction of hypnotist and subject involved in a sexual act are likely to change as a function of the kinds of factors that we illustrate in our cases and link to the literature (see also Laurence and Perry, 1988, and Perry, 1979).

Motivation to Use Hypnosis

The question "Why hypnosis?" has been not addressed fully in the literature on the forensic setting, although Orne (1979; Orne et al., 1984) has pointed to various reasons associated with the inappropriate use of hypnosis. It needs to be acknowledged that the motivations for using hypnosis are not always clear and may be quite different from what is stated formally. The forensic system is one in which motivations are often not what they seem, and professionals should be alert to the temptation to accept things at face value. This caution can be applied to police who want to introduce hypnosis into their investigation of a crime; witnesses, victims, and sometimes suspects who want to be hypnotized to assist them to meet particular goals; and also to some experts in the field who use hypnosis in the forensic setting in a relatively routine way. The reasons for using hypnosis often work out in practice to be different from official ones. "Police" motivation, for example, is complex and the expert should be alert to this. Invariably, also, one narrative or rationale is reinforced by official reasons for its use, but several different kinds of motivation can be evident in actual practice, and such motivations can differentially serve the interests of hypnotist, client, police, and others alike.

In dealing with a wide range of cases involving the hypnotic enhancement of memory, it seemed to us that more often than not the motivation for hypnosis was associated with a poor understanding of the real effects of hypnosis on the one hand, and a desire for a simple solution on the other. As our cases demonstrate, this question needs to be answered effectively and sensibly before hypnosis is introduced into the forensic setting. There are some clear instances in our cases and in the literature of inappropriate motivations for hypnosis, and procedures must be put in place to guard against them (for discussion, see Orne, 1979). The needs of the hypnotist also require attention, especially since they have been linked to possible facilitation of memory distortion in work reported elsewhere (Barber, 1994; Yapko, 1994).

For example, on the surface, the motivations of hypnotists who attempt to use hypnotic procedures to facilitate sexual involvement may appear to be straightforward. A more detailed analysis of those situations (see also Barber, 1994), however, points to complexities involved in the personal interactions of people who have multilayered needs. Similarly, although one is tempted to make the assumption that the motivation of the subject in these situations is to seek professional assistance rather than engage in sexual involvement, a more detailed analysis of the matter suggests a degree of greater complexity that forces one, for example, to draw distinctions between irresponsible, unprofessional, and coerced behavior (see also Perry, 1979). Motivations can change also during hypnosis, and although the shift may be transient, it is complicated. To understand the patterning of motivations of hypnotist and client in these situations helps us to appreciate more fully the meaning of cases handled by the legal system.

Meaning and Feeling in Hypnosis

When hypnosis is used to enhance memory, the material to be remembered is often highly charged with meaning, the witnesses or victims are often experiencing complex emotions, and the conduct and outcome of the hypnosis sessions frequently have substantial impact on the witnesses or victims themselves, and on the investigation as a whole. Personal meanings and emotions involved when hypnosis is used forensically have not been discussed fully in the literature, although they have been pointed to (e.g., Scheflin & Shapiro, 1989; Udolf, 1983). For the most part, the literature has argued that the emotional content of the forensic hypnosis session is one of the major reasons why the hypnotist should be a mental health professional rather than a law enforcement professional. Whereas this is a legitimate argument, this focus has led the literature to underestimate the full relevance of the different components of investigative questioning and to limit consideration of the range of emotions that is likely to be involved when hypnosis is used to influence memory.

To work effectively in the practical setting, there is a need to understand the interactions between emotional and memory processes, and especially to understand the role that hypnosis may play when it is introduced into this constellation. The communication of information as memory may be as important to the needs of the individual as it is to the needs of the investigation, and that point is compellingly apparent in several of the cases we consider. As can be inferred from the work of Spence (1982, 1994), the needs of the individual and the needs of the investigation may not be congruent in the gap that can exist between narrative truth and historical accuracy. The story being told may serve the needs of the client, and indeed the purposes of therapy, but may not reflect what happened in fact. As Spence has demonstrated so cogently, therapy can genuinely advance on the basis of reconstructions of events that are simply not true. Of course, legal proceedings cannot and should not advance on this same basis.

When hypnosis is used to influence sexual involvement, the emotion of both the hypnotist and the subject is likely to be highly charged and very complex. The subject abused in the hypnotic setting is likely to experience the emotions of any victim of sexual assault, and our evaluation of cases in which such abuse has occurred highlights particular aspects of the care needed by such people. Moreover, our research highlights the duty that the field as a whole has to try and ensure that misuses and abuses of hypnosis are minimized, and that situations are handled responsibly when abuse occurs.

Ethical and Professional Issues

Ethical and professional issues lie at the heart of most of the issues involved in the interaction of hypnosis and the forensic setting (Sheehan & McConkey, 1993). The nature of the forensic system often pushes and pulls experts to step outside their professional boundaries to assist in meeting the aims of a criminal investigation. These forces are powerful in their influence on the professional and acquiescing to them may be rewarding in the short term. In the long term, however, acquiescence is damaging to the professional, to his or her profession, and to the forensic system as a whole. A critical part of the checks and balances of the forensic system is the requirement that competent professionals engage in ethical conduct (e.g., Blau, 1984; Brodsky, 1991; Freckelton, 1987; Weiner & Hess, 1987). The well-being of the client should be a major touchstone for ethical practice, and competent professionals must always assess their actions on that basis. In some of the cases we consider, strong threats to ethical and professional conduct are highlighted, and some of the procedures to guard against those threats are evaluated and discussed. Although various comments on the ethical issues involved in interacting with the forensic system can be found in the literature (e.g., Fitch, Russell, & Wallace, 1987; Hess, 1987; Rogers, 1987; Slovenko, 1987), the literature has not given sufficiently explicit indication of the possible problems that professionals encounter when hypnosis is involved. Following earlier work on this theme (Sheehan & McConkey, 1993), we discuss these issues when presenting the selected cases in this book.

One area in which the ethical and professional responsibilities of those who use hypnosis are highlighted occurs when allegations of the misuse of hypnosis have been made. Breaching the trust of a client by attempting to meet one's own needs rather than the needs of the individual is apparent in some of the cases considered. Although one might try to understand these breaches in psychological terms, there is no basis for excusing the behavior that is shown by the hypnotists involved. Psychological analysis can explain, but should never excuse, acts that are unethical and unprofessional. In the field that we cover, ethical issues are far from simple and are often difficult to put into practice, but ethical standards are necessary.

Theoretical and Practical Implications

Theory and practice should move interactively, and this book attempts to draw out especially the relationship between theory and practice in considering hypnosis, memory, and behavior in the forensic setting. Our major theoretical approach is one that emphasizes the idiosyncratic character of responding to hypnosis, the variable nature of memory reports, and the complexity of the interpersonal context in which hypnotic response occurs (see also Sheehan & McConkey, 1982). The material that we present allows us to comment also on the nature of hypnosis and its relationship to memory.

AN OVERVIEW OF THE PROGRAM OF INQUIRY

Before turning to the cases considered in this book, we would like to comment about some general aspects of the program of inquiry from which the cases were taken. In the context of our research program into forensic hypnosis (McConkey, 1988, 1989, 1992; McConkey & Jupp, 1985; McConkey & Roche, 1989; McConkey, Roche, & Sheehan, 1989a, 1989b; McConkey & Sheehan, 1988a, 1988b, 1989; Sheehan, 1988c; Sheehan & McConkey, 1988, 1993), and in the context of general discussion about forensic hypnosis in Australia (e.g., Burrows, 1981; Kapelis, 1987; LePage & Goldney, 1987; MacLeod, 1988; Odgers, 1988a, 1988b; Walker, 1988), we indicated to police services that we were interested in either conducting or evaluating hypnosis sessions with victims or witnesses of crime, and evaluating any alleged criminal uses of hypnosis, such as sexual assault. That brought a number of cases to our attention in one way or another, and specific parameters were adopted to decide whether we would become involved.

We advised generally against the use of hypnosis when there were reasons to believe that the relevant information may not have been encoded in the first place or when significant factors may have interfered with the storage of the information in memory. For instance, we advised against the use of hypnosis in cases where the subject had suffered organic brain damage during an incident. We also cautioned against the use of hypnosis with young children, even when there were no particular contraindications for its use. The literature is uncertain, for example, about whether children are easily led, accept suggestions more readily than adults, and are unreliable witnesses (see Hembrooke, 1994). We are aware that in many of these cases, the investigating officers contacted other individuals, who conducted hypnosis sessions with some of the subjects. In a number of these cases, we were approached subsequently to evaluate these uses of hypnosis to enhance memory; typically, we declined to do so.

We were approached to conduct hypnosis sessions in some cases, and for a variety of reasons these sessions did not proceed. In some instances, the investigating officers themselves decided not to proceed; in others, we decided not to conduct the session after evaluating the possible subject. For instance, in one case we had not been informed (despite asking) that the subject had a history of abusing prescription medication and had at least one psychiatric admission. Prior to the hypnosis session, the subject made a comment to the hypnotist about another psychologist with whom she was in therapy to help deal with the incident that she had observed. The hypnotist contacted that other psychologist immediately, discovered the history of the subject, and discovered also that her psychologist was not aware that the subject had agreed to participate in a hypnosis session in an attempt to assist the criminal investigation. The session with the subject was terminated before the induction of hypnosis began, and the subject was advised to contact the psychologist with whom she was in therapy. The investigating officers were then advised (strongly) against the use of hypnosis with this subject.

In another case, we agreed to conduct the hypnosis session with the victim of a major crime, and laid out for the investigating officers the guidelines that we would follow in the conduct of this session. Although the officers agreed to these guidelines, they were clearly ambivalent about some aspects of them (see Chapter 3 for their definition), such as the videorecording of the session and constricting the kind of setting in which we intended to conduct the session. It seemed to us that simple compliance was being sought by the police in this case. The investigating officers did not respond to messages left for them to confirm the time of the session, and they did not arrive for the session that was scheduled. Around that time, however, we read newspaper reports of a "hypnosis expert" being brought from another part of Australia to hypnotize the person. The newspaper reports also indicated that the police expected a major breakthrough in the case. Informally, we were advised by a senior police officer that the investigating officers were unhappy about the "restrictions" we placed on the conduct of the hypnosis session and had found someone who would "do it the way [they] wanted it done."

Turning to cases that we evaluated rather than conducted, it is relevant to note that we decided against evaluating the use of hypnosis in some cases, and in other cases our evaluations were rejected by those who sought them. In terms of the cases that we decided against evaluating, the major reason was the lack of information to evaluate. In the context of our program of inquiry, we decided to accept only cases in which there was material to assess. We declined invitations to evaluate the use of hypnosis, when what was requested was a bald statement that hypnosis either should or should not be used with witnesses or victims of crime under any circumstances, or stark positions that hypnosis either did or did not allow the control of a person's behavior during sexual contact. In terms of the cases in which our evaluations were rejected, the major reason for this seemed to be that we had not made, and were not willing to make, a strong enough statement for the adversarial nature of the forensic system. Our evaluations attempted to give a balanced perspective, and that was not always appreciated. Our position was to try and avoid rhetoric, and when it was taken seriously, we found that the influence of our evaluations was substantial.

In this book, the cases in which we have been involved have all involved the police. Hypnosis obviously has key relevance in criminal investigations conducted by the police, and in this introductory chapter, it seems appropriate to comment on the analysis of policy and practice of police in Australia who are associated with the use of hypnosis in criminal investigations. It is also relevant to review some of the key legal decisions in which hypnosis has been involved.

HYPNOSIS AND THE AUSTRALIAN FORENSIC SYSTEM

A Survey of Forensic Hypnosis

We analyzed the use of hypnosis in criminal investigations in Australia (see McConkey & Sheehan, 1988b) by a survey of police departments throughout the country. The survey aimed to provide data about police use of hypnosis in criminal investigations, to canvass policy and practical issues, and to index the extent and nature of forensic hypnosis and its perceived value in criminal investigations. The majority of those who responded were police officers. They held the rank of sergeant or above and were involved in criminal investigations. A minority were medical practitioners or psychologists working within police departments. Most respondents were male, around 40 years of age, and had at least 20 years of service. The data indicated a general awareness of the issues involved in the use of hypnosis in criminal investigations, but pointed to areas in which a more detailed consideration of issues is needed by police departments and the criminal justice system.

Findings indicated that there was a substantial increase in the use of forensic hypnosis in Australia from 1981 to 1987, and pointed to the use of hypnosis in investigations of major crimes such as murder, manslaughter, serious or violent assault, and rape. The data further showed that hypnosis had been used mostly with adult victims and witnesses who were female. There was confusion and inconsistency about any guidelines to be used when hypnosis was introduced into criminal investigations. No police department in Australia had then developed specific guidelines that were recognized formally. This was clear from the data which indicated that various people were typically present during the hypnosis sessions; there was no set procedure for testing memory reports prior to the induction of hypnosis; and there was no set procedure or understanding of the importance of recording (either audio or video) the hypnosis session. Findings pointed also to only a rudimentary understanding of the clinical aspects surrounding the use of hypnosis.

Our survey indicated that the information obtained during hypnosis was thought to assist the investigation in about half the cases in which it was used, and it was not seen to have hindered any of the investigations. Respondents indicated strong support of the view that information obtained during hypnosis should only be accepted if it was confirmed by independent evidence. Consistent with this, respondents were relatively cautious and conservative in their views about hypnosis. Moreover, and related to issues we take up in detail in Chapter 8, strong support was given to the view that medical practitioners and psychologists should serve as hypnotists. There was little support for the view that police officers or lay hypnotists should act as the hypnotist in criminal investigations. There was strong endorsement, however, of the need for the hypnotist to have an understanding of police methods of investigation.

Most respondents indicated that hypnosis should be used for "investigatory" purposes (i.e., to provide leads), whereas less than half reported that it should be used for "evidentiary" purposes (i.e., to elicit testimony for court). However, many respondents were prepared to accept information obtained during hypnosis as reliable without independent corroboration, even though there was general recognition of the possibility of problems if this was done. Finally, the majority of respondents reported that the courts should decide on a case-by-case basis whether information obtained during hypnosis should be admissible as evidence.

The opinions expressed in the data highlighted a range of issues that we pursue further in Chapters 7 and 8. For example, there is a definite need for the consideration of appropriate qualifications and roles of the hypnotist in forensic hypnosis. A consistent set of guidelines needs to be put in place, covering legislation, the qualifications of the hypnotist (viz., the most appropriate person), the type of crime and type of subject (viz., to ensure the protection of the rights and well-being of the subject), the decision to use hypnosis, and procedural aspects regarding the conduct and analysis of the session. We set out such guidelines in Chapter 3, and these guidelines were applied in most of the cases that we discuss in the chapters that follow.

Some Key Legal Decisions

Although the forensic use of hypnosis had been debated earlier (e.g. Burrows, 1981; Grant, 1977; Griffiths, 1982; Purnell, 1981; Watkins, 1982), the article by Kirby (1984) focused important attention on the legal issues involved in Australia. Kirby highlighted the fact that hypnosis was being used increasingly as an aid to enhancing recall of critical circumstances, and he noted that although there were success stories, there were also serious dangers of confabulation and false memory. He argued that there was a need to look to psychologists, psychiatrists, and the police for assistance in the approach that should be proposed to courts, and emphasized that definite safeguards should be imposed on the use of hypnosis in the forensic setting.

A range of relevant issues have been considered in the Australian legal system in relation to the forensic use of hypnosis, and we comment selectively now on some of those issues and cases here. A major issue concerns the use of hypnosis in the court itself. In *Van Vliet v. Griffith* (1978), the counsel for the plaintiff requested the use of hypnosis in the court so that the judge could determine for himself the relevancy of the information obtained during a previous hypnosis session. The judge did not allow this, and said that to do so would risk the introduction of new or extraneous information that would supplant the legitimate material that was being considered. The judge, however, did allow the hypnotically influenced evidence of the plaintiff to be admitted and indicated that he was satisfied about the reliability of the evidence following cross-examination of the witness and expert evidence given by the psychiatrist (who conducted the hypnosis session).

A second case raised issues concerning both the amount of memory available for recall and the adequacy of the procedures used in the hypnosis session. In *R. v. Speechley* (1984; Aboud, 1985) the judge directed that the jury acquit the accused following expert testimony about the use of hypnosis with a woman who allegedly had been assaulted. She acknowledged that she had been substantially intoxicated at the time of the event. The woman had undergone hypnosis to remember the alleged assault and to identify her attacker. During hypnosis she identified the accused as the attacker. However, expert evidence indicated that because of the amount of alcohol and drugs that the woman had ingested on the evening of the attack, her memory would have been almost certainly unreliable and imperfect. Moreover, expert evidence indicated that the hypnosis session, which had been videorecorded, had been unsatisfactory in a number of other respects. Most notably, attention was focused on the lack of qualifications of the hypnotist and the use of unduly suggestive procedures. In another related Australian case, the use of hypnosis to confirm previously given information was considered. In *Wentworth v. Rogers* (1986), the appellant in a civil case sought to have a hypnosis session that she had arranged introduced into evidence. Her counsel argued that the use of hypnosis proved the accuracy of the statements that she had made previously to another court. The appeal court ruled that the videotape of the hypnosis session was inadmissible, because it was irrelevant to the legal issues being considered. Moreover, the court noted that there were no "fresh facts" involved, and the material in the hypnosis session was "self-serving material by which the appellant was seeking to corroborate her own version of the facts from her own mouth."

Other court decisions (e.g., *R. v. Geesing*, 1984, 1985; *R. v. Horsfall*, 1989) have considered relevant psychological and legal material, as have various articles (e.g., Odgers, 1988a, 1988b). However, two recent cases have provided very specific and influential directions. These cases are *R. v. Jenkyns* (1993) and *R. v. Haywood, Marshall, and Roughley* (1994). In *R. v. Jenkyns*, the evidence of a witness, LS, was challenged on the basis that he had undergone hypnosis to enhance his memory of detailed aspects that concerned his seeing the accused wearing certain clothing shortly before a person was murdered; the detail of the type of shoe was central to the identification of the assailant. The information provided by LS during hypnosis with a police officer was that the accused was wearing "Reebok Phase One" shoes hours before the murder. Physical evidence indicated that it was likely that this type of shoe had been worn by the assailant at the time of the murder. The judge decided that there were many areas of concern in relation to the reliability of the hypnotically induced evidence of LS: namely, the implied suggestions made by the police hypnotist that LS could see what he was told to see (but could not see); the emphasis placed prior to and during the hypnosis upon the importance of the footwear worn by the accused; the police hypnotist's lack of independence from the police force; the presence of an investigating officer during the hypnosis session; and the significant discrepancy between the recollection of LS during the hypnosis session and his subsequent hypnotically induced statement and evidence. Notably, it was recognized by the court that there was no real reason for LS to have perceived the detail about the accused's footwear in the first place. The judge decided that "these concerns prevent me from being satisfied that the hypnotically induced evidence given by LS is sufficiently reliable as to provide a prima facie reason for admitting it, and that evidence is rejected." This decision, in particular, highlighted the importance of carefully explicating guidelines, and of not assuming that hypnosis can enhance memory for detail that is likely to have been beyond the ken of the witness.

In *R. v. Haywood, Marshall, and Roughley* (1994), the accused were charged with multiple crimes associated with the gang rape of a 16-year-old female, JO. She had been unconscious during part of the attack; she also said that during the time that she was conscious, she was trying to blot the events that were occurring out of her mind. With the agreement of a sexual assault counselor, JO sought hypnosis to recover memories of the events. She approached a medical practitioner to undertake the hypnosis session; the police were aware that hypnosis was to be used, and did not object to its use. JO underwent four sessions of hypnosis with the hypnotist, but only the first of those focused on her memory of the events. The judge considered that it was unlikely that the second, third, and fourth sessions had any effect upon her memory of events. Also, he saw nothing in the evidence that would justify concluding that hypnosis may have contaminated her memory enough to make it unsafe for her to testify as to the relevant events. Nevertheless, following a close consideration of other relevant cases in the Australian legal system, the judge ruled that the prosecution "has an obligation to satisfy me that it is safe to admit the challenged posthypnotic evidence in the particular circumstances of [this] case." The judge went on to comment that "there is very considerable danger in embarking upon hypnosis of a complainant or other witness prior to a criminal trial." He argued:

> It would be highly regrettable if in future a victim of crime were to be rendered incompetent to testify by reason of an ill-advised attempt to enhance his or her recollection by hypnosis. I recognise that in some cases an investigation will be unable to proceed to prosecution unless hypnosis is employed on the investigative process, and that, in other cases, proper treatment consideration will suggest that hypnosis is imperative for the future mental health of the victim. However, in circumstances other than these I recommend great caution and the need to obtain proper legal advice before proceeding in this way.

This decision puts the weight of responsibility on the side that seeks to introduce the hypnotically influenced testimony and says that it should demonstrate that the testimony is not unreliable. As before, the importance of articulating and following specific guidelines is underscored in the decision.

The cases reported in this book were conducted in a situation in which relatively few legal decisions have been made about the use of hypnosis in the Australian forensic setting, but in which the issues are beginning to be appreciated (e.g., Freckelton, 1987; Kirby, 1984; Odgers, 1988a, 1988b; *R. v. Geesing*, 1984; *R. v. McFelin*, 1985; *R. v. Speechley*, 1982, 1984, 1985; *Van Vliet v. Griffiths*, 1978). As can be seen in Evans and Stanley (1994), more and more cases in Australia are cross-referencing to legal decisions elsewhere, and common issues are increasingly being highlighted, particularly relating to judgments in New Zealand and the United States (whose decisions have been very diverse; Scheflin & Shapiro, 1989). In *R. v. Haywood, Marshall, and Roughley* (1994), for example, reference was made to *R. v. McFelin* (1985) and the California Evidence Code. Similarly, the judge in *R. v. Jenkyns* (1993) decided:

> There is no inflexible rule that hypnotically induced testimony is inadmissible. The onus lies upon the party seeking to introduce such evidence to establish that it is safe to admit it in the particular

case, in the sense that it is sufficiently reliable as to provide a prima facie reason for admitting the evidence.

Here, the judge ruled that "until directed by an appellate court or the Legislature to the contrary, the trial courts of New South Wales should follow the guidelines put forward by the New Zealand Court of Appeal in *R. v. McFelin* (1985)." He then went on to give an elaboration and discussion of those guidelines, and a consideration of the obligations of those who seek to introduce hypnotically induced evidence. The procedures outlined in this judgment were designed to achieve two things: (1) to limit the likelihood that the hypnotized person may be inadvertently influenced by suggestions or other cues from the hypnotist or the setting, and (2) to assist the courts to determine whether confabulation has occurred, whether confidence in recall has been strengthened or artificially created, and whether any lessening of the ability to cross-examine the person has taken place. These are sensible aims of any guidelines, and are consistent with those we present in Chapter 3.

We turn now to consider the first of the cases analyzed in this book. In the cases discussed in Chapter 2, no set guidelines were practiced and major problems occurred partly in result. Our analyses of these cases and their problems begins to isolate themes that occur also in other cases in Chapters 4–6, and that we review critically in Chapters 7–10.

Revelations and Practices in Hypnosis

In this chapter, we sample cases that convey some of the problems that can occur in the interaction of hypnosis and the forensic system. Our focus is primarily on the procedures involved, and the complications that can arise quickly when hypnosis is introduced into a criminal investigation that is, in itself, complex. The issues that we pick up reach out to address the appropriateness of introducing hypnosis into the cases, the procedures employed when hypnosis is used, the qualifications and expertise of the hypnotists, and the impact of the use of hypnosis on the individuals and the investigations. These issues (and others) are raised to anticipate suggested guidelines for professional practice, which are formalized in the next chapter, and which guided our practices in cases to follow in which we took a more active part.

The three cases reported in this chapter go wrong and fail to use adequate procedures. At the outset, however, it is important to note that no one is immune to making mistakes and misjudgments, and we recognize that the police and hypnotists involved in these cases did not intend for things to go amiss. At the same time, they perhaps did not fully appreciate that the potential costs of introducing hypnosis into a criminal investigation can be high, and the potential benefits can be low.

This chapter attempts to provide enough detail to reinforce at the outset the fundamental importance of laying out adequate procedures for the interaction of hypnosis and the forensic setting. The broader context of hypnosis, memory, and behavior can only really be properly understood when specific guidelines are applied and standard procedures put in place. These are outlined in formal detail in the chapter that follows. To lay the foundation for the guidelines, cases are discussed with major recommended procedures in mind.

THE CASE OF BT

This case involved the use of hypnosis in 1991 with a 21-year-old woman, BT, and focused on events that she reported happening in 1980–1986, when she was between the ages of 10 and 16 years. During this time, her father allegedly was sexually abusing her older sister (for a fuller discussion of recovered memories, see Chapters 3 and 9), and BT eventually made a statement to police about various events that she said she witnessed. The father had left the family in 1986 and the allegations had been made to police by the elder sister in 1991. Four hypnosis sessions were conducted by a lay hypnotist at the request of BT's mother, and the audiorecordings of these sessions were made available to the police by the mother. The police were not aware at the outset that BT was undergoing hypnosis to assist her memory of the events that her elder sister had told her she had witnessed. The session was not properly recorded, no systematic inquiry into prehypnotic memories was conducted, and the case provides copious illustration of potentially suggestive and seriously distorting influences at work.

The context and content of the hypnosis sessions and of the allegations against the father appear to have been discussed at length by the lay hypnotist, BT's mother, and both her older and younger sisters. It seems clear that they all hoped that certain details would emerge from the use of hypnosis with BT. The exact content of those hypnotist and family discussions was not recorded in any way. The procedure followed by the hypnotist breached an essential guideline for the conduct of forensic hypnosis sessions formalized in Chapter 3. This guideline is that the hypnotist should have minimal information about the to-be-remembered material, and should have minimal interactions with any person other than the subjects of the hypnosis session. Moreover, the fact that four hypnosis sessions were conducted makes it seem likely that the hypnotist moved toward a particular construction of the to-be-remembered material, and this narrative construction was communicated both explicitly and implicitly to BT and her family. To do so infringes on the basic rule that the hypnotist should explore in a nonleading way the recollections reported by the subject. It is also likely that the family discussed the sessions outside the presence of the hypnotist. Such discussion would have further shaped the memory of BT during the hypnosis sessions. In many ways, then, there was ample opportunity for preconceptions, expectancies, and personalized constructions to shape (and distort) BT's memory reports.

The four hypnosis sessions in February and March 1991 contained a substantial amount of material that appeared in the formal statement that BT made to police in August 1991. The hypnosis sessions contained some routine aspects of hypnotic induction, maintenance, and deinduction, but it is not clear how much BT's natural proclivity for responding to hypnosis was carefully assessed. When attempting to elicit memories from BT, the hypnotist used various procedures of direct suggestion, indirect suggestion, memory revivification, affect bridging, and age regression. He attempted to keep these procedures relatively general, but these attempts broke down for two major reasons: (1) many of his questions became highly convoluted and confusing (suggesting to us that all communications, although as nonsuggestive as possible, should be clear and direct), and many of his questions conveyed and reinforced the notion that anything can be recalled accurately if people "feel secure" about doing this. This created procedural difficulties for us in that the methods used seem to have conveyed the impression that particular memories would be recalled by BT, and it was the client's insecurity that was not allowing those memories to be expressed fully. Guidelines are needed to militate against such impressions being formed.

Although the balance between probing for possible memories and suggesting particular memories is a difficult one to maintain, it seems likely that the memory enhancement procedures used by this hypnotist shifted the balance toward suggesting particular memories, and reinforcing specific thoughts and feelings that BT may have had prior to her involvement in the hypnosis sessions. Across the four hypnosis sessions and the subsequent statement made to police, it appears that BT moved from either no recall or a vague sense of particular events to reported memories of very specific events that were communicated with certainty. Given this situation, one could argue either that genuine memories were brought forward by the hypnosis session, or that false memories were created. The reasons for arguing one way or another lie essentially with the adequacy of the procedures associated with the hypnosis sessions, and the material that is available to index changes in memory and/or confidence in memory, assuming, of course, that there was no independent corroborative material available, and there was not. Our guidelines in Chapter 3 address these issues by outlining specific responsibilities for a hypnosis coordinator, whose task it is to help ensure that safeguards against distortion are in place; they also outline specific and detailed procedures for minimizing suggestive influences.

In this case, the procedures associated with the hypnosis sessions are in no way adequate. In our opinion, this case is so compelling in its presentation of therapeutic errors and their consequences that we have quoted extensively from the transcript of what was actually said. The case forcefully underscores the need to adopt for professional practice stringent and detailed guidelines that reach out to address all aspects of conducting forensic hypnosis. This is despite the fact that in a statement to police the hypnotist said: "During my sessions with [BT] great care was taken when asking general questions and I am very aware of the problems which may arise from asking leading questions." However, he also said:

> As a result of these sessions conducted with [BT] I had discussed with her sister . . . and more so with her mother . . . allegations made by [BT] of a sexual assault committed by [BT's] father . . . upon her elder sister . . . These conversations with [BT's mother and sister] took place generally before or after the sessions were concluded.

In this case, the material illustrates many potential problems of the conduct and interpretation of using hypnosis to enhance memory, there being no controls on pre- or postexploration of memory. To illustrate these and other problems, we present selected material from each of the sessions and provide comment that highlights the problems.

Session I

In the first session, a lengthy induction procedure was given and the hypnotist (H) indicated the purpose of the hypnosis sessions. Immediately, questions were asked which were suggestive, leading the subject to report particular kinds of events. This infringement of the guidelines, set out in the next chapter, picks up pace and emerges even more clearly as the sessions progress:

H: Are you aware that in the case of your elder sister, RT, in her relationship with her father, that there are various charges being brought about against him?

BT: Yes.

H: Right. As RT's sister, I am asking you now, as to whether you are a witness in the past to any impropriety that your father may or may not have committed toward your sister RT?

BT: No.

The hypnotist continued to ask suggestive, multifaceted, and confusing questions about the father and his interactions with BT, her sisters, and her mother, and eventually BT commented in response to a long question about her father and "impropriety":

BT: It was RT.

H: It was RT. What do you see now? What have you been withholding? What do you want to reveal?

BT: I walked in on them in bed.

H: Right. You walked in on them in bed. And how old are you? If you picture that time, what do you see and how old are you?

This excerpt sees the hypnotist pressuring the subject and tacitly (at least) beginning to structure BT's recall. At this stage, the interaction focused on BT's age, the ages of her sisters, the location of the house, and the location of people within the house on this occasion. BT's comments were brief and relatively general, and the hypnotist typically asked questions a number of times before BT gave a specific enough response for the hypnotist to move to another question. The hypnotist also explored the emotional meaning of this occasion and whether there were other occasions when BT observed her father and RT.

H: Could I ask you as to whether there are any other occasions besides that Saturday afternoon where you are aware of some impropriety between your father and some other person in the family?

BT: No.

H: Are you only aware for the moment at this your first subconscious session, are you only aware of that occasion when you walked into your father's room on a Saturday afternoon and was suddenly aware that RT was in your father's bed with him under the blankets and sheets? Is this the only occasion that you noticed your father was not at all acting out the proper fatherly role?

BT: Yes.

Session 2

Here, the hypnotist structures and essentially suggests a particular interpretation. He begins to also deal overtly with memories associated with possible sexual abuse. The importance of this area is such that we consider it necessary to formulate particular guidelines in this area, and they follow in Chapter 3. In the second session, the hypnotist became much more directive and forceful, and seemed to use other information obtained from outside the sessions in his interactions with BT. Moreover, the hypnotist appeared to answer on behalf of BT a number of times, presumably after seeing head movements by BT. The hypnotist had become involved and committed, it seemed, to the development of a particular narrative. For instance:

H: You noticed on one occasion as you stepped into his room. There was a shock, was there not, when you noticed that RT was in his bed? Is this true?

BT: . . .

H: Right. You're acknowledging yes. Does it surprise you at all that RT attests to the fact that there were other occasions too when you were present?

BT: . . .

H: It doesn't surprise you. You see, it doesn't surprise you because there were other occasions. You are setting out now to find and scan through the information that you have in your subconscious now. There is some other occasion when something quite bizarre is happening in his room. First of all, you're scanning for information at a particular time. The place is probably located already. It's in your father's room. Nod your head when you see some type of occasion, some other instance . . . Take your time. You're following through that extraordinarily big data bank of yours. You can feel sure that even as your sister attests to the fact that you were present on some other occasion that your father and her were doing something together, and you were there, you were watching. When you see something just nod your head . . . It may not be something that you like at all. But you're prepared for that. Something might even shock you. A tripod, a camera setup, or even if it isn't there, anything significant. When you see it, when you recall it, just nod your head . . . You can consider whilst you are searching and scanning the information that is stored in your subconscious; you might be a little bit scared. There's a bridge to cross before you get to the other side, but it's worth it. If there is significant information there that stirs up emotion in you, then believe in the way that your mother would have you believe. It's worth it to expose whatever information is there that you've been through. Or something that your father could have put RT through. It's as though you are the third person, an observer, made to observe . . . Something that you previously, possibly, probably blocked off from your mind. Tried to ignore, but for RT's sake, for your sake, and strangely enough for your mother's sake, you don't want to ignore it anymore. If there is something you saw, something that your father imposed on another member of the family, particularly RT, and you can see it being done in your father's room. You can see it now. When you see it, nod your head.

Here the hypnotist is clearly informed about allegations in the case. There should have been a hypnotist coordinator who exposed this hypnotist to minimal information about the case. None of the exchanges here were videorecorded; if they had been, it is likely that that would have strengthened the impression that suggestive cues were being given.

BT: . . .

H: You're nodding your head, and that took great courage. You've earned the right to relax. (*Here the hypnotist gives suggestions for relaxation and a sense of security, and then continues.*) It's still a particular place, a particular spot. Do you see yourself witnessing something in your father's room?

BT: . . .

H: Right. You're acknowledging yes. Is it an incident that you have tried to ignore?

BT: . . .

H: You're acknowledging that it is. What do you see? You can verbally say what you see now, without being afraid. You're secure in here. You can externalize and say what you see.

Here, the hypnotist is trying to facilitate recall of past memories of witnessing sexual abuse. Guidelines need to alert the hypnotist to potential harm, and the possibility that false memories can be created through suggestion. The hypnotist and BT then discussed in detail the layout of the room and its contents, including a video camera at the foot of the bed, and the position and movements of her father and her sister. The hypnotist continued to seek detail, and returned to points whenever BT provided general rather than specific comment. Perhaps because of the reported location of the video camera in the room, the hypnotist decided to use this as a technique to then help BT remember the events at her current, rather than her age-regressed, age. He did this as follows and again the cues led to a particular response:

H: Alright. Instead of you being there, I'd like you to imagine that whatever the video has filmed, you're going to replay it. It might be in a room on your own. You've got the opportunity to look through this video, not to satisfy yourself by what's on the video, but to scan over evidence of what might have happened that day. I don't want you to think that it is that day now. I'd like you imagine yourself older, wiser, and you are looking over this video, the film tape that your father took that day. I want you to stick in into a machine, and you are doing that now. Can you see this?

BT: Yes.

H: Yes. You're in a room, on your own, and you do not feel at all intimidated, because nobody can walk in on you. You have the controls to the video itself. You are about to press a play button that is going to show you what happened that day. You are going to see what happens as your father kneels over your sister on the bed.

The hypnotist then asked a series of questions about the interactions of the father and the sister, and those questions were detailed and sexual. Some of the questions (e.g., about the precise positioning and movement of the father's hands and genitals) presumably would not have been answered meaningfully by anybody, because they could not be seen. Thus, the hypnotist was conveying that BT had extraordinary ability to remember and report on very specific details that likely would have been hidden at the time, even if they had occurred. Although it was over 6 years since the time of the alleged event being discussed, and although BT did not report the event herself but eventually agreed with her sister and the hypnotist that she was a witness, the hypnotist tried to elicit answers to detailed questions. Moreover, he did this with BT as an adult watching the videotape rather than as BT as a child personally viewing the event. Here and elsewhere, the hypnotist violates the major guideline of exploring in a nonleading way, structures recall rather than facilitates the subject's own narrative of events, and allows the subject relatively little opportunity to comment on the hypnotist's interpretations.

Session 3

The theme of the third hypnosis session was the importance of BT recalling the event as an adult:

H: You can feel good, you can feel safe, you can feel more secure that you can feel happy with what your subconscious mind already knows, because it has lived through events that may have been to some people very shocking, to you at the time even more shocking, to such an extent that you for years have buried these thoughts. And now is the time to exhume some of these thoughts, so that you can face them, and get away from the childhood psychological defense mechanisms of avoiding. I would like you now to cast your mind back, casting your mind back to a situation, without avoiding the situation at all, where you have been summoned to your father's room. You wouldn't go there voluntarily to see what you are about to see, not to enjoy it. You were summoned to even sit in a particular spot that's next to the video camera.

BT: . . .

H: You do recall being summoned to the room.

BT: Vaguely.

H: Vaguely. So, you do at least remember yourself once more being seated next to the camera at the foot of the bed. Can you see yourself?

BT: Yes.

H: Can you nearly see what the video would be seeing?

BT: No, it's very blurry.

These excerpts indicate that the client is uncertain, but memories appear to be shaped by the structure that the hypnotist supplies rather than the experiences of the subject. This is a central issue in the recovered memories debate, which our guidelines (Chapter 3) specifically aim to address. The hypnotist attempted to make the picture clearer by suggesting that the room become lighter and things brighter. Because BT was only partially receptive to this approach, the hypnotist returned to the technique of BT viewing the videotape of the events, rather than the events themselves.

H: I would like you now to picture yourself taking out the videocassette. That you've got this chance, not to gleefully look over the tape, but to confront issues that you've got stored in your subconscious mind there. To trust your conscious mind to know what your subconscious mind or memory bank does know and has lived through. Are you prepared for such a journey?

BT: Yes.

H: You are quite prepared at your level of maturity to put your videocassette that no one knows you've got into a player, and you and an analyst might be sitting there viewing through a representation of what your subconscious mind has seen. And you're going to review what did happen so many years ago.

The hypnotist then asked a series of detailed questions about the father, the sister, and their interaction. A new element in this session concerned questions of force by the father and resistance by the sister. Each time, the narrative suggested by the hypnotist becomes more explicit, and the vagueness of the subject gives way to greater certainty. For instance:

H: Right. Where are his hands? Where are they moving, if they are moving at all?

BT: They are holding her down.

H: They are holding her down. Are there any muffled sounds coming out from underneath him?

BT: No.

H: Is there crying or whimpering?

BT: No.

H: Is there silence?

BT: Yes.

H: There is silence. What do you then see happening?

BT: She is moving her legs, kicking the covers off.

H: She's kicking and trying to get him off.

BT: Yes.

H: And he's still holding her down?

BT: Yes, and he's got his hand over her mouth.

H: A hand over her mouth. Is this the left hand or the right hand, as you see it on the video now? You can trust your subconscious mind to reveal. What do you see the hands doing? One hand over the mouth, and the other?

BT: I think they're both on her mouth.

H: Both on her mouth. She's still kicking away?

BT: Yes.

H: Is she trying to get out from under the bed covers?

BT: No, they're off.

H: The bed covers are already off. Is she succeeding or failing in getting away from him?

BT: Failing.

H: She's failing. And what then happens?

BT: I don't want to look at it any more.

The hypnotist allowed BT to rest at this point, and then returned to elicit further information about the struggle between father and daughter that BT was describing during hypnosis. After a further interaction in which explicit detail was reported, the hypnotist seemed to move to end this third session, but suddenly shifted back to elicit more material.

H: Right. How do you feel right now as you have been watching this video? What emotion do you feel?

BT: Sadness.

H: Sadness for whom? Yourself?

BT: My sister.

H: For your sister? What do you feel toward your father?

BT: Nothing.

H: Nothing? Is there a hint of anger that you feel toward your father?

BT: No.

The comments of the hypnotist then indicated that he was not ready to end the session, and he returned to the videotape technique.

H: I'd like you to let the play mode go on, and when you see something else come onto the screen, I would like you to immediately start talking. Allow your subconscious to feel secure and safe whilst you and an analyst look over the pictures coming on the screen. You can actually state what you see. You can let yourself reveal what the subconscious mind has known for a long, long time.

BT: It's my sister in my father's room.

H: It's your sister in your father's room. Are you older than the time before, or younger?

BT: Older.

H: But maybe not that much older.

BT: No.

H: No. And allowing yourself to trust yourself to reveal to your conscious mind what your subconscious mind already knows, what are you prepared to let yourself see on this video now?

The session at this point deals centrally with uncovering memories of sexual abuse and one might argue at this stage (see Barber, 1994; Bloom, 1994; Yapko, 1994) that the subject is more vulnerable to suggestion than before. In response to questions from the hypnotist, BT at this point described a sexual interaction between her father and sister and gave these descriptions in an explicit and detailed manner. The hypnotist established through questioning that this was a different occasion from the other two that she had reported. Moreover, the hypnotist sought to establish consistency with the reports that RT had given of BT's presence on a number of occasions of sexual interaction with her father. After BT detailed this interaction, the hypnotist moved to end the session in a way that he presumably thought was therapeutically appropriate.

At this stage, one notes especially the monosyllabic replies to the hypnotist/therapist, whose suggestive frame of reference now broadens to focus on the responsibilities of the client. In this sense, it is important that guidelines on recovered memories establish limits for the therapist to accept responsibility for both diagnosis and treatment (see also Bloom, 1994), and recognize the particular vulnerabilities of clients exposed to abuse scenarios, suggested or real.

H: Now you are 21 years old, you're 20 years old. Around this age, and having known your father, and that he's done this to your sister and you, because it's psychologically upon you that you had been a victim and now a survivor. Do you feel feelings toward your father at this time, knowing that your conscious mind wants to handle what your subconscious mind has known for a long time?

BT: No.

H: There's no emotion at this point in time?

BT: No.

H: Are you ready some time in the future, to objectively look at what your feelings should be toward a man who has perpetrated acts like this? Do you feel that you are ready to look at that at some time in the future?

BT: Yes.

H: Yes, okay. If there are other situations that have come up, your videocamera can reveal all as a representation of your subconscious mind. Your subconscious mind is a memory bank, and you can entrust a third party to help you resolve all that you've seen, all that you've experienced, all that you as a Christian have been coerced to be witness to, when perpetrated acts against your sister by a man named [BT's father] and a person or spirit much stronger than you or I, and that is God. You may feel some satisfaction as you leave here, that your prayers to resolve issues that you've seen can be answered. You are a Christian, are you not?

BT: Yes.

H: Yes. So through Jesus Christ, you can pray for this, that these issues be resolved for yourself, as a previous victim and now a survivor, for your sister, the victim but hopefully a survivor, through the grace of Jesus Christ. And you can say, "Amen."

BT: Amen.

H: I'm going to count up from zero to five. On the count of five, you will be wide awake, feeling really good. Really alive on the count of five. Knowing that through courage, through revelation, you can proceed on with your life.

Session 4

In the fourth and final session, the hypnotist went over the material that had been dealt with in the first three sessions, but BT was much more direct and specific now in her responses than she had been in those sessions. Substantial certainty in what was being recounted by BT is now evident. In fact, the hypnotist rarely repeated a question or asked for more detail. BT answered questions clearly, and immediately. The session presents evidence that what the hypnotist suggested before was now, in fact, accepted and elaborated upon by BT. The hypnotist reinforced the value of BT doing this by comments such as the following:

> You can allow now your subconscious to convey what it already knows. You can let your conscious mind know, what you feel for the last few weeks now, that there's a strong urge to reveal, to get things off your chest, because you're a survivor, you're no longer a victim, you see.

The hypnotist went over, in particular, the material that indicated that the father used physical force and the sister attempted to resist the sexual contact by the father. Just as he had broadened his closing comments in Session 3 to include Jesus Christ as a powerful authority figure associated with truth and redemption, the hypnotist broadened his comments in this final session to include other people also.

H: And taking yourself away from the situation now, and then look back, do you understand now that your father is sexually perverted and ill, and mentally ill? Can you see this?

BT: Yes.

H: Do you feel that any man has the right to treat a wife, let alone a daughter, or any other female that way?

BT: No.

H: Do you feel happier now, to know that there are some males in the world who not only can romance his loved one, his wife or his girlfriend, but does it make you feel all the more secure to know that a man, even under pressure, with a wife or with a girlfriend can still treat her with the dignity she deserves?

BT: Yes.

H: Do you feel that before, some months before now, it was very hard to trust anyone?

BT: No.

H: But nevertheless, do you feel that you can trust some men more now, now that you are able to let out what you know, to get off your chest what has happened as fact in your own childhood experiences?

BT: Yes.

After repeating this material a number of times, the hypnotist ended his four-session-long interaction with BT in the following way:

> Right. And by letting out lots of things that you have known and felt forced to harbor, you can with people that you trust let out the information. It doesn't have to be here. It doesn't have to be with your own counselor. But at least you can feel secure knowing that should there be a time or a need to reveal information, that anyone that you trust, you can do it just like today.

BT subsequently made a formal statement to police that detailed her believed-in memory report of observing sexual assaults on her sister by her father. That statement did not mention hypnosis. Many of the details in that statement can be traced back to either the first, second, third, or fourth hypnosis session. Following our analysis of the hypnosis sessions, which was undertaken at the request of the prosecution, the prosecution decided that the material elicited from BT during those sessions should not form part of the evidence in the prosecution of BT's father for allegedly assaulting BT's sister. The prosecution came to a view that the trial judge would probably not allow BT's testimony to be admitted because of the way in which it was elicited during hypnosis. There were very few guidelines, in fact, that could be said to be satisfied by this case. For example, the general issue was clearly at stake that the use of hypnosis was not consistent with clinical and legal safeguards designed to ensure the well-being of the subject. There was no one to monitor the extent of exposure of the hypnotist to details of the case. The hypnotist was not appropriately qualified, nor had he any understanding of investigative and legal issues relevant to hypnosis. No prior recollections were specifically assessed. Technically, the events of the four sessions were not fully reproducible, and no clinical follow-up was provided. Arguably, damage was done to BT by the hypnotist, although his intentions were presumably sound. If the guidelines suggested had been practiced, the outcome may have been different.

THE MR. BUBBLES CASE

The second case also illustrates hypnosis that went wrong. Guidelines were not practiced and many of the specific issues highlighted in the first case appear again. We have already commented on how easily suggestive influences can define the content of treatment. This case presents another situation in which that same problem occurs.

This case involved allegations of sexual assault of 17 preschool children by adults who were associated with the child-care center that the children attended. As part of the criminal investigation, hypnosis was used with one 3-year-old girl who was at the center of the allegations, and the material presented here focuses on that use of hypnosis and on the prehypnotic interview. Setting aside the problems with the investigation as a whole, we believe that hypnosis should not have been used with a child of this age under any circumstances, and the case suggests to us the necessity of establishing firm guidelines relating to type of subject (as well as to the type of crime). In this case, when hypnosis was used, the session breached common sense, let alone any recommended guidelines, for the conduct of a forensic hypnosis session. The case serves primarily as a forceful illustration of what can happen when eagerness overwhelms the hypnotist and the investigating officers. Although it is difficult to determine the full impact of the prehypnotic and hypnotic interviews with the girl (NF), it is likely that they were instrumental in creating a construction of particular memory reports that was then accepted by her, infringing again on the basic rule of minimizing suggestion.

Prehypnotic Interview

The prehypnotic interview involved a female police officer (PO), NF's mother (M), and NF. Although most discussion was between the officer and NF, the mother intervened a number of times in a way that was directive and reflected (understandable) emotional concern. Thus, it seemed that the mother was structuring the subject's response to some degree. The police officer was highly leading in her interaction with NF and appeared to have a particular scenario in mind. For instance, she said, "We'll talk about it like we did with [various other children]," and this could have led NF to believe that she should give the same information as given by the other children. The mother adopted the same position in her own interventions. For instance:

M: Who told you that you and _____ were going to die?

NF: I don't know.

M: You do too. I do too. And you've got to keep telling us who it is so that we can be sure.

This case, like the last one, establishes the need for a coordinator who can serve as a link between the hypnotist and the investigating authorities and who has well-defined tasks and responsibilities. The police officer employed a variety of strategies in the interview, but these appeared to be both contradictory and confusing. Early in the interview, the police officer acted as if she was one of the children at a party that "Mr. Bubbles" attended; Mr. Bubbles was the name given to a man at the child-care center who allegedly dressed as a clown and bathed the children in a bubble bath.

PO: Do you know the bubble man? I think you do. He's a friend of mine. I don't really like him though. He's not a very nice man. He took me to a party once, but I didn't want to go. And _____ was there, and he was crying because he didn't want to be there either. Everyone was there. And they told me that if I talked about it, something bad was going to happen.

Later in the interview, the police officer acted as if she were one of the offenders at the party:

PO: Who's over there?
NF: NF.
PO: I've put you in the bath, haven't I, NF?
NF: No.
PO: With all the bubbles.
NF: No.
PO: I did.
NF: No.
PO: Took your clothes off and put you in the bathtub.

NF was asked other questions that were highly directive and placed substantial pressure on her. For instance:

PO: But you have to say something sensible. You have to talk about the bubble man.

Moreover, the police officer falsely stated that she personally saw things involving NF.

PO: I saw you. I was there that night. Didn't you see me?
NF: No.
PO: I was watching you.
NF: I didn't see you.
PO: Remember how Mr. Bubbles takes your photo. You were showing us how he does that, weren't you?

There are many other instances in this prehypnotic interview that could appear to convey to NF that the police officer and the mother knew certain things, and that it was NF's task to simply confirm this knowledge. In addition, there were some responses of NF's that suggested that she was engaging in a game during the interview. For instance:

PO: Are you telling me the truth?
NF: No.
PO: Is your name NF?
NF: No.
PO: What's your name?
NF: Suzy. [This was not NF's name.]

There are instances, however, when NF's comments should have been considered more closely. For instance, at one time NF said to the police officer, "Did a wee on your back." Rather than respond to this in a sensible manner, the police officer virtually shouted back and the following interaction occurred:

PO: Who did a wee on my back?
NF: Nobody?
PO: You just told me they did.
NF: Tricked ya.

Thus, the apparent lack of experience in dealing with 3-year-old children and the apparent overreaction by the police officer meant that the impact of a spontaneous comment by NF that may have had significance was lost; also, it appeared to cause NF to avoid any further discussion of her comment, which may or may not have had clinical and forensic significance.

Hypnotic Interview

Following this interview, there was another interview in which hypnosis was used by a male police officer; the female officer and the mother were present as well. The information given to NF and her mother about hypnosis, the induction procedure, and any suggestions were not recorded on the audiotape (a videotape was not used, making it impossible, as in the previous case, for events to be fully reproduced); also, any discussion of the hypnosis session with NF and her mother was not recorded.

The audiotape began with the hypnotist asking NF who she could see at a party. The hypnotist asked NF to describe what was happening to the "princess" at the party. (It seems that the hypnotist told NF that he would refer to her as the "princess.") Most of the procedures of the hypnosis session would not meet the criteria of acceptability under proper guidelines for forensic hypnosis, for the reasons that we stated in the previous case and that were summarized in our concluding remarks. Suggestive influences were clearly operating. There was no controlled exploration of prehypnotic memories, the roles appeared confused on the part of both hypnotist and subject, and hypnosis was not undertaken with sufficient caution considering the age of the subject.

Given the age of the child and the extremely direct approach of the hypnotist, it is very plausible that the questions asked during hypnosis influenced strongly the memory reporting of NF in a way that led to substantial contamination. Not surprisingly perhaps, NF initially adopted a negative orientation during the hypnosis session, but this seemed to make the hypnotist only more directive and eager to obtain a positive response to his leading questions, which raised further problems. For instance:

H: Do you think the bad guy would hurt the princess?
NF: No.
H: What has the bad guy been doing to the princess?
NF: I don't know.
H: You don't know? Take a close look there and tell me what the bad guy's been doing to the princess.

And later:

H: Who's taking the photographs now?
NF: Nobody.
H: Where's the camera?
NF: I don't know.
H: Can't you see the camera? Where have they put the camera?
NF: I don't know.
H: Did they move it?

The hypnotist also asked questions about particular people in a way that was leading, suggesting particular embellishments of a structured narrative. As in the last case, the situation again deals with accessing memories of abuse. This case also indicates the necessity for adopting special prescribed guidelines for uncovering memories associated with abuse.

H: Is Miss _____ there? Can the princess see Miss _____?
NF: No.
H: Is she in the other room?
NF: No.
H: Is Mr. Bubbles there?
NF: No.
H: Where's Mr. Bubbles?
NF: I don't know.

In asking questions like this, the hypnotist targeted the individuals that he believed were involved in the sexual abuse of the children and seemed to ignore comments by NF that indicated anything to the contrary. For example, at one point, NF repeatedly attempted to tell a story about a "bad guy" with a suitcase on an airplane. For the most part, however, the hypnotist ignored NF's story and drew her back to direct questions and answers about the party. Clinically and forensically, it would have been better for NF if she had been allowed to tell the story she wanted. Eventually, NF responded positively, but in doing so she relied upon, and used, stereotypes. For instance, after NF agreed with the hypnotist that there was "a bad guy" at the party, she indicated that he had "black all over him." Later, she spontaneously indicated that the bad men were all wearing black and the bad ladies were all wearing silver. Examples of NF's eventual desire to give correct answers and her inconsistency in giving these answers can be seen in her description of the "baddies' hair" as variously black and white, black and red, or purple and pink. Similarly, in moving from resistance to apparent acquiescence to the hypnotist, NF variously indicated the number of people in the bathtub at the party as none, 1, 4, and 15. The hypnotist appeared to settle on 4 as an appropriate number of people to be in the bathtub, and NF agreed. Thus, it seems that the hypnotist had a scenario in mind and asked questions in a way that encouraged NF to report critical aspects of that scenario. Moreover, some of the questions of the hypnotist who was a police officer and the lay

hypnotist could be argued to move from being leading questions to being framed as specific hypnotic suggestions. For
instance:

H: Does the princess like having her photograph taken?

NF: Uh.

H: Does she? Who's taking the princess's photograph? Just see
the princess there now. Tell me who's taking the princess's
photograph.

This moves from a simple inquiry about whether the princess, NF, likes something to a direct suggestion involving a
hypnotic hallucination that the particular thing is occurring in
the situation being discussed. Similarly, some of the questions by
the hypnotist could be said to have led NF to report events that
she may not have reported previously, procedures infringing
many of the guidelines we recommend. For instance, during
hypnosis the hypnotist asked, "Is the princess sore anywhere?
Does she have a hurt or a pain?" Plausibly, this could have led
NF to report that hurt or pain was happening.

Overall, this case is a striking example of the inappropriate
use of hypnosis and the application of deficient procedures.
Proper guidelines were not followed and the use of hypnosis was
flawed. The ultimate effect of hypnosis was of little benefit to
either NF or the investigation of the alleged offenses and the
corroboration of many events was not at all possible. Although
a man and three women associated with the child-care center
were charged with over 50 counts of sexual and indecent assaults
on 17 children aged 3 to 6 years, the case did not proceed past
the pretrial, committal hearing. In that hearing, the use of
hypnosis was condemned by the expert witnesses, and the
potential damage that it had done to NF was highlighted; it was
argued that this particular use of hypnosis was morally, ethically,
and scientifically unacceptable. We agree. The charges against
the accused were dismissed and they were eventually awarded
an amount of money to cover the substantial legal costs that had
been associated with their defense. Lives were left in ruins,
however, after the public ignominy surrounding the case, and
this highlights one of the major issues that drive our set of
guidelines in Chapter 3; namely, a concern for the welfare of the
person hypnotized must be seen as primary and procedures need
always to carefully address that person's needs. Also, the lives of

other children and their families were damaged, and this addresses the matter of concern for the consequences of a case. Finally, the community was left with the uncertainty about what, if anything, had occurred, and also with considerable anger about the nature of the police investigation that had been conducted and the interviewing techniques (including hypnosis) that had been used.

THE BLACKBURN CASE

This third case illustrates some difficulties that are common to the previous two cases, but highlights additional issues. Our discussion is focused around why the legal process warned against the use of hypnosis, and this is discussed by us in the context of no formal guidelines having been adopted or practiced.

In July 1989, a 59-year-old recently retired police officer (Harry Blackburn) was arrested and charged with 25 offenses involving sexual assault, assault, and robbery over the periods from October 1969 to July 1970 and August 1985 to December 1988. The strong reputation of this man, his decorated police service, the nature and extent of the crimes, the manner of his arrest in a public place, and the active involvement of the media meant that this case became a public spectacle. This was especially so when the prosecution offered no evidence at the pretrial, committal hearing, and all charges were dismissed.

To deal with the legal and political situation that arose from this case, the State government established a Royal Commission of Inquiry (similar to a grand jury inquiry) into the arrest, charging, and withdrawal of all charges. The Royal Commission called 78 witnesses whose questioning led to about 6,500 pages of transcript, and considered 565 exhibits comprising approximately 5,500 pages of written or printed material. The Royal Commissioner submitted a report of over 600 pages, and made 18 specific recommendations. One of those recommendations concerned hypnosis, because it emerged that hypnosis had been used with a number of witnesses and victims in the course of the investigation (see Lee, 1990). Moreover, hypnosis had been seen to be a critical factor by the investigating officers in the so-called identification of the "target suspect" (Blackburn) by one of the witnesses. In the huge complexities and inadequacies of this case, the use of hypnosis could be said to be of relatively small moment; however, it was important enough for the Royal Commissioner to comment on specifically and for the Police Commissioner to then endorse that comment. The relevant formal recommendation of the Royal Commissioner was as follows: "I recommend that police should be warned not to indulge in hypnosis until reputable expert opinion on that subject can positively rule out any risks that comments made under hypnosis are, or could be, unreliable" (Lee, 1990, p. 315). The Police Commissioner supported this recommendation and said that action had already been taken to ensure that under no circumstance would police arrange for victims or witnesses to be hypnotized. The action that he was referring to was taken after the Mr. Bubbles case; after that case, the use of hypnosis by police officers had been banned by the Police Commissioner in that State because of legal and ethical concerns. Notably, however, 4 years later, a new Police Commissioner lifted the ban, and hypnosis is being used again in that State. The thrust of that removal was in partial response to the judgment in *R. v. Jenkyns* (1993), which recognized that hypnosis should only be used when compliance with specific procedures could be guaranteed.

We turn now to summarize the essential elements of what led the Royal Commissioner and the previous Police Commissioner to adopt such a strong position against the use of forensic hypnosis. We focus on the use of hypnosis by the police on two occasions with the same witness. On the first occasion in January 1989, the witness (MI) was hypnotized in an effort to reveal the registration number of a vehicle that was used in the abduction and sexual assault of a woman in August 1985, that is, about $3\frac{1}{2}$ years before the hypnosis session. Potentially (for reasons discussed by us in Chapter 9), it was thought that the recall of a specific, salient detail could have been aided by the application of hypnosis.

On the evening of the attack, the witness was getting into his vehicle near the victim's home when he saw a van come out of the nearby school grounds. A couple of days after the attack, MI contacted police and gave them a description of the van. He said that the first letter of the registration number of the van was definitely "K." The route that the van traveled after it passed him and the route that MI traveled in his vehicle was the same for some distance so he had the opportunity to observe it. In his statement, MI noted that he thought it was strange for the vehicle to be coming out of the school grounds at 6:30 P.M., and said also that he would have written the registration number down but did not have a pen or pencil to do so.

In January 1989, MI was hypnotized by a police officer who aimed to assist him in remembering the registration number. The witness did not produce any further information about the number, but indicated that he was sure, as he always had been, that the first letter was "K." In his original statement in August 1985, MI had said that he had seen the driver and had described him in that statement. During the hypnosis session, the witness described the driver of the van as a "small man," but this description was not pursued by the hypnotist. One reason for this may have been that the target suspect, Blackburn, was a big, tall man, and this fact was known by the hypnotist who was involved centrally in the investigation. However, this detail highlights an important issue for guidelines that we take up, in drawing attention to the need, where possible, to independently corroborate reported events. Corroboration is defined by us formally in Chapter 3.

The police notes on this hypnosis session indicated that MI said that the driver was in the headlights of his vehicle at one stage, but MI made it clear, in fact, that this was not the case. The second occasion in which hypnosis was used with MI was in May 1989. The details of that hypnosis session are unclear, because either an audiorecording was not made, or an audiorecording was made but subsequently lost. Like the previous two cases, events were not fully reproducible. During the hypnosis session, 3 years and 9 months after the event, MI was shown a folder of photographs, and one of those was of Blackburn. In a formal statement made immediately after the hypnosis session, MI stated:

> I indicated photograph number 9 [Blackburn] as a male person I believe to be the driver of a Nissan vehicle which was leaving the grounds of the school about 6:30 on Wednesday, August 7, 1985. I believe this to be the man I saw driving that vehicle, although I would have to say I am 80 percent certain because of the time element.

In a subsequent statement in August 1989, after the arrest of Blackburn, MI referred to the hypnosis session and said:

> I am 80 percent sure that the man I saw in the folder of photographs that [the hypnotist] showed me is the person I

saw driving the van. . . . I would like to add that I cannot positively identify this person because of not only the time limit, but also I do not have a photographic memory.

In his testimony to the Royal Commission, MI said:

My best recollection is that I said the gentleman I had identified appeared similar in a lot of ways to the man I had seen driving the vehicle that night. I think in the statement it says that I was 80 percent sure and the reason was (a) it was so long ago, and (b) I don't have a photographic memory. I wouldn't be able to pick someone out after four years.

When asked, "Did you ever tell the police it was a positive identification?" MI answered, "No, I did not. They basically told me what to write down."

The notes of the investigating officers paint a very different picture of the hypnosis session and the subsequent statement by MI. Immediately after the hypnosis session, the police notes stated that "the witness . . . indicated that photograph number 9 in that folder was the driver of a Nissan van that he saw leave the school grounds." About a week later, in an assessment of the evidence to that time, the police notes indicated that MI "has now identified the driver as the target." About a month later, in a summary of the investigation prepared for senior police, the notes stated that MI "positively identified the suspect." The fact that hypnosis had been involved in the identification of the target suspect was not included in the assessment of the evidence or in the summary of the investigation that was prepared for senior police. The careful use of a hypnosis coordinator (see Chapter 3) in this case might have alleviated this problem. Not only would the procedures involved have been better managed, but the choice of later details to be communicated might also have been different.

Although the use of hypnosis probably did not influence the memory or confidence of MI, it seems that its use changed the weight that the investigating officers placed on the "identification." MI made it quite clear at all times that there were similarities between the photograph and the driver of the van, but that he was not making a positive identification. In the eyes of the investigating officers, however, the fact that this identification had been made during hypnosis seems to have added considerably to the 80% confidence expressed by MI in his identification of the man in the photograph.

In the inquiry into this case, the Royal Commissioner stated:

I would not leave the topic of hypnotism without sounding a strong warning that police should not indulge in hypnosis of witnesses until reputable expert opinion on that subject can positively rule out any risks that statements made under hypnosis are, or could be, unreliable. For until that happens there is every likelihood that courts will not accept such statements and will even reject other evidence not obtained under hypnosis but thought to be tainted by it. The consequences of this could be the total failure of a prosecution and the waste of time and resources, in perhaps a long and painstaking investigation. (Lee, 1990, pp. 171–172)

CHAPTER 3

Suggested Guidelines for Practice

The three cases summarized in Chapter 2 point to many problems involved in the use of hypnosis in the forensic setting when proper procedures are not employed. Overall, they highlight the need for clear professionalism and the adoption of standard procedures when hypnosis is used in an attempt to enhance memory. They focus, in particular, on how easily suggestion can operate to influence what is said. Another overarching issue is the matter of the qualifications of the hypnotist; appropriate qualifications for using hypnosis forensically must be a central concern of any set of guidelines.

Issues of who should use hypnosis in the forensic setting and how it should be used have been debated in the literature, and a variety of guidelines have been available (e.g., Ault, 1979; Orne et al., 1984; *R. v. McFelin*, 1985; *R. v. Jenkyns*, 1993; Scheflin & Shapiro, 1989) to guide our own reformulation of procedures. Two of the more significant statements about the issues have been those produced by the International Society of Hypnosis (1979) and the Council on Scientific Affairs (1985). These statements influenced the series of case analyses that we conducted. However, we considered that more detailed guidance was needed, and more issues should be highlighted. Accordingly, we developed a set of procedures that aimed to be comprehensive and relevant to the issues we personally (and professionally) consider to be important on the basis of the research that we conducted. At the same time, they attempt to operationalize in a reasonable way the sentiments and concerns expressed in the general (nonhypnotic) literature about professionalism and the need for application of ethical practices.

The guidelines that we adopted in the cases to follow are set out in this chapter. The full set can be compared by the reader with other existing sets. However, it seems instructive at the outset to summarize the major features that differentiate them from other guidelines that are available, particularly with respect to their greater detail and explicitness.

Under this new set, prime focus is placed on the welfare of the subject, this issue being addressed at several different points in our guidelines: the roles of the hypnotist and the coordinator of the session are defined and demarcated more closely, the hypnosis coordinator being seen to be a useful additional mechanism; the skills that health professionals who are police may bring to a forensic setting are highlighted more obviously; procedures are related more broadly to the forensic system as a whole (e.g., the flow-on consequences of forensic procedures are recognized), and offer particular guidance on interactions with police and the legal system; greater attention is paid to the rights of all participants (including the subject); special attention is paid to the status of the person hypnotized and to the possibility that such status (e.g., victim, witness, or defendant) may change during a forensic session; more guidance on procedures is given relating to the obligations remaining for the hypnotist after the session has concluded. Finally, the scope of technological requirements for conducting a well-recorded session are outlined more specifically. We return to discriminating features in Chapter 10.

GUIDELINES FOR THE FORENSIC USE OF HYPNOSIS

General Issues

1. The use of hypnosis should be consistent with existing government legislation relevant to hypnosis.

2. The use of hypnosis should be consistent with significant legal judgments relevant to hypnosis in the country in which hypnosis is practiced.

3. The use of hypnosis should be consistent with clinical and legal safeguards designed to ensure the well-being of the subject and others involved.

4. Hypnosis should not be used with very young children.

5. The use of hypnosis primarily assists an investigation by eliciting additional information that can be followed up. Its use is not to elicit material that cannot be corroborated in any way, such as emotions, feelings, opinions, and guesses. Independent corroboration is defined as evidence that confirms in a clear and unequivocal way the fact that the crime at issue has been committed and/or that the accused has committed it. In some instances, corroboration is required by case law, whereas in others it may be required by statute law. Corroboration can take the form of a document, or other material evidence, but may encompass witness testimony provided such can be shown to be reliable. Verbal testimony, where clear cut and reliable, is acceptable (but it should be noted that the evidence of accomplices is likely to be unreliable, as also is the evidence of very young children).

6. The primary client in forensic interactions involving the subject is the person being hypnotized.

The Hypnosis Coordinator

1. The hypnosis coordinator should be professionally trained in a relevant discipline and should be familiar with hypnosis and its use in the forensic setting. He or she should serve as the link between the investigating officers and the hypnotist, and primarily should be responsible for ensuring that all guidelines are followed and all safeguards are in place. Most police forces do not have a coordinator and it is recognized that hypnosis may have to be practiced when the hypnotist is alone.

2. The hypnosis coordinator should have access to senior officers inside the police department and to hypnosis experts outside the department. He or she should have no involvement in the particular investigation, other than coordinating the use of hypnosis, and have no conflict of interest in the case by way of being employed by any associated institution or agency.

3. The hypnosis coordinator should be able to provide a clear statement of the rationale for using, or not using, hypnosis

and of the investigative and legal limitations and complications of using hypnosis in any particular case.

4. The hypnosis coordinator should establish with the investigating officers that all standard investigative procedures have been employed in the case prior to considering the use of hypnosis with any particular subject.

5. The investigating officers should contact the hypnosis coordinator about the use of hypnosis. The hypnosis coordinator should make an initial assessment about the use of hypnosis in the case.

6. The hypnosis coordinator should contact the hypnotist and provide a written summary on the case and the subject in relation to the goals of the hypnosis session. This summary should contain only enough detail for the hypnotist to make an informed decision about involvement and/or procedures to use. It should not contain so much detail that it is likely to influence the specific features of the hypnosis session or lead the hypnotist to suggest possible information or misinformation to the subject.

7. The hypnosis coordinator should contact the investigating officers and arrange for the subject to attend for a hypnosis session. The hypnotist should have no contact with the investigating officers or with the subject prior to the hypnosis session.

8. The hypnotist should consult with the hypnosis coordinator as to whether hypnosis should be used.

The Hypnotist

1. The hypnotist should be a qualified and registered medical practitioner or psychologist.

2. The hypnotist should have specific training and experience in hypnosis that is consistent with the requirements for full membership of the Australian Society of Hypnosis (or its national equivalent elsewhere).

3. The hypnotist should have a detailed understanding of the investigative and legal issues relevant to the use of hypnosis and have training and experience, if possible, in the application of forensic procedures.

4. The hypnotist may, as a health professional, be a member of the police department or may be independent of the depart-

ment. However, he or she should have no involvement in the investigation other than the use of hypnosis.

5. The hypnotist should be satisfied that the use of hypnosis is appropriate. The final decision to use, or not use, hypnosis should be made by the hypnotist following an assessment of the suitability of the subject during a prehypnotic interview.

6. The hypnotist should have the ultimate right to terminate the session at any time in respect of the needs of the subject rather than the needs of the investigation. The well-being and legal rights of the subject should be the overriding factors in any decisions that the hypnotist makes before, during, or after the hypnosis session.

7. Discussion should occur with the subject about who he or she considers an appropriate hypnotist. Such discussion should encompass issues such as gender and perceived similarities between the hypnotist and the accused.

8. The hypnotist should declare any perceived or real conflict of interest. If such exists (i.e., there is conflict of interest), another person should take over the role of the hypnotist.

9. The formal allegiance of the hypnotist should be understood clearly at the outset of the case.

Type of Crime

1. The use of hypnosis should be considered in the investigation of major crimes only, and only after existing leads and standard investigation procedures have been followed. Endorsement of the use of hypnosis in minor crimes will lead to a proliferation of the use of hypnosis when hypnosis may not at all be necessary, alternative procedures being more desirable.

2. The use of hypnosis may be considered when it is thought likely that the subject can provide additional information that could assist the investigation in a meaningful way. For example, when an effort at the scene of the crime has been made to try and remember information, hypnosis may provide additional motivation to enhance retrieval.

3. Hypnosis should not be used in the investigation of any crime (e.g., child sexual abuse) if it is seen at the outset that its use will add substantial complications to the investigative and/or legal proceedings. When evidence exists, for example, to confirm that sexual abuse has occurred, the introduction of hypnosis may confound investigation by confusing fantasy and reality.

Type of Subject

1. The use of hypnosis should be considered usually with victims and witnesses of crimes; only under unusual circumstances should it be considered with suspects or defendants. If a witness appears to change status during a hypnosis session, then the session should be terminated. Hypnosis should be terminated, for example, if a witness signals culpability of the crime during the hypnosis session.

2. The use of hypnosis should be undertaken with great caution when the victim or witness is a juvenile.

3. Hypnosis should not be used with infants or young children under any circumstances. Testimony by young children can be especially unreliable.

4. The subject should have no history of significant medical or psychological conditions that contraindicate the use of hypnosis (e.g., depression). The subject should not have been experiencing any significant abnormal physical or mental effects (e.g., hallucinations) at the time of the to-be-remembered event, because that would make it unlikely that the event had been adequately encoded or stored in memory. At all times, the hypnotist should follow reasonable procedures to minimize the possibility that the use of hypnosis will have an appreciable negative effect on the subject.

5. The subject should be able to give informed consent to the use of hypnosis (see suggestions for its use later in this chapter) and should be informed about his or her clinical and legal rights. This should be done at the outset of the session, and the subject should have a clear understanding that he or she can withdraw from the session at any time.

6. The well-being and legal rights of the subject should be a major concern of the hypnotist. At all times, he or she should take care that the investigative intent of the hypnosis session does not place the well-being or legal rights of the subject in appreciable jeopardy.

Procedures of the Hypnosis Session

1. The hypnosis session should be conducted in a relatively quiet, comfortable setting. All interactions between the hypnotist and the subject should occur in that setting, and should be

videorecorded; this should apply to interactions before, during, and after the actual hypnosis.

2. Normally, only the hypnotist and subject should be present in the setting, but there may be exceptions, depending on the special circumstances of the case. It may be necessary, for example, for a parent or guardian to be present if the subject is a juvenile. It may be permissible for others (e.g., police artist, recording technician) to be present during the hypnosis session, but only for brief periods and never without the hypnotist.

3. The hypnosis coordinator and investigating officers should be able to view the hypnosis session through a one-way screen or via a videomonitor. Other persons (e.g., legal representative) may view the session if special circumstances require this. In some circumstances, it would also be permissible for the hypnosis coordinator to communicate with the hypnotist through an earpiece worn by the hypnotist. The hypnosis coordinator should, however, minimize comments to the hypnotist, and should also make a written record of the time and content of those comments.

4. At the beginning of the session, the hypnotist should begin the videorecording and state the date, time, place, name of subject, and his or her own name. The hypnotist should then wait for the hypnosis coordinator to accompany the subject to the hypnosis setting and introduce the hypnotist to the subject.

5. Initially, the hypnotist should outline the structure of the session to the subject, indicate that the session is being videorecorded, and obtain a written and videorecorded informed consent from the subject for the session to proceed. The hypnotist should make it clear that the subject is not required to proceed with hypnosis, and that the subject may request that the hypnosis session be terminated at any time.

6. The hypnotist should conduct his or her own assessment of the subject's medical and/or psychological suitability for the use of hypnosis.

7. The hypnotist should conduct an assessment of the subject's recall of the to-be-remembered events by asking the subject to give a free narrative of those events. The hypnotist should explore in a nonleading way the recollections reported by the subject. The hypnotist should use nonhypnotic techniques (e.g., repeated recall) to facilitate the subject's recollections at this point.

8. The hypnotist should then make a final decision to use, or not use, hypnosis. If the hypnotist decides to use hypnosis,

then he or she should elicit the subject's expectations and preconceptions about hypnosis and the effect of hypnosis on memory. The hypnotist should clarify any misconceptions and indicate to the subject that hypnosis may or may not facilitate recall of the to-be-remembered events.

9. The hypnotist should use an appropriate hypnotic induction procedure (one that employs a standard procedure for induction and tests responsivity to suggestion across a range of hypnotic tasks varying in difficulty). The subject's responsiveness to hypnosis should be tested on selected hypnotizability tasks of known difficulty level.

10. Following this, the hypnotist should assess the subject's general recall of the to-be-remembered events by asking the subject to give a free narrative of those events. The hypnotist may choose to do this with or without the use of a suggestion for age regression, or other suggestions for memory enhancement. The hypnotist should explore in a nonleading way any recollections reported by the subject.

11. After exploring the narrative offered by the subject, the hypnotist should ask specific but nonleading questions. The hypnotist should indicate to the subject that the response "I don't know" is an acceptable one to his or her specific questions.

12. After asking specific questions, the hypnotist should give the subject the opportunity to comment on anything that he or she wishes.

13. The hypnotist should use appropriate procedures to cancel any suggestions given during the session, and should use an appropriate deinduction procedure to end the hypnosis session.

14. Following hypnosis, the hypnotist should ask the subject to comment on his or her recall of the to-be-remembered events during hypnosis. The hypnotist should determine what impact the subject thinks hypnosis may have had on his or her recollections of the target event.

15. At the end of the session, the hypnosis coordinator should enter the setting and escort the subject to the investigating officers. The hypnotist should finally state the date, time, place, name of subject, and his or her own name, and then end the videorecording.

16. The hypnotist should follow reasonable procedures to ensure that any clinical follow-up needed by the subject is arranged. However, the hypnotist should not provide that clinical follow-up.

Technical Issues

1. An appropriate high-quality video system should be used to record the hypnosis session. The minimum equipment is a videocamera, videocassette recorder, a videomonitor, and microphones for both the hypnotist and the subject. Preferably, two videocassette recorders should be used, so that two copies of the videotape (one for the hypnosis coordinator, and one for the hypnotist) can be made while the session is being conducted. It is essential that the microphones be of high quality, and preferably be lapel microphones.

2. An appropriate communication system between the hypnosis coordinator and the hypnotist may be needed in some circumstances. A transmitter for the hypnosis coordinator and a small receiver and earpiece for the hypnotist would be suitable if needed.

3. The lighting and noise levels of the hypnosis setting should be such that they do not interfere with the recording of the session.

4. The time should be recorded onto the videotape either through electronic means in the videocamera itself, or through the presence of an appropriate clock, with seconds display, in the setting. Both the hypnotist and the subject should be present in the scene being recorded and should be recorded at all times when together.

5. All technical aspects of the session should be checked in advance of the hypnosis session by an appropriate technician. They should be checked also by the hypnotist and the hypnosis coordinator immediately prior to the session.

6. The hypnotist should not proceed with the session unless satisfied that all guidelines are being met and all safeguards are in place.

Evaluation of the Hypnosis Session

1. The hypnosis coordinator should discuss the hypnosis session with the investigating officers and ensure that they understand the limitations of any additional material that is reported by the subject. The need to approach this additional material as leads, rather than as either facts or fantasies, should be emphasized.

2. The hypnotist should prepare a written report of the hypnosis session that provides details on the rationale and limitations of the procedures and techniques used. The hypnotist should note especially any deviations from these guidelines, and should record the reasons for any such departures.

3. The hypnotist should ensure that his or her copy of all materials associated with the hypnosis session are stored in a secure location.

4. It should be a matter of informed judgment as to whether a copy of the videotape of the session be forwarded to the subject when the session has concluded. This release recognizes the rights of the subject, but there are risks involved in the subject being subsequently exposed to events that may be stressful.

5. In overall evaluation of the session or interactions with the subject, care should be taken to determine whether the hypnotic reports of the subject are genuine or faked.

6. The hypnotist should prepare a formal statement on the use of hypnosis if such a statement is subsequently required in any legal proceedings.

7. The hypnotist should attend court and testify if required to do so in any legal proceedings.

GUIDELINES RELATING
TO RECOVERED MEMORIES

Specific guidelines are also needed to set forth information and recommendations designed to assist clinicians who are dealing with reports of recovered memories. Their relevance and importance were signaled earlier by us in the case reported in Chapter 2. In many respects, guidelines for procedures related to recovered memories can be regarded as a subset of the procedures we have advocated previously in our general guidelines for forensic hypnosis. For example, procedures in common are those related to informed consent, guarantee of proper qualifications and training, avoidance of leading suggestions, evaluation of susceptibility to hypnosis, as well as maintenance of proper records of what occurs in the sessions. Listed next are matters that relate specifically to recovered memories associated with especially strong emotion and those related to the distant past. In formulation of these guidelines, however, we have anticipated the relevance of the experimental evidence reviewed by us in Chapter

9. The guidelines in the form in which they appear here were the basis of those adopted by the Australian Psychological Society (1995; see also McConkey, 1995) and have been used in legal cases in Australia in 1994 and 1995. Our commentary is embedded into the guidelines to emphasize their rationale.

Overview

Generalizing across from the guidelines for the forensic use of hypnosis to these guidelines relating to recovered memories, it is particularly important to obtain informed consent regarding the therapeutic procedures, record intact memories at the beginning of therapy, be familiar with research in memory and hypnosis, clarify with a subject that he or she is responsible for the reported accuracy of memories (not the therapist), and be aware of possible biases in this area regarding the accuracy or inaccuracy of recovered memories of traumatic events. In making these comments, we are aware that research is needed to understand more about trauma-related memory, techniques to enhance memory of the distant past, and techniques to deal effectively with childhood sexual abuse. Further comment on this is given in Chapter 9, where relevant evidence is reviewed in some detail.

A Scientific Perspective on Memory and Abuse

Memory is a constructive and reconstructive process. What is remembered about an event is shaped by what was observed of that event, by conditions prevailing during attempts to remember, and by events occurring between the observation and the attempted remembering. It is important to note that memories can be altered, deleted, and created by events that occur during and after the time of encoding, during the period of storage, and during any attempts at retrieval.

Memory is integral to many approaches to therapy. Repression and dissociation are processes central to some theories and approaches to therapy. According to these theories and approaches, memories of traumatic events may be blocked out unconsciously, and this leads to a person having no memory of the events. However, memories of these traumatic events may become accessible at some later time. Although some clinical observations support the notion of repressed memories, empirical research on memory generally does not. The scientific evidence does not allow global statements to be made about a definite relationship between trauma and memory.

"Memories" that are reported either spontaneously or following the use of special procedures in therapy may be accurate, inaccurate, fabricated, or a mixture of these. The presence or absence of detail in a memory report does not necessarily mean that it is accurate or inaccurate. The level of belief in memory or the emotion associated with the memory does not necessarily relate directly to the accuracy of the memory. The available scientific and clinical evidence does not allow accurate, inaccurate, and fabricated memories to be distinguished in the absence of independent corroboration.

It is established by scientific evidence that sexual and/or physical abuse against children and adults is typically destructive of mental health, self-esteem, and personal relationships. It is also the case that people who suffer these experiences may use various psychological mechanisms to reduce the psychological severity of the painful events in an attempt to help them cope with the experience and its consequences.

Just as clinicians should be familiar with this evidence, so should they recognize that reports of abuse long after the events are reported to have occurred are difficult to prove or disprove in the majority of cases. Independent corroboration of the statements of those who make or deny such allegations is typically difficult, if not impossible (see general guidelines for definition of corroboration). Accordingly, clinicians should exercise special care in dealing with clients, their family members, and the wider community when allegations of past abuse are made.

Clinical Issues

1. Clinicians should evaluate critically their assumptions or biases about attempts to recover memories of trauma-related events. Equally, they should assist clients to understand any assumptions that they have about repressed or recovered memories. Assumptions that adult problems may or may not be associated with repressed memories from childhood cannot be addressed by existing scientific evidence.

2. Clinicians should be alert to the ways in which they may unintentionally overlook or minimize reports of experiences of

abuse or other events that may have had a significant impact on a client. They should also be alert to the ways that they can shape the reported memories of clients through the expectations they convey, the comments they make, the questions they ask, and the responses they give. Clinicians should be alert to the fact that clients are susceptible to subtle suggestions and reinforcements, whether those communications are intended or unintended. Therefore, they should record intact memories at the beginning of therapy, and be aware of any possible effects from outside the therapeutic setting (e.g., self-help groups, popular books, films, and television programs).

3. Clinicians should be alert not to dismiss memories that may be based in fact. Equally, they should be alert to the role that they may play in creating or shaping false memories. At all times, they should be empathic and supportive of the reports of clients while also ensuring that clients do not jump to conclusions about the truth or falsity of their recollections of the past. They should also ensure that alternative causes of any problems that are reported are explored. It should be recognized that the *context* of therapy is important as is its *content*.

4. Clinicians should not avoid asking clients about the possibility of sexual or other abusive occurrences in their past if such a question is relevant to the problem being treated. However, clinicians should be cautious in interpreting the response that is given. They should not assume the accuracy or inaccuracy of any report of recovered memory.

5. The needs and well-being of clients are the clinician's essential focus, and therapeutic interventions should be designed accordingly. Relatedly, it should be recognized that therapeutic interventions may have an indirect impact on people other than the client being treated. Clinicians should seek to meet the needs of clients who report memories of abuse and should do this quite apart from the truth or falsity of those reports. They should be cautious about conveying statements about the accuracy of memory reports given by their clients. In particular, it is necessary to understand clearly the difference between narrative truth and historical truth, and the relevance of this difference inside and outside the therapy context. Memory reports as part of a personal narrative can be helpful in therapy independent of the accuracy of those reports, but to be accepted as accurate in another setting (e.g., court of law), those reports will need to be shown to be accurate.

Ethical Issues

1. Clinicians treating clients who report recovered memories of abuse are expected to observe the ethical standards of their professional association and licensing body. In particular, they should obtain informed consent at the beginning of therapy in relation to the therapeutic procedures and process.

2. For any client who reports recovering a memory of abuse, it is necessary to explore whether that report is an accurate memory of an actual event, an altered or distorted memory of an actual event, or a false memory of an event that did not happen. Clinicians should explore with the client the meaning and implications of the memory for the client, rather than focus solely on the content of the reported memory. They should explore with the client ways of determining the accuracy of the memory, if appropriate.

3. Clinicians should be alert particularly to the need to maintain appropriate skills and learning in this area, and should be aware of the relevant scientific evidence and clinical standards of practice. When appropriate, they should refer the client to a colleague who is especially skilled and experienced in dealing with issues in this area. Specifically, it is necessary to guard against accepting approaches to abuse and therapy that are not based in scientific evidence and appropriate clinical standards.

4. Clinicians should be alert also to the personal responsibility they hold for the foreseeable consequence of their actions.

Legal Issues

1. Childhood or adult sexual abuse, or abuse of any kind, should not be tolerated in any way. Clinicians should ensure that their services are used appropriately in this regard, and should be alert to problems of deciding whether allegations of abuse are true or false. They should be alert especially to the different demands and processes of the therapeutic and legal contexts in dealing with such allegations.

2. Some approaches and writings concerning abuse and recovered memories urge people who report recovered memories to pursue legal action of various types. Given that the accuracy of memories cannot be determined without corroboration, cli-

nicians should use caution in responding to questions from clients about pursuing legal action.

3. Clinicians should be aware that their knowledge, skills, and practices may come under close scrutiny by various public and private agencies if they are treating clients who report recovering memories of abuse. They should ensure that comprehensive records are maintained about their sessions with clients who report recovering such memories.

AN EXAMPLE OF INFORMED CONSENT PROCEDURES

Relevant to both our general guidelines and the guidelines related to recovered memories are procedures associated with informed consent. They are an important part of any forensic session. There are many possible varieties of pro forma procedures for informed consent and the exact form that is used will need to reflect the particular setting in which hypnosis will be conducted. All pro forma procedures, however, should attempt to cover or address the following points:

1. The client should be informed regarding the aim of the session being conducted. The client should have a clear understanding of why hypnosis is being used and what is the reason the hypnotist, in particular, is using hypnosis.

2. The client should be asked to indicate by signature whether he or she is willing for hypnosis to be used.

3. The client must be free to withdraw from the session or stop the session at any time. Consent relates not only to the session commencement, but also to its progress through time.

4. There should be a clear understanding on the client's part of all technical aspects of the session, for example, who is watching the session (and why) and the procedural aspects of the communication that has been established (e.g., the hypnotist can communicate with viewers at any time and vice versa).

5. The uses to which material collected in the session may be put should be understood by the client at the outset. He or she should know, for instance, that police may have access to what is reported, as also may those involved legally in the case.

6. It should be understood by the client before hypnosis is introduced that the prime concern of the hypnotist is with the welfare of the subject.

7. Before the hypnotic session commences, the client should understand that set procedures are being followed in the case, and that the conduct of the session will be in accord with a formal code of ethical professional conduct.

Finally, other issues also need to be canvased in therapists' interactions with their clients. These include possible negative legal effects if hypnosis is used, the rights of the parties involved and the conditions of release from liability, the nature of the provision of clinical follow-up, and the formation of a mutual understanding on fees.

We move now to discuss two cases in which we conducted the hypnosis sessions, and in which we attempted to apply the guidelines summarized in this chapter.

Motivation and Manipulation in Hypnosis

In the cases presented in this chapter, we conducted the hypnosis sessions following a formal request from the police physician who had evaluated the cases and the possible use of hypnosis prior to contacting us. As will be seen, both of the cases highlighted difficulties and unanticipated events. There are many choices that need to be made by the expert who enters the forensic system, and those choices do not always sit comfortably with the decisions that the expert may make when operating outside it. The rules change when one enters the forensic system, and knowing those rules and how to operate under the formal and informal structures that turn those rules into forensic practice is critical.

THE CASE OF HL

HL was murdered in August 1988, when he arrived home around midnight after attending a dinner party with his wife (BL). After parking the car in the garage, HL took the garbage to the street and BL entered the house. At the front of his house, HL was shot in the back at point-blank range and died within 10 minutes without speaking.

He was a semiretired businessman and had been married to BL for approximately 25 years. They had three adult children

and were active members of the Italian community in the city in which they lived. They spoke Italian at home and with other members of the Italian community; they spoke English when interacting with others. HL had been associated with various businesses over the years and was still associated with a group that invested in diverse business ventures.

Apart from the assailant, there were no witnesses to the shooting. The first person to reach HL after the shooting was his wife, and the second person was their son (PL). Neighbors and another son were also on the scene within minutes. However, the "witnesses" to the events immediately before and after the crime were BL, who had driven onto the property with her husband, and PL, who was in the kitchen of the house when his mother and father arrived home.

Approximately 6 weeks after the murder of HL, the investigation of the crime had virtually come to a halt. The investigating officers had interviewed HL's family members and business associates in an attempt to establish motives and leads. They had also interviewed neighbors and door-knocked the neighborhood in an attempt to determine whether anyone had seen unfamiliar people or vehicles in the area, either in the days preceding, or on the night of the murder. The officers had exhausted all their usual avenues of inquiry.

The officers approached the police physician to ask whether hypnosis could help BL recall additional information about the night of the murder. They reported that BL had recalled only general information about the night, and was having difficulty remembering and/or relating details that were associated with various things that she had seen or heard. For instance, she had recalled seeing an unfamiliar car parked in a street near their home, and had thought it unusual for that time in a neighborhood where people typically parked in garages; however, BL had not been able to recall any details of the car. The officers were interested also in whether hypnosis might help BL remember more details of a visit at home by one of her husband's business associates (KB) and his wife approximately 3 weeks after the murder. The officers were interested in this because, although BL had described the visit in general terms, she had become distraught when trying to relate the details of the visit.

The physician reviewed the file on the investigation, discussed with the officers the possibility of using hypnosis with BL, reviewed the medical and psychological information available about BL, and recommended that hypnosis be used in an attempt to assist her to recall information that might be relevant to the investigation. We were contacted and requested to undertake investigative hypnosis. The hypnosis coordinator was given the details of the crime and some personal details of BL. On the basis of this information, a brief memorandum was prepared for the hypnotist. It was then agreed to conduct the session on the understanding that all interactions with BL would be videorecorded and that all decisions about what to do and say in the session would be the responsibility of the hypnotist.

The Hypnosis Session with BL

Six weeks after the murder, the hypnosis session was conducted in a room that was designed for the videorecording of clinical or forensic sessions. Only the hypnotist and BL were present in the prehypnotic, hypnotic, and posthypnotic parts of the session. The investigating officers, an assistant to the hypnotist, and a technician were in an adjoining room and watched the session on a videomonitor. The assistant could speak to the hypnotist through an earpiece that the hypnotist was wearing.

Almost immediately upon being introduced to the hypnotist, BL became distraught and displayed strong emotion at the mention of her husband. She said, "It would be easier to be with my husband, and not have to go through all of this. I can't stand the pain any more." This comment set the stage for the establishment of a close relationship between BL and the hypnotist. It was clear from early in the session that not only was BL seeking to assist the investigation, but also she was looking to the hypnotist for clinical support and guidance. In response to this, the hypnotist presented the session as a chance to "do something to ease the pain," as well as an opportunity to "help out the police." Throughout the session, the hypnotist was often placed in a situation in which he had to provide clinical support when BL was relating emotionally upsetting information.

The hypnotist and BL discussed three major events: (1) the car parked in a nearby street; (2) the shooting of HL; and (3) the visit of KB. These events were discussed before hypnosis, during hypnosis, and after hypnosis. We turn now to consider these events, summarize the essential information, and point to major themes reflected in the information.

Before hypnosis, BL reported that she thought an unfamiliar car was parked in a street not far from her house. However, she commented, "I was asked by the police if there were any cars on the road . . . so this could all be in my imagination." Before hypnosis, BL gave little detail about this car, other than it was smaller and darker than the car that her husband drove. In contrast, during age regression to the time when she and her husband were driving along that street, BL provided numerous details about the size and shape of the car, the size and shape of the headlights and the taillights, and the colors of the car. For instance, she said:

> I think the top was a different color, a lighter color, a lot lighter on top than on the bottom. I think it was brown on the bottom, and a lighter color, not white, on top; maybe light brown or cream. There was something about the wheels, funny wheels, spoked wire wheels. I can't remember if they were shiny.

This additional detail needs to be considered in light of BL's comments after hypnosis, however, when she repeated the details but added that she had "seen a similar car since" that night and noted that the subsequent car was a "funny looking" one. She also commented that during hypnosis, the car and all the details about it "came to mind as if I was just driving past it," although she commented also that the "car must have been there for me to have noticed [it]." In this sense, BL appeared to have been acknowledging both the possible reality and fantasy aspects of her memory of the car. It is this possibility that in part justifies the practice of the guidelines set out in Chapter 3 that insist on a prehypnosis test of recall. If prehypnosis and hypnosis are the same in mixing fantasy and reality, then occurrence of such a mix in hypnosis cannot, in fact, be attributed to hypnotic processes per se.

Before hypnosis, BL described the drive home from the dinner party and commented that they were both relieved to arrive home. After parking the car, her husband took the garbage to the street for collection and she went inside the house, where she found her son in the kitchen preparing his lunch for the next day. BL recounted how they heard a loud noise and they both ran outside. She said that she saw HL on the ground and shouted to her son, "Call an ambulance, your father's had a heart attack!" She added that her son "ran out to the back gate," and so she again shouted, "Go and call an ambulance!" BL described how she then went to her husband. Her next memory was of a police officer taking her inside the house about 20 minutes later and telling her that her husband had been shot.

During hypnosis, BL's behavior in recounting this event was characterized by extreme emotion that was abreactive in nature. She spoke in the present tense, and often did not appear to be aware of the presence of the hypnotist. During age regression, she described driving onto the property, and said, "Thank God we're home." BL went on without direction or input from the hypnotist, who let her continue without interruption during this compelling display of hypnotic regression. As she entered the house, she said to her son, "Put the light on for your father. Your father's coming inside in a minute. Did you get your lunch?" She then physically startled, and shouted out, "Your father's had a heart attack!"

Crying, BL said, "HL, HL, wake up darling . . . wake up, the ambulance is coming . . . wake up darling," and reached out as if to stroke someone. After BL shouted for her husband a couple of more times, the hypnotist intervened in an attempt to assist her with the emotion that she was experiencing, and gave a number of supportive suggestions for coping with the loss of her husband; BL then quieted considerably. Although this ventilation of feelings may have had some therapeutic benefits, it provided no additional information about the shooting.

In the prehypnotic interview, the comments of BL were characterized by general statements about the visit of KB, an associate of her husband. In explaining why she was upset about the visit and thought that "he should have come earlier," BL explained that she and her husband often referred to KB as *compare*, which she said was a term that was used as a "sign of respect for someone who is closer than a close friend." During age regression to the time of the visit, BL reported events in substantially more detail, using both the present and the past tense and speaking in both English and Italian. BL reported that while KB's wife was giving displays of affection for HL, by crying and saying things like, "Everybody loved him, everybody respected him. How could anybody do it?", KB took her to one side and asked a number of questions. When reporting these questions and answers during hypnosis, BL spoke in Italian (which the hypnotist could neither speak nor understand) in the same manner that she and KB had spoken at the time of the visit. KB asked BL if she knew anything about who had shot HL or why he had been shot, and he also asked her what the police had said to her about the shooting.

While describing the visit during hypnotic regression, BL also spontaneously mentioned the funeral of her husband and commented on two aspects of it. First, she was angered that KB had not attended the funeral, especially when HL had been on a 2-day trip with KB a few days before he was shot. KB's absence from the funeral confused her about her feelings toward KB and his involvement with her husband. Second, she repeated for the hypnotist some advice that her husband's brother had given her immediately after the funeral, when those who attended the funeral were gathered at her house. She reported that he had said, "We don't know who did this to HL. Don't say nothing to nobody. Don't trust anybody, don't talk to anybody. The animal who did this to him could have been at the funeral. He could be in this house. He could have come up and shook my hand. Don't say anything except to the police. Don't tell anyone anything the police tell you."

Evaluation of the Hypnosis Session with BL

BL was a cooperative subject who was keen to assist and was capable of vivid, intense involvement, which was triggered by feelings of anguish that were nearly always at the threshold of expression. The overall degree of detail that was evident in BL's recall was notable, whether hypnosis was involved or not. Strikingly, it seemed that the context of the session as a whole, the expectations of BL, and the clinical approach of the hypnotist allowed BL either to recall or to relate more detail than she had reported to the investigating officers.

The accuracy of this detail, however, is a separate matter, and there is strong reason to doubt the reliability of some of it. For example, although BL reported additional details about the car parked in the nearby street, she was not sure that the car as reported by her was actually seen by her. She commented, for instance, that she may have imagined it in response to the police asking her questions about cars in the area. Her recall of the car was complicated further by the fact that she saw a car afterward that she said looked the same. Although BL reported additional details of the car during hypnosis (e.g., size and shape of headlights and taillights, spiked wheels), the interpretation of this detail is quite problematic. BL had at least three impressions (the car in the street, thinking about the car when asked by police, and seeing the car afterward) and these impressions potentially competed with and interfered with each other. The problems of interpreting the information about the car were compounded further by the fact that BL was uncertain even after hypnosis. Although hypnosis can reduce uncertainty and promote confidence in remembered material at times (for review of the evidence in this respect, see Chapter 9), enhanced confidence was not at all evident in BL's comments about the car.

A high level of emotion characterized BL's memory reporting overall, and especially her recall of the death of her husband. The possibility of some overplaying the role of distraught widow, or even simulation of the emotion, cannot be discounted. For instance, when commenting during hypnotic regression about her husband's death, BL tracked through the sequence of events and reported information almost "frame by frame" as if the events were occurring in the immediate present. Verbally, and in some aspects, physically, BL presented an instance of age regression to a traumatic event as if it were occurring in the present. In contrast, BL's recall of the visit of KB was characterized by a narrative reporting rather than a presentation of sensorily immediate events, and her recollections were reported in a relatively passive way. This difference in style of reporting may have been either because of her different involvement in these hypnotic regressions, or because of the different role that was played by the hypnotist. For the shooting, the hypnotist allowed BL to describe the events in an uninterrupted manner and provided clinical support. In contrast, for the visit, the hypnotist asked a series of questions to assist BL to recall the conversation that occurred during the visit of KB. In describing this visit, BL showed relatively little emotion and her recall was relatively depersonalized.

Perhaps the most striking difference between BL's recall of the shooting and her recall of the visit was her use of Italian. (After the session, we had the Italian translated to English to allow analysis.) When BL started speaking in Italian, the hypnotist did not interrupt but permitted her to continue with this mode of communication. The hypnotist did not communicate to BL that he could neither speak nor understand Italian. Rather, he responded to BL in English by using nonspecific phrases (e.g., "What happened then?"; "Go on"; "Tell me more about that"). The shifting of BL to Italian raised the possibility that this gave her protection from the scrutiny of the hypnotist, reduced the pressures for compliance by distancing her from the specific questions of the hypnotist, and allowed her to be as involved as she was ready, willing, and able to be. The style and nature of her recall about the visit of KB indicated that some degree of defensiveness was present in reporting the association of her husband and KB. However, the situation was structured by BL in a way that partially resolved this defensiveness. Namely, BL achieved involvement by speaking in Italian, and this possibly satisfied a felt need for cooperation and for relatively uninhibited comment to be made. It is arguable that much less detail about the visit would have been offered by BL if the hypnotist had not allowed her to speak in Italian.

BL's hypnotic recall of the visit appeared to provide more detail than that of the shooting of her husband, and this was probably because the emotion surrounding the shooting was so extreme. The hypnotic recall of the shooting and the visit, however, did not assist the investigation in any major way. For the shooting, BL's expression of deep feeling was the major aspect of her reporting and no additional information that would offer leads for the investigation seemed to be produced. Clearly, a distinction can be drawn in this case between emotionally driven memories and memories that are driven in other ways. It is interesting to speculate whether the same scenario that unfolded here would have unfolded if the hypnotist had spoken or understood Italian, and this fact had been recognized by BL. It is likely that a very different kind of hypnotic interaction would have then occurred. Perhaps, also, a greater knowledge of Italian culture would have assisted the hypnotist in structuring the session, and such knowledge might have helped the hypnotist respond to the information given by BL during the session. It is an open question, of course, as to whether this strategy would have led to additional information being provided by BL. In hindsight, it is also important to consider that the hypnotist used in this case should have been fluent in Italian. In that instance, interactions with the subject might well have been different and might have elicited other information.

This case illustrated a general need to specifically inform the hypnotist before the session commences about relevant details of the case as a whole, rather than simple factual information about the major events. Such information should not encourage the hypnotist to hold any single hypothesis about the events to be remembered, but it would allow him or her to have sufficient background to explore multiple possibilities in a meaningful way. For instance, it would have been useful in this case for the hypnotist to have had some information about which aspects, if any, of the visit of KB to explore in more detail. Also, further background about the multiple roles that BL had to fulfill (e.g., good wife, dutiful wife, witness to a shooting, and good hypnotic subject) and any possible conflict among those roles might have assisted the hypnotist in shaping his method of interacting with BL.

Although the hypnotist did not test BL on any standard measures of hypnotizability because of her extreme emotion, she gave a display of hypnotic regression that seemingly pointed to a capacity for intense role involvement and absorption in emotionally engaging events. The nature of this display stemmed very probably from a motivation to meet therapeutic needs to abreact, and her performance in the session overall was characterized by her ready disposition to relive the trauma of her husband's death, which was something that she had not yet worked through at a personal level. At the end of the session, there was a clear need for therapeutic follow-up, which was arranged by the police physician who was overseeing the use of hypnosis in the case as a whole. At the end of the session, BL showed signs of unresolved grief and emotional lability and was still deeply distressed by her husband's death. She continued to express conflict about her own feelings, and appeared to lack the capacity and social support to resolve her personal situation without professional assistance.

The Hypnosis Session with PL

Approximately 6 weeks after the hypnosis session with BL, the son who was in the kitchen at the time of the shooting approached the investigating officers with a request that he be hypnotized so that he could remember more details of the night of the shooting. Up to this point in the investigation, PL had provided little information about the night of the shooting, but the information he had provided was consistent with that offered by his mother. When he approached the police at this stage, however, PL appeared to be convinced that he "knew more" than he could remember, and that he wanted hypnosis to bring that information to light. His expectation was that hypnosis would help him remember information that until this time he could not remember at all. PL said, in fact, that if the police did not arrange a hypnosis session for him, then he would arrange one independently so that he would remember information that would "help [the police] solve their case."

This was an unexpected turn of events, driven presumably by particular motives of PL. The exact nature of those motives, however, was unclear. As with BL, the investigating officers discussed the request for hypnosis with the police physician, who subsequently discussed it with us. PL had specifically requested that the hypnotist who had seen his mother be the one to conduct the session with him, because his mother had said that she trusted him. Argument can be made that hypnosis should not have been used with PL, because there was no indication that he had any additional information to report, and the use of hypnosis could have allowed him to either confabulate or alter his confidence in information that he wished to convey. Relatedly, the argument can be made also that the hypnotist who conducted the session with BL should not have conducted a hypnosis session with PL, because it was likely that his views of the case as a whole had been shaped by the information that he had been given by BL; moreover, PL could, in turn, have been influenced by his aware-ness of his mother's previous interactions with the investigative hypnotist. Despite these caveats, however, our view, and the view of the police physician, was to conduct a hypnosis session with PL. This decision was influenced in part by the fact that the investigation had not proceeded any further as a result of the information that had been provided by BL. It was influenced also by the fact that PL made it clear that he would arrange his own hypnosis session if his request was not granted. The realities of the forensic system are that difficult choices often have to be made. A consideration of the potential costs and benefits asso-ciated with undertaking hypnosis with PL suggested that the session should proceed, although PL's overall motives in wanting hypnosis remained somewhat unclear.

The location and structure of the hypnosis session with PL was the same as with BL. The same personnel were involved in both sessions, except that a different assistant to the hypnotist was involved. Shortly after being introduced to the hypnotist, PL stated that he had wanted hypnosis to be used with him so that he could "help the police" and specifically that, with hypnosis, he "might be able to remember hearing a noise or a sound or something. As far as I can work out the person [who shot my father] was probably there when I walked through the back gate [when I arrived home shortly before the shooting]." PL presented to the hypnotist with an apparent wish to convey a knowledge of crime and of being "street-smart." He was superficially aggressive, threatening, and demanding in his initial interactions with the hypnotist. For instance, PL commented, "He [the assailant] might have pulled the trigger on me, thinking

I was my father." The hypnotist and PL discussed two aspects of the evening: (1) the car parked nearby earlier in the evening; and (2) the shooting of HL. These aspects were discussed before hypnosis, during hypnosis, and after hypnosis.

In his prehypnotic interview, PL described how he had returned home about 45 minutes before his parents, and had noticed a car parked in front of a house a short way down the street. He said that it was an unfamiliar car, and after going inside his house, he watched as it drove slowly along the street and met a young woman who came out of a house on the opposite side of the street. PL said that he did not recognize the young woman or the man who was driving the car. He said that he then did some chores around the house and that he was in the kitchen preparing his lunch for the next day when he heard his father's car turn into the driveway. His description of the events from the time that his mother entered the kitchen were essentially similar to those given by BL. PL added, however, that he thought he "heard a car taking off just as I got to Dad" after he had been shot.

The behavior of the hypnotist with PL was strikingly different from that with BL. Whereas the hypnotist was gentle, sympathetic, and nondirective in his interactions with BL, he found himself more forceful and directive in his interactions with PL. In a number of ways, this behavior mirrored the behavior of the subject, and this was partly because PL seemed responsive only to a firmly authoritative approach. Following a standardized induction procedure, the hypnotist administered a suggestion for arm lowering. PL did not respond at all to this suggestion, however, until the hypnotist made further hypnosis contingent upon the subject displaying the experience of arm lowering; PL's arm then lowered immediately and quickly. The hypnotist then administered a suggestion for arm levitation and linked that suggestion to increased depth of hypnosis: "As your arm moves up more and more, you go deeper and deeper in hypnosis, further and further, more and more." The rapid speed with which PL responded to this suggestion could be said to have indicated that he was now eager to follow instructions, rather than to be experiencing any suggested effects. Moreover, it appeared that PL believed that responding quickly would convince the hypnotist that he was deeply hypnotized.

The hypnotic age regression of PL had none of the compelling qualities of that of his mother. PL, for example, talked quickly and in a relatively impersonal way. It appeared that he had almost a rehearsed script to follow. He seemed annoyed, for instance, when the hypnotist attempted to involve him more in the experiences of age regression by asking him about the movie he had seen before returning home on the night of his father's shooting. PL pointed out sharply that he could not remember anything about it, including its name or where he saw it. When talking about seeing the parked car, PL gave some additional information about the vehicle and about the people associated with it. He commented specifically and in detail on its color, shape, make, and likely model. Moreover, he gave five of the six characters that he said made up its registration number and indicated that he was certain about four of these five characters. The detail of this material was conveyed very confidently.

When talking about the shooting of his father, PL gave essentially the same information that he had given in the prehypnotic interview, but he was unemotional in his comments and some inconsistencies emerged. For instance, PL now said that his mother first attempted to call the ambulance, and that he made a second call to the ambulance and the police. PL provided relatively little information about the car that he thought he heard drive off shortly after his father was shot. He simply said, "I remember hearing a car taking off when I first got to my father." When the hypnotist asked PL to tell him more about that, PL said, "It sped off really quickly, it didn't screech when it took off. It just took off really quick. I can't remember if it was a car that was coming around the corner at the time, or if it was the person that did what they did to my father." The only impact of the hypnotic procedures on this aspect appeared to have been some degree of firming in PL's confidence that he had heard a car at that time. Before hypnosis, he thought he had heard one; during and after hypnosis, he now believed that he had heard it. Given that it seems unlikely that PL was experiencing hypnosis at the time, it is likely that this would have occurred following any procedure that legitimized, as it were, a shift in the confidence associated with memory reporting.

Evaluation of the Hypnosis Session with PL

PL's overall behavior during the hypnosis session did not convey a strong impression of involvement in hypnosis. He was distanced personally from his comments on the events, and he provided a narrative that was seemingly rehearsed and flat in affect. Given the overall approach that PL had to the hypnosis session and the nature of his interactions with the hypnotist, it is difficult to see the information that was provided by him as indicating anything other than confabulation. In essence, PL's hypnosis session appeared primarily to meet his needs, whatever those needs were, rather than to assist the investigation.

Implications for Theory and Practice

The murder of HL remains unsolved. The investigation has not advanced beyond what was known before hypnosis was used with BL and PL. The information that BL provided about the visit of KB did not assist the investigation into the murder of her husband. No car could be found that fitted the description that BL gave of the vehicle that was parked in a nearby street; anyway, it was a vehicle that she was never confident she saw. The additional information that PL gave of a car proved to be fruitless. No car could be found that fitted the description, or that had the four characters he felt sure were in the registration number.

In a number of significant ways, and this is the major point of the case as a whole, the hypnosis sessions seemed to meet the needs of BL and PL rather more so than the needs of the investigation. BL derived therapeutic benefit from her interactions with the hypnotist, and PL appeared to communicate that he was doing all he could to assist the investigation. A special feature of the use of hypnosis in the case was the different reactions of the subjects and the consequential different interactive styles of the same hypnotist. The characteristics that emerged as especially relevant were BL's use of the present tense compared with PL's use of the past tense, BL's sensorily vivid reporting of all events compared with PL's structured narrative of central material only, and BL's degree of affective responding compared with PL's relating of the shooting of his father. BL and PL used the hypnosis sessions to meet apparently different needs. The most distinctive feature of BL's involvement in hypnosis was the emotionality that she displayed. Her expression of these emotions and her reporting of the events associated with her husband's death may have been influenced also, of course, by cultural factors.

An especially instructive aspect of this case was the contrasting styles of both witness reporting and hypnotist interaction that occurred for the one hypnotist and two witnesses of the same crime. The issue of the veracity of memory report is not the main issue raised by this case. Complex interactions occurred between the needs of the witnesses and the style and behavior of the hypnotist, and this complexity must be understood in any attempt to interpret the data forensically. In this case, there were no major inconsistencies across the memory reports of the two witnesses, but there were grounds for doubting the genuineness of the hypnotic experience of at least one of the witnesses.

Our consideration of the forensic use of hypnosis does not focus only on the accuracy of memory reporting. Rather, we are interested as well in interpreting witness's behavior and reported experience in the wider social context, and it seems evident that there is a need to respond to witness behavior clinically as well as forensically. There is evidence throughout this book of how good clinical practice can be at odds with the purposes of criminal investigation. There were times in this case, for example, when the hypnotist might have probed more intensively to clarify the reasons for anxiety or perceived concern. Such probing would perhaps have indicated whether the personal distress was related to as-yet-undiscovered and relevant aspects of the crime. For BL, the content of her speaking in Italian at a time of stress needed to be explored. And for PL, we might have learned why it was so important to report convincingly information that was essentially misleading. To do so, however, might have led to misinformation or put the witnesses at some risk.

THE POLICE KILLINGS

In this complex, very public, and highly emotional case, two young police officers were killed in an ambush that had been set in the early hours of one morning in October 1988. A stolen motor vehicle with its lights on and doors open had been left in a leafy street of an exclusive suburb, and the officers were responding to a telephone call about this vehicle. When they arrived, they were both killed by shotgun blasts to the head at close range. There were no witnesses to the killings, although there were witnesses that either saw or heard some people running through a lane immediately after the shooting. The darkness and the clothing worn by these people, however, made it impossible for any meaningful description to be given or identification to be made.

The closeness in time of this ambush killing of two young police officers to the shooting by other police officers of a person they had been trying to arrest led the criminal investigation in a particular direction, and that direction involved the police questioning DS. During questioning, DS said that two of his associates had come to his place very early on the morning of the killings, had been wearing clothes with blood on them, and had told him that they had "shot some police." The three of them had then taken a taxi to another location. The investigating officers were keen to interview the taxi driver, but their attempts to find him proved unsuccessful. DS was placed in protective custody, and the possibility of using hypnosis to assist him to recall any details of the taxi or the taxi driver were discussed with the police physician. Following a recommendation by the police physician and an assessment of the information that was made available to us by the investigating officers, we agreed to conduct a hypnosis session. Perhaps because police officers had been shot, the investigating officers clearly limited the information they gave to us; moreover, the overall management of the investigation of this case was on a "need to know" basis. Professionals involved in such cases are typically assumed to need to know very little; such an assumption can be a mixed blessing, however.

We turn now to consider the nature of the information that DS gave to the hypnotist, and the manner of his interactions with the hypnotist. We focus on his reported memory of the taxi ride, and on the behavior that he displayed in what was a difficult situation for himself and for the hypnotist.

In the prehypnotic interview, DS told the hypnotist (H) about the taxi ride as follows:

H: What kind of a taxi?

DS: A taxi's a taxi. You've seen one taxi driver you've seen them all. I just got out, didn't look at the driver. I didn't want him to recognize me sort of thing.

DS was obviously very nervous and ill at ease. For instance, when asked what he had been thinking about the events of the period in question he replied:

DS: I don't want to think about them anymore. I have nightmares about them.

H: How do you feel about hypnosis going over these events again?

DS: (*Head down, arms folded.*)

H: What are your worries, about hypnosis?

DS: Not very worried.

H: Would you prefer not to go into hypnosis?

DS: Yes.

This interaction was typical of much of the engagement between the hypnotist and DS, who was reluctant to get involved in remembering the events in question in any great detail. He interacted infrequently with the hypnotist, and seemed to prefer to keep his head down, avoid eye contact, and answer questions with a "yes" or "no." He was unwilling to elaborate on anything. The hypnotist obviously found it extremely difficult to establish a relationship with the subject, who did not appear to trust him, or anyone. When the hypnotist asked DS what he particularly wished to recall, he replied, "The taxi driver." DS said that he would not discuss any details concerning the actual killings or his knowledge of them, and asked the hypnotist about the specific questions that he would be asked during the hypnosis session. He appeared to be concerned that he would not have control and could be influenced perhaps to say more than he should about the killings when he was experiencing hypnosis. It is unlikely that he experienced hypnosis at all, because his whole manner was one of resistance and anxiety. For instance:

H: Anything else about the night that you'd like to tell me before we try hypnosis?

DS: (*Shakes head.*)

H: Anything at all?

DS: I don't want to talk about the night.

H: When you say you don't want to talk about it, are you happy to have hypnosis and maybe go over that taxi ride again?

DS: About the taxi, yes.

H: Okay, what are the parts you don't want to talk about?

DS: All the rest except the taxi driver.

H: The rest being what happened at the shooting?

DS: (*Nods.*)

H: Anything else you don't want to talk about?

DS: No. Except just talk about the taxi driver.

H: Do you want to be able to remember the taxi driver?

DS: Yes. I remember everything else except the taxi driver.

In the hypnosis session, DS provided a substantial amount of detail about the taxi, the driver, and the events of the taxi ride. However, his behavior during the session was entirely inconsistent with any notion that he was experiencing hypnosis. During the induction, DS had a pained, anxious expression on his face. The hypnotist attempted a number of induction procedures, but it was clear that DS was finding it impossible to focus his concentration in the way the hypnotist requested. Moreover, DS appeared to be resisting actively any likelihood of being influenced by the hypnotist, and this was apparent throughout the entire session. DS was not hypnotized throughout the session. Although he provided additional details about the taxi ride, he did not report any meaningful, new information. Although he gave some extra description of the taxi and the driver, it was not clear whether this was the result of remembering more or simply elaborating on what had been remembered previously.

Overall, the hypnosis session with DS was limited in its scope and usefulness. DS placed constraints on what could be explored during hypnosis and also resisted the hypnotist's attempts to gain information or establish a useful relationship. Understandably perhaps, given his status as a protected witness, DS presented as unwilling to "give in" to the requests or questions of the hypnotist. Interestingly, at the end of the session DS claimed not to be able to recall anything that was discussed during the hypnosis session.

H: Can you remember what we've been talking about?

DS: (*Shakes head.*)

H: What have we been discussing?

DS: Can't remember.

H: What's the last thing you remember?

DS: Feeling relaxed.

H: What then?

DS: Counting.

H: Anything you'd like to ask me about the session?

DS: What did I say?

H: Just talked about the taxi driver. Do you remember about the taxi driver?

DS: Sort of.

Overall, the hypnosis session had no noticeable impact on the recall of DS. Virtually no new information was provided, and it is likely that DS was faking his reports of any experience of hypnosis (e.g., feeling "deep" and "strange"), as well as his reports of amnesia for the hypnosis session.

The motivations of the police in wanting hypnosis in this case were clear. They were dealing with the ambush killing of two of their fellow officers, and DS had named two associates as being involved in those killings. At the time, the investigating officers saw it as critical that the taxi driver be found in the hope that he would be able to provide relevant information. Although we were aware that DS was in protective custody at the time of the hypnosis session, we had not been told that he had initially been charged with the killings and that those charges were going to be dropped in return for his assistance in the inquiries surrounding this case. This was an aspect that we did not "need to know," at least in the view of the investigating officers. The factors involved in the case overall were many, and the place of hypnosis was small. There was a long investigation and a lengthy trial of the accused, who included the associates named by DS. However, the men accused of the crime were not convicted and the case has been closed.

The case raised serious issues for us about the amount of information provided to us about the status of DS and about the way he attempted to limit the hypnosis session and manipulate the hypnotist. Clearly, DS had rights and the hypnotist had rights; however, in an investigation such as this, the rights of individual participants are sometimes lost in the intensity of the search to bring some correction to the wrongs that have been done. More generally, this case highlighted the very real limits on involvement of the expert in the forensic system. The knowledge and skill of the expert are often needed, but the way in which this knowledge and skill is used can be limited inherently by the nature of the forensic system itself. In relation to the guidelines specified in the preceding chapter, it seems reasonable to argue that the coordinator or the hypnotist involved should have made a specific point of asking at the commencement of proceedings whether the witness had made a deal with the police. After the event, the problem became known, and the case highlights the need to clarify the status of any individual in advance, if at all possible.

SUMMARY COMMENT

Both of the cases reported in this chapter highlight the ambiguous position of the expert who becomes involved in the forensic system. The role that the expert is expected to play may be different for each participant in the system. For instance, the witnesses and the police involved can seek to use the expert to meet their own needs and ends, and the expert needs to be vigilant and assertive to ensure that his or her rights are not abrogated by the system. The intentional or unintentional manipulation of the expert by the forensic system must be guarded against. In our case, there were instances of particular information not being given to the hypnotist by the investigating authorities, and of information being given to the hypnotist that was intended perhaps to shape the individual behavior of both the hypnotist and the investigating authorities.

The overriding message from both cases is the importance of interpreting the motivations of those with whom hypnosis is used, and of making sure that enough information is in the hands of the hypnotist to allow him or her to make decisions that are consistent with professional rights and responsibilities. Criminal investigations often, and understandably, operate on a "need to know" basis. In some cases, however, the expert has a professional responsibility to know more than the forensic system can perhaps accommodate comfortably.

Damage and Dreams in Hypnosis

This chapter analyzes two cases that involved allegations of sexual assault. In these cases, the young women experienced functional amnesia for the time surrounding the incidents, and hypnosis was used in an attempt to overcome their memory blocks. In each case, additional information was provided either during or after hypnosis, and that information led to arrests being made and charges being laid; each case went to pretrial, committal hearings, and the defendants were committed to stand trial. In one case, the prosecution withdrew the case at the beginning of the trial; in the other case, the jury acquitted the defendant after the prosecution had presented its case in the trial. In contrast to the cases discussed in Chapter 4, the use of hypnosis was a matter of detailed discussion in the legal proceedings of both of these cases. The cases are complex and raise important questions about the clinical and forensic responsibilities of persons involved in such cases. As we note elsewhere in this book, the balance of those responsibilities is critical to the display of expert and ethical involvement in the forensic system.

The use of hypnosis in these cases highlights also the dilemmas of ensuring appropriate procedures in cases in which there is little, if any, chance of the corroboration of further information provided either during or after hypnosis (for further discussion of this issue, see Chapter 7; for definition of corroboration, see Chapter 3). Moreover, the cases also raise important questions and provide useful data concerning the consistency of memory

reports, and the substantial personal and emotional impact of sexual assault. Both cases also raise issues about the duty of care of persons working within the forensic system.

One of the cases had the added complication that the accused allegedly had used hypnosis in his attempted sexual involvements with various young women, including the woman who claimed he had sexually assaulted her. Detailed information on the "modus operandi hypnotic" of this person was obtained through an analysis of his attempted hypnotic seduction of an undercover policewoman; this attempt was recorded covertly and this recording was made available to us. This case links also with the material in Chapter 7, and picks up on a variety of issues concerning the use of hypnosis for the purpose of sexual contact.

A VICTIM OF ABDUCTION
AND SEXUAL ASSAULT?

AP was an 18-year-old woman who lived with her divorced mother and younger brother. Because her mother and younger brother had been away for an extended period of time, a friend of AP's, TY, who was also 18 years old, was living with her in the family house. AP and TY had been friends through school, and since completing high school they had been either unemployed or working in casual and part-time positions in restaurants and fast-food outlets.

Just prior to the incident under investigation, AP and TY had worked briefly as waitresses at a restaurant co-owned by two men (RL and DF). AP reported that during that period one of the owners, RL, was "grabbing us each time we walked past, putting his arms around our waists, and things like that," and also that "RL would touch my breasts and try and kiss me and was always talking about sex." AP indicated that DF did not engage in any of this behavior, although he was sometimes present when RL would make sexual advances to her. AP and TY stopped working at this restaurant after 4 days. They were not paid for their work during that period, although RL had given one of them a small amount of money for their travel home one night when they did not have taxi fare. AP reported that she and TY took the matter of the sexual approaches of RL and the nonpayment of wages to the employment agency that had arranged the jobs for them, and that agency subsequently put

them in contact with the government body that considered complaints of sexual harassment in the workplace.

In the few days between the time when AP and TY stopped work at the restaurant and the incident came under investigation, AP reported that she received a number of threatening telephone calls from either RL or DF. She reported that in some calls they identified themselves, and in others, the male callers made statements similar to those made when they identified themselves. AP reported these threatening telephone calls to her local police prior to the occurrence of the incident considered here. The local police advised her that they "couldn't do anything until something actually happens." In her initial statement to police after the incident considered here, AP indicated that in these telephone calls the men were:

> threatening us because of us leaving and also saying that we owe them money [$20 for taxi fares], and that if we don't pay we are going to be dead. . . . They keep telling us that they are going to kill us or take us away so that no one will ever find us. . . . They also said that if we don't drop the police matter [presumably the sexual harassment complaint], that our lives wouldn't be worth living.

The incident considered here occurred one night when AP was on her way to meet TY and then go to the dance club they attended regularly. AP reported that she dressed and prepared to leave her house in time to catch a bus at a stop that was a short walk from her house. She said that when she was waiting at the bus stop, a car drove up and she was forced into it by DF. Initially, AP provided very little information to police about what occurred at the bus stop, and could not provide any information about what occurred while she was in the car. She reported that she subsequently "woke up" when she was shaken by three people who found her lying naked in a park in the city. AP reported that she then "must have" dressed but couldn't "remember getting my clothes on," and then walked to the dance club, where she found TY and other friends. AP, TY, and another female friend returned to the house, because AP "didn't want to go to the police. I just wanted to go home. I wanted to forget about it." After arriving home, TY contacted a friend's father, who was a police officer, and he advised her about the course of action that AP should take. TY then contacted the police sexual assault unit and AP's local doctor; when the police arrived they took AP to the sexual assault clinic of a major hospital, where medical examination revealed that semen was present in AP's vagina, and bruising on her upper arms and forehead.

In her initial statement to police, AP was not able to provide any information about what occurred in the car. However, she stated that it was DF who had approached her at the bus stop and forced her into the car. AP said, "Even though I don't know what has happened, I think DF and RL were responsible for what happened to me on that night. I think that's how I got to that park. DF and RL dumped me there."

The Investigation

In the week following the incident, AP attended counseling sessions with a clinical social worker at the sexual assault clinic. However, virtually no progress was made in terms of her remembering whatever events occurred when she was in the car. The investigating officers subsequently sought advice from senior police about the possibility of using hypnosis in the case. We were contacted, and following consideration of a number of factors (e.g., AP had not ingested any drugs or alcohol on the night in question, and had not suffered any serious physical injuries during the incident), we indicated that hypnosis might be helpful in this case that appeared to be functional amnesia associated with sexual assault. This diagnosis of AP's apparent memory loss had been made independently by the medical staff at the clinic she was attending for counseling.

The hypnosis session with AP took place 12 days after the incident and was conducted in an interview room that was specially designed for videorecording. The hypnotist and AP were alone in the room for the majority of the session and were joined after hypnosis by the clinical social worker. The investigating officers, the clinical social worker, and an assistant to the hypnotist were in an adjoining room and viewed the session on a video monitor. The assistant was able to communicate with the hypnotist through an earpiece that the hypnotist was wearing. The entire session between the hypnotist and AP was videorecorded.

The Hypnosis Session with AP

Prior to the session, the investigating officers gave detailed information about the case to the assistant, and he provided a written outline of the incident to the hypnotist, who did not meet AP until the beginning of the session. The hypnotist initially explained the general procedures of the session to AP, and asked her about her expectations of hypnosis and the session. He asked about a number of matters typically associated with rape trauma syndrome (e.g., see Frazier & Borgida, 1985, 1988, 1992). He discussed some of the emotions that AP had been experiencing and commented on ways to think about and deal with those strong emotions. The hypnotist then asked AP to recall and describe as much as she could of the incident.

Following AP's description of various events that she believed to be related to or part of the incident, the hypnotist administered a hypnotic induction procedure and used selected hypnotic test items to formally index her hypnotic responsiveness. AP's performance on these items suggested that her hypnotizability was in the high-medium range. The hypnotist then used an age regression suggestion to regress AP to the day of the incident, and asked her to freely recall the events of that evening.

During her recall, AP displayed an emotional reaction that was essentially abreactive in nature. The hypnotist provided supportive and reassuring comments while AP ventilated her emotions. After the abreaction passed, AP oriented herself and the session continued. Specifically, AP said that she remembered a good deal of material that she had not reported prior to the hypnosis session. Some of this material she reported to the hypnotist, some of it could be inferred from her comments during the abreaction, and some of the material, AP said, she did not want to communicate. She said that she now knew exactly what had happened in the car, but she did not spell out to the hypnotist what had occurred.

Following a deinduction procedure, AP continued to display a strong emotional reaction and the hypnotist asked the clinical social worker to join them. After a brief discussion among the three of them, the hypnotist left AP and the clinical social worker together. She provided clinical care to AP and arranged to see her at a later date at the sexual assault clinic.

It is instructive to comment on the reactions of the investigating officers and the social worker, who were watching the hypnosis session on a video monitor. Their comments, questions, and reactions were noted unobtrusively by the assistant who was in the room with them, and we considered that material to better understand the overall social context of the place of hypnosis in this investigation. Our analysis indicated that the officers were impressed by what seemed to have been achieved during hypnosis and the apparently impressive effects of simple hypnotic suggestions; they later asked the hypnotist, "What other tricks do you have that we could use?" The officers repeatedly questioned the assistant on "how far under" hypnosis AP was, and their comments implied that the "farther under" she was, the more accurate they believed the reported material to be. The officers were eager for the hypnotist to ask direct (and leading) questions during hypnosis, and they commented on the investigative ineptitude of the hypnotist in allowing free recall with follow-up questions rather than "asking questions directly."

When AP was displaying the abreaction, the officers wanted the assistant to tell the hypnotist to "push harder" for the names of the assailants; however, the assistant decided not to convey this to the hypnotist. The officers were impressed by the abreaction, and seemed to assume that such strong emotion would be associated with a truthful and accurate account of the incident. They were also keen to learn exactly what techniques the hypnotist had used "to make her break down," because they thought they might use those techniques in other investigations. In stark, and necessary, contrast with the position of the investigating officers was the position of the clinical social worker. She expressed concern about attitudes toward rape victims and concern that the hypnotist was male and involved in the case via the request of the investigating officers.

The assistant, who was a clinical psychologist, and the clinical social worker discussed the events of the hypnosis session as they were occurring, and the social worker picked up on a number of matters to explore and resolve in further counseling sessions. She commented that more was coming out in the hypnosis session than in any of the previous counseling sessions and eventually saw the hypnosis session as a positive event for AP in that it provided material for them to work on in further counseling sessions. The social worker was upset at the strength and content of AP's abreaction but was pleased that the hypnotist asked her to join himself and AP after the hypnosis session was over. She commented that although she was reluctant initially to let her client undergo hypnosis, she was pleased that "the personal needs of AP were placed ahead of the police needs" during the hypnosis session.

Approximately two weeks after the hypnosis session and after two more counseling sessions with the social worker, AP made a formal statement to police that detailed the events of the incident. She indicated how four men had assaulted her in the car, and she named two males (RL and DF) as sexually assaulting her; she said that she did not know who the other two men were. Although AP had named RL and DF as being involved in other matters, she had not named them previously to police as being responsible for the sexual assault. That statement led to the arrest and charging of these two men. To understand the impact of the use of hypnosis in this case, we comment on the consistency and inconsistency across AP's memory reports at various times.

Consistency and Inconsistency in Memory

We considered four sources of memory reports by AP: (1) the initial statement to police, (2) the prehypnotic interview, (3) the hypnosis session, and (4) the final statement to police. We considered six major aspects of the information that AP gave at one or more of these times: (1) working in the restaurant, (2) receiving the telephone calls, (3) preparing to go out, (4) waiting at the bus stop, (5) being in the car, and (6) waking in the park. These six aspects will be considered in turn, with an emphasis on the consistencies and inconsistencies across the different times that information was given.

Working in the Restaurant

A description of the events at the restaurant (e.g., getting the job, being sexually harassed by one of the owners, leaving the job, and the dispute over wages) appeared in both the initial statement to the police and the prehypnotic interview with the hypnotist. Probably because they became somewhat less relevant to the incident as time progressed, these events were not mentioned in the hypnosis session or in the final statement. As will be seen, however, these events were critical to the eventual outcome of the case. The description of this material at these two times was consistent, and much the same detail was reported on both occasions. There were virtually no discrepancies between the two reports of working in the restaurant owned by RL and DF.

Receiving the Telephone Calls

The incidents of telephone harassment were not dealt with during the hypnosis session, nor were they reported in the final statement. However, they were described in both the first statement and the prehypnotic interview. AP was clear and consistent on both occasions, and identified the callers as RL and DF. The conversations attributed to the callers were practically identical in both accounts. There was congruence in AP's story about this aspect of the events.

Preparing to Go Out

The events that occurred when AP was preparing to go out on the night of the incident were discussed during the prehypnotic interview and during the hypnosis session. There were no reports of these events in either the initial or the final statement to police. This is probably because the police considered these events irrelevant to the occurrences later in the evening. AP's narrative of events in the house, when she was preparing to go out, was consistent from the prehypnotic interview to the hypnosis session, although more detail was given during the hypnosis session. This may be due to AP's recalling this material in more detail during hypnosis, or it may be a consequence of the hypnotist eliciting more information about this aspect during hypnosis in order to assist AP to reinstate her sense of the general physical and psychological context of the evening of the incident. What is especially interesting about the description of this material during hypnosis is that it gave an indication of AP's apparent fear after the threatening telephone calls. In commenting on this aspect, AP explicitly linked her fear at the time when she was preparing to go out to her fear generated by the telephone calls from RL and DF. This suggests that she may have linked in her own mind the later events with the threatening telephone calls, regardless of what actually happened. AP's reported fear at this time had not been mentioned previously, and its emergence during hypnosis underscores the tendency of hypnotized individuals to more readily experience emotion that is meaningful to them. Whether this fear was actually occurring at the time, or whether it reflected a projection or transposition of her fear during the incident is a question that cannot be answered. It may be that hypnosis leads people to transpose emotional material in a way that makes it consistent with their developing personal narrative. It is important to recognize, however, that although hypnosis can lead people to transpose emotional material in ways that fit with their personal narrative, people can do this without hypnosis. The phenomenon of providing a coherent, albeit not necessarily accurate, cognitive and emotional narrative is not a necessary artifact of being hypnotized. Hypnosis, however, can contribute to this phenomenon, just as other forms of questioning also contribute to it.

Waiting at the Bus Stop

The investigation into the alleged assault began essentially at the bus stop. Consequently, AP's description of the events at the bus stop appeared in all reports. It is with this aspect that major inconsistencies began to arise across the reports. The greatest amount of detail about this aspect was given during the hypnosis session and in the final statement. AP's reports in the initial statement and the prehypnotic interview agreed on what took place, although the extent of the detail that AP provided was relatively limited. In both of these reports, AP talked about seeing a car, seeing DF standing next to her when she turned around, and seeing DF holding a bottle of some sort. No mention was made of the actions or involvement of RL or the two unnamed men, nor was there any explanation given as to how AP was taken from the bus stop. The prehypnotic interview differed slightly from the initial statement, in that AP mentioned some possible witnesses (e.g., a man jogging on the other side of the road), and the time that AP first saw the car seemed to have altered.

Major inconsistencies occurred in the description of these events in the hypnosis session and in the final statement. In both of these reports, more detail was given about the interaction with DF (e.g., his grabbing AP), and a clear explanation of how AP was taken from the bus stop was offered. The novel information in the reports during the hypnosis session and in the final statement concerned the descriptions and actions of RL and the two unknown men. During hypnosis, RL was said to have gotten out of the car and helped DF grab AP and push her into the back of the car. In the final statement, RL was not reported as getting out of the car; rather, one of the unnamed men "with streaks in his hair" was said to have helped DF grab AP and force her into the back of the car.

There were inconsistencies also about when AP reported first seeing the car: as it drove slowly past the bus stop (initial statement), when it was stopped behind the bus stop (in the prehypnotic interview and hypnosis session), and after being grabbed by the assailants (final statement). AP's reporting of the use of a "weapon" at the bus stop also shifted across the four reports: in the initial statement and the prehypnotic interview, AP described a bottle being held by DF in a threatening way; during hypnosis, she said that DF was not holding a bottle, but rather a knife was being held by RL in a threatening way; and, in the final statement, AP did not report any weapon being held by anybody at the bus stop.

It is not clear why AP changed her version of events from the hypnosis session to the final statement to police. There were major consistencies in what actions took place (e.g., her arms were grabbed and she was forced into the car), and in what was actually said (e.g., "Get her into the car"). But there were also major inconsistencies, particularly in terms of who did and said what at different times. The extent of inconsistency indexes considerable unreliability in memory reporting.

Being in the Car

Prior to the hypnosis session, AP reported no memory of the events that occurred in the car. Consequently, there was no mention of this aspect in either the initial statement or the prehypnotic interview. Although some of the events were mentioned generally during the hypnosis session, AP's description contained relatively little detail and was interspersed with strong emotional displays. Comparison of the reports during the hypnosis session and the final statement revealed a great deal of congruence, even though a lot less information was given during the hypnosis session. The major inconsistency lay in the positions of the four males in the car. However, AP said that she was facedown on the back floor of a car after being abducted and was surrounded by men speaking in another language; such a situation could be expected to give rise to some confusion about exact details. Although AP was inconsistent about these precise details, in the final statement she conveyed strongly the identity of two of the four men that she said were in the car. The exact details of the sexual assault were not touched on in the hypnosis session, but they were recounted in the final statement. Arguably, greater detail was given in the final statement, because AP needed time after the apparent lifting of the amnesia to emotionally assimilate the remembered material. Also, and perhaps more practically, the questioning of the police during the final statement most likely encouraged her to give explicit details.

Waking in the Park

The information about AP waking up in the park was included in most reports. AP was very consistent in her description of this occasion across the initial statement and the prehypnotic interview: where she was woken, by whom, and in what state, were identical in each report. Likewise, in both reports she was equally uncertain of the particulars regarding how she came to be there. However, she either stated explicitly (in the initial statement) or implied (in the prehypnotic interview) that DF and RL had something to do with her waking up naked in the park. This preconception of the involvement of these two men could mean that any memories she reported during hypnosis or thereafter were not true recollections, but rather a cementing of the preconceptions that she held.

The final statement included a lot more detail and gave a detailed account of how AP came to be in the park. She stated clearly that she was dropped there by DF, RL, and the two unknown men. The only discrepancy in this report, when compared with the previous one, concerned her state of undress when woken in the park by the passersby. In the first two reports, AP said that she was naked when woken, but in the final report, AP described herself as wearing a skirt and bra at this time. This was a discrepancy in her report, but why it changed was not clear. It is possible that the final report was more accurate, considering that in the first two reports AP described herself as being naked and then having dressed, but she was unable to remember doing so.

The Committal Hearing and the Trial

The committal hearing of DF and RL was held approximately 1 year after the incident. The prosecution called to testify the senior investigating officer, the medical practitioner who examined AP following the incident, and the hypnotist. The defense did not call any witnesses. The hypnotist was cross-examined by the legal counsel for RL, but was not cross-examined by the legal counsel for DF. DF and RL were both committed for trial on charges of abduction, rape, and assault.

The trial of DF and RL was scheduled to be held approximately 2 years after the incident. The prosecution planned to call the hypnotist, and the defense planned to call another psychologist who was expert in hypnosis. The trial was to be by judge only. On the morning of the trial, however, the prosecution obtained a summary of the interview that AP and TY had had with the government body about their claims of sexual harassment when they were working at the restaurant owned by DF and RL. The investigating officers had never sought to obtain this material. When reviewing the case and the investigation immediately prior to the trial, the prosecutor decided that he should see this material and obtained it directly. In the material, AP was reported as saying that a consequence of the harassment at the restaurant was that she had dreamed that DF and RL had kidnapped her in a car and raped her. At the beginning of the trial, and as required by law, the prosecutor brought this material to the attention of the judge and the defense (which also had not sought to obtain it). After considering this new material, and after a discussion among the judge, the prosecutor, and the defense attorneys in the judge's chambers, the prosecutor indicated that he did not wish to proceed with the case.

The judge had indicated that because the victim had reported a dream about an incident essentially similar to the alleged sexual assault and had reported this dream before the alleged assault had occurred, then he would have to find in favor of the defense unless the prosecution could provide strong physical evidence. The prosecution had not obtained any such evidence. Thus, AP's report to the government body of dreaming about a similar incident involving DF and RL prior to the occurrence of the alleged assault became the critical factor when the case went to trial. The judge said that he would have taken this position about the importance of the reported dream whether or not hypnosis had been used with AP. In his view, the use of hypnosis was irrelevant to the legal position that he adopted. The judge's opinion, in this case, reflects the observation we made earlier that hypnosis does not necessarily cause contamination of memory.

This case raises particular questions about the exact status of memory reports in and of themselves, and their forensic meaning and value, especially when hypnosis is involved. At the outset, the clinical indicators in this case suggested that it was appropriate to use hypnosis. A young woman reported that she had been sexually assaulted and could not remember critical aspects of that assault. The use of hypnosis appeared to assist her to remember those aspects. However, approximately 2 years after the assault, it emerged that AP had reported a dream about being abducted and sexually assaulted by the two men before the incident occurred. The medical indications were that AP had sexual intercourse that evening. However, the question remains as to who committed that assault.

The memories of AP were critically important to her, and those memories have haunted her since. The assault changed her life dramatically, and in the 2 years between the assault and the trial, she abused alcohol and drugs, and attempted suicide. Her memory reports were accepted as veridical by the clinical counselors she saw, but rejected as unsafe by the legal system. The use of hypnosis helped her access and/or construct particular memories, but the forensic system played no role in her ongoing personal care. The importance of finding a balance of clinical and forensic responsibility was very apparent in this case. The hypnotist veered toward the side of clinical responsibility, but that responsibility was not necessarily consonant with meeting the technical needs of the forensic system. And the criminal investigation missed a piece of information that changed entirely the legal outcome of the case. Notably, AP never mentioned to us the dream that she had had 2 weeks before the event. If she had, we would not have used hypnosis because of the possibility of increasing confusion between her memory of the dream and her memory of the event of the sexual assault.

A VICTIM OF HYPNOTIC SEDUCTION AND/OR SEXUAL ASSAULT?

One evening in April 1988, JD, CK, and other friends around the ages of 18–20 years took a taxi to the apartment of JD, which she shared with some of those friends. They invited the taxi driver, LG, in for coffee. While he was there, LG claimed expertise in hypnosis and demonstrated hypnotic induction procedures. He offered to hypnotize JD to help her learn to relax and sleep more easily, and she accepted. JD and LG went into her bedroom, where he administered a hypnotic induction. JD reported that she almost fell asleep. JD and LG then returned to the living room and engaged in general conversation with her friends for a while. JD said that she was feeling tired and was going to bed, and LG offered to help her get to sleep. She accepted, and JD and LG went into her bedroom a second time. LG asked her to rearrange her clothing and massaged her upper body while administering a hypnotic induction. JD said that she remembered LG talking about her fingertips and then "vaguely remembered" sitting on the kitchen floor amid broken glass and talking to her friends; she said that she had a feeling that she had "smashed things" while "feeling as though [she] was in a trance." JD's friends said that LG was in the bedroom with her for about 20 minutes, then came out and left after saying that JD was asleep. JD then came out of her bedroom, walked around apparently without awareness of her friends, and broke various things on the coffee table, in the kitchen, and in the bathroom. Her friends said that they eventually calmed her and she went to sleep.

On the following evening, LG came to the apartment when JD, CK, and another friend were there. LG, who was approximately 35 years older than these young women, provided them with information about hypnosis and demonstrated various hypnotic inductions and suggestions with JD and CK, in particular. When CK indicated that she was going to leave, LG offered to drive her to her apartment, and she accepted. Upon arrival, LG offered to help CK carry her bags of groceries into her apartment. CK reported that she walked into her flat at approximately 8:30 P.M., and LG was behind her. She said that she heard him place the grocery bags on the floor of the kitchen as she went to her bedroom to put some personal belongings away. She heard the door close, thought LG had left, and lay on her bed fully clothed to rest for a few minutes. She reported not remembering "anything else after that" until she "heard the door close." She looked at her watch, and it was 9:30 P.M. The bedclothes were messed, she was naked, and she felt wetness around her vagina. She then dressed, checked the security of her apartment and her personal belongings, went to a neighbor, and telephoned her friends. JD and the other friends arrived, the police were contacted and they took her to a police station and a hospital. Medical examination indicated that sexual intercourse had occurred.

As part of the criminal investigation, we agreed to conduct hypnosis sessions with both JD and CK. The aim of the hypnosis session with JD was to assist her in trying to recall aspects of the second time that she went into her bedroom with LG. We thought that she might have been asleep for some or all of this period, or that she might have difficulty remembering this period because of whatever events occurred, or that she might have been given specific hypnotic suggestions to forget this period. The hypnotist received no indication whether sexual assault had (or had not) occurred.

This posed an interesting issue in relation to application of the guidelines. Although no evidence had indicated that intercourse had occurred, the details of that evidence needed to be kept from the hypnotist to minimize subsequent suggestive influence (see Chapter 3). Facts that are salient forensically may nevertheless operate as cues that produce later distortion.

The primary aim of the hypnosis session with CK was to assist her to remember the period from 8:30 to 9:30 P.M. As with JD, we thought that she might have been asleep for some or all of this period, or that she might have difficulty remembering this period because of whatever events occurred, or that she might have been given specific hypnotic suggestions to forget this period. Evidence showed that sexual intercourse had occurred during this period. Before considering the hypnosis session, it is useful to set forth some issues that we considered at the outset of this case. These related to clinical concerns, forensic issues, and the possible professional and ethical dilemmas that were involved in using hypnosis with these two women in particular. We comment on these matters in turn.

Clinical Concerns

From a clinical perspective, it was easy to see the need to resolve the memory gaps that were being experienced by both young women. Both had reported that they were asleep or deeply relaxed in bed at the time. Both were aware that LG had been with them just before the target time, but neither of them had a memory of the specific events that occurred during those periods. Clearly, the women needed to work out what had happened during those periods in order to integrate those events with their perception of themselves. Both women were experiencing personal difficulties and were reporting negative feelings toward themselves; their comments and behavior reflects the observation that negative self-image can be associated with incidences of sexual assault (Frazier & Borgida, 1985, 1988, 1992). Clearly, it was important clinically to recognize the adaptive significance of doing whatever was appropriate to help them change their self-perceptions and increase their feelings of self-worth.

The precise role of hypnosis, both in creating and in resolving the events in question, also seemed clinically important to us. Hypnosis may have played some role in facilitating sexual assault, and we were cautioned by that possibility. Clinically, it seemed to us that it might be significant to use hypnosis also in an attempt to resolve the conflict that the possible use of hypnosis by LG may have produced, at least in part.

Forensic Issues

One major forensic issue was the legitimacy of the memory gaps that both women reported. The question here revolved around whether the women's failure to report was a genuine memory loss or a motivated unwillingness to report. The investigating officers appeared to believe strongly that something relatively bad must have happened for the women not to be able to talk about it, for whatever reason. Another major issue was the question of why the investigating officers were so eager for the use of hypnosis, even after we had laid out the potential difficulties that could be associated with its use in this case. Predominantly, they wanted hypnosis to retrieve the memories of the periods that the women could not recall. Moreover, it seemed that one possibility was that the women had been given a suggestion of some sort to forget certain events. It appeared that the women and the police all believed that LG, as a hypnotist, had the skill to do this both unobtrusively and effectively. The investigating officers recognized that a potentially serious risk of the use of hypnosis was that it could lead to confabulation or to concretizing the women's suspicions about what had happened. Despite this potential risk, they were interested in attempting to gain access to the assumed material in memory. It is also important to note, with respect to this concern, that the officers considered that some checking of any events reported in hypnosis could be provided by other investigative and forensic work that was occurring. A further complicating factor in this case was the fact that the women were close friends, and this raised the issue of whether the story of one was being reinforced wittingly or unwittingly by the story of the other. Moreover, it was unclear at the outset whether both women were victims of sexual assault or whether one was a victim and the other was perhaps an intended victim.

Professional and Ethical Concerns

There were various professional and ethical dilemmas in this case. For instance, the use of hypnosis to investigate an event that may have been linked in its creation to a misuse of hypnosis warrants some caution. There are risks, for example, in producing false memories in the circumstances of this case. If used correctly and professionally, however, hypnosis does have the potential to reveal aspects of the women's memories that could help them both as individuals and also help the criminal investigation. Relatedly, however, we were aware that the use of hypnosis for an investigative rather than clinical purpose might be a difficult thing to achieve when the real depths of the women's traumatic reactions to their experiences were not clear.

With these issues in mind, and following consultation with the investigating officers and an arrangement with an independent clinical psychologist to provide counseling and ongoing support, if necessary, immediately after the hypnosis sessions, we made a decision to proceed with the use of hypnosis for several reasons. For instance, the investigation was oriented around a possible use of hypnosis by LG, and information about the women's hypnotic responsiveness was considered in itself to be both relevant and useful. Also, because there was a possibility that the women's apparent memory loss may have been due to posthypnotic suggestion, it seemed plausible that a reinstatement of memory might be possible through the application of hypnosis in a safe setting.

Our decision was influenced also by the fact that neither woman had obtained any counseling or other therapeutic help regarding the events in question, although they clearly were distressed by those events. They were both positively oriented toward the notion that hypnosis could be used to help them understand more about those events and hence enable them to ultimately regain their self-esteem and feelings of competence and control. Finally, the investigating officers agreed to follow any guidelines that we set and to provide any information that we asked for. They acknowledged that we had full professional control of the hypnosis session. Interestingly, this was something of a double-edged sword: by yielding control to the "experts," the police also protected themselves, in that any problems that occurred either immediately with the women, or subsequently in the legal proceedings, could be attributed to the experts.

The Hypnosis Session with JD

The focus of the session with JD was intended to be recall of the events that took place in her bedroom. However, every strategy that the hypnotist employed to have JD consider that 20-minute period was unsuccessful. Rather, she commented on her destructive behavior after the target period. This behavior obviously upset JD, and she adopted a paranormal explanation for it; namely, she reported that she had been "possessed" during that time. In addition to talking about this destructive behavior, she spent time talking to the hypnotist about being sexually assaulted by another person about one year previously. She had not mentioned this previously to anyone. Because of the psychological vulnerability of JD and the clinical signs of her unresolved feelings, the hypnosis session was truncated, and JD accepted an offer to discuss immediately her feelings with the clinical psychologist who was available. After seeing JD's behavior, the investigating officers decided that it would be unrealistic to pursue any further investigation of the possibility that JD was a victim of sexual assault by LG. The hypnosis session with JD then was of little positive value to the forensic investigation. However, the hypnosis session with CK was a different matter.

The Hypnosis Session with CK

The hypnosis session with CK took place in June 1988, and was conducted in accordance with our guidelines for the use of hypnosis in criminal investigations. The hypnotist had been provided with a memorandum that summarized the events on the night in April that CK had reported to the police. The memorandum indicated that the purpose of the hypnosis session was to assist CK to remember the period on that evening from when she arrived at her flat with LG until when she went to see her landlady.

Prior to hypnosis, the hypnotist asked CK about her expectations and experiences of hypnosis. He also conducted a pre-hypnotic inquiry into her recall of the events of that evening. Following this, the hypnotist administered a hypnotic induction and tested the susceptibility of CK to hypnotic suggestion. This indicated that she was highly responsive to hypnotic suggestion. The hypnotist conducted an inquiry into CK's recall of the events during hypnosis, and she reported material that she had not reported prior to hypnosis. This additional material was very specific about what had occurred in the period 8:30 to 9:30 P.M. CK reported that LG had sexual intercourse with her during this period, and she reported in detail what LG had said and done.

CK also indicated that during this period LG had been talking in a way that was consistent with the style of communication typically associated with hypnotic suggestion. When she was reporting this material, CK displayed a strong emotional reaction that included feelings of distress, disgust, and anger. After the hypnosis session, the hypnotist discussed with CK her experience of hypnosis and her memory of the events. She continued to report the additional material, and continued to show a strong emotional reaction.

Analysis of the Memory Reports of CK

We analyzed the memory reports of CK and focused on the events that she apparently remembered only during hypnosis. In her initial statement to police CK said:

> I remember walking in the front door of my flat, it was 8:30 P.M. LG was behind me. I put my things on the floor and I heard him place my other things on the floor behind me. I just looked around and started griping about the things that I had to do. I heard the door close and I thought that LG had gone. So I lay on the bed facing the wall. I was fully clothed. I remember turning the light off, and then I don't remember anything after that.

In her prehypnotic interview, she told the hypnotist: "We carried stuff in; he was behind me. I said just dump it anywhere. I heard the door shut; I thought he went. So I lay down on the bed and crashed out. I thought he'd gone but he hadn't."

The report during hypnosis was very different. During hypnosis, CK said:

> He carries in a box of garbage and plastic bags. I turn on the light, and say dump it anywhere. Then I heard the door shut, and I thought, "Yeah, well he's gone, I can get some sleep." I fall asleep with my pillow under my arm. I had all these funny thoughts but I think I'm asleep.

CK then went on to say that she heard a voice saying, "Everything's going to be all right. Don't worry, I'm not going to hurt you. It's okay, don't worry. Relax." CK said that this was LG's voice, and that he was saying these things as he was taking her clothes off. She added, "I can't wake up and do anything about it." CK reported that as LG started to stroke and caress her body, she thought to herself, "I can't do anything about it." She added, "It's hard to comprehend. I don't know if I'm dreaming. I'm scared. Why would I feel like this otherwise? It must be happening. It scares me a lot.

CK reported that she lay on her back with her arms above her head, and that LG had sexual intercourse with her. When he ejaculated, she reported thinking to herself, "I don't believe it, but I feel it. I'm scared that I'm going to die." She reported that LG said, "Thank you," kissed her, and then left her flat. CK said that she "woke up" when she heard the door close. She saw that the bedclothes were in disarray; she was naked and she felt wetness and stickiness around her vagina. She said to the hypnotist that it was only then that she realized what had happened.

Emotional Reactions

Before the hypnosis session, CK had remarked, "I feel violated, and I hate it." Thus, she conveyed at the outset the strong emotional nature of the events, and she showed a very strong affective response to the material that she reported during hypnosis. In giving this information, CK showed feelings of disgust, anger, and helplessness. After saying that the image of the assault "popped" into her mind during hypnosis, the hypnotist (H) asked:

H: Are you frightened to talk about this?
CK: Yes, I don't like it. I put a block up against it. I wanted to forget. I felt bad.

After hypnosis, the hypnotist asked CK how she felt about the session.

CK: At least I can remember what happened.
H: Do you remember now?
CK: Mm.
H: How do you feel about what you remembered?
CK: I'll probably have nightmares about the bloody thing.

CK continued to show strong emotion to the material and commented spontaneously about the event, "Sometimes I felt like I wanted to cry, or I wanted to shake, but I didn't." She also talked about the impact of the incident on her personal relationships (e.g., with her boyfriend) and explained some of her ongoing reactions to the event (e.g., nightmares). As with many victims of sexual assault, CK tended to blame herself entirely (Frazier & Borgida, 1985, 1988, 1992). For instance, she commented, "It makes me think that I'm bloody stupid for letting it happen in the first place. I blame myself. It shouldn't have happened; you should have been thinking, you shouldn't have trusted someone so quickly." Similarly, toward the end of the session when she appeared to be "resigned" to the memories retrieved during hypnosis, CK said, "I blame myself anyway."

Use of Hypnotic-Like Communications

A possible link to the use of hypnosis, or at least hypnotic-like communications, by LG at the time can be seen in a number of ways. During the hypnosis session, for instance, CK leaned back and put one arm back over the chair. This position was maintained for the entire session. Similarly, CK appeared not to have moved during the sexual assault. She described her position during the assault as being on her back with her arms above her head. When asked about her arms being above her head, CK replied that LG had put them there. During his demonstrations of hypnosis, LG apparently had told JD and CK that arms are difficult to move during hypnosis because they are so heavy. When recounting the assault, however, CK did not report any explicit suggestions that resulted in her arms feeling heavy and her eyes not being able to open.

H: Why are your arms so heavy?

CK: I don't know. I sort of wanted to move them. They felt like lead, and they were numb, 'cause they didn't want to move.

When the hypnotist asked about her arms being heavy during hypnosis, CK stated, "He said we wouldn't want to move them when he hypnotized us before."

It seemed that the communications used by LG during the alleged sexual assault were entirely consistent with hypnotic suggestions. The reported state of CK during this time also resembled hypnosis, at least in part. For example, she commented repeatedly on her inability to distinguish whether the events were real or a part of a dream. A difficulty of interpretation arises because it is not clear whether the events in her apartment were hypnotic in any way, even though some aspects of LG's communications during that time, as reported by CK, appeared to be hypnotic-like. Moreover, CK claimed that she experienced inexplicable sensations, such as her arms not being able to move, but at no point did she report that any specific suggestions were given during this time. Although the communications of LG were similar to those used during a hypnotic procedure, CK did not recall an induction procedure, nor any specific suggestions that made her unable to resist what was occurring. Perhaps her inability to move her arms could be attributed to a posthypnotic suggestion given during the earlier sessions, yet CK did not report any such suggestions. More parsimoniously, perhaps, it could have been fear that led CK not to speak and not to move during intercourse.

Analysis of Attempted Hypnotic Seduction

As part of the investigation of the alleged sexual assault and the misuse of hypnosis by LG, a young, female undercover police officer, PO, made contact with LG in a social setting. In his conversation with PO, LG offered to help her give up smoking and also to help her learn how to relax. LG indicated to PO that she must be nervous because she was smoking, and that he could help her overcome both problems. PO told him that she was only visiting the city for a few days and was staying in a local motel; also, she said that she would like to give up smoking and learn to relax more. LG offered to drive her to the motel and help her in these ways, and PO accepted. They drove to the motel where their conversation was audiorecorded by the investigating officers who were in the next room of the motel. Our analysis of that conversation highlighted the nature of the relationship that LG attempted to establish, the nature of the suggestions that he used, and the overriding sexualized aspects of his interaction with PO. Notably, however, testimony concerning this aspect of the investigation was not permitted by the judge because he ruled that it was not relevant to the charge of LG sexually assaulting CK.

The recording indicated to us that LG attempted to hypnotize PO, and he attempted also to engage in hypnotically facilitated sexual contact. His "modus operandi hypnotic" was clear and competent, and he showed considerable skill in the use of both hypnotic and nonhypnotic techniques of suggestion and interpersonal manipulation. These techniques aimed to establish a context for sexual activity, and his communications aimed to place PO in a position of easy acquiescence. For instance:

LG: Do you want to know how it feels to be completely and utterly relaxed?

PO: Um, I like to be relaxed.

LG: Fine, all right move over there.

PO: Where, on the bed?

LG: Yeah, on the bed.

PO: Why, what's wrong with a chair?

LG: Because it's impossible, I need the muscles in a certain position.

PO: The muscles in a certain position?

LG: Yeah, do what you're told. I promise you won't be hurt.

PO: I can't sit up like this on the chair?

LG: I want you lying down.

PO: Lying down?

LG: Lying down.

PO: Can I sit up? I want to sit up.

In the conversation, LG worked hard to shift the nature of his relationship from a stranger to that of either a friend (viz., by describing how caring and trustworthy he was) or an authority figure (viz., by describing himself as a doctor and expert on hypnosis). He spoke in either a friendly or an authoritative way, and his communications appeared to convey that he cared about PO, that he knew what was best for her, and that she would benefit by following his communications. For instance:

LG: Now you're completely relaxed, would you like to relax even further? Would you like to relax even more and become even more relaxed, even further? Would you like to know the complete satisfaction of relaxation?

PO: Mm.

LG: To be able to do that you have to do as you are told. You are completely and utterly safe. And what we are going to do now is a massage to relax those muscles. We will do that because you want to do that.

Throughout the conversation, and especially when PO indicated some resistance or disagreement, LG emphasized his greater knowledge and ability in medical and psychological matters. He indicated that he could assist PO with her problems of relaxation and smoking, but that she would have to follow his directions. These statements about helping her were sexualized (e.g., "You have a beautiful body and you want to look after it"). Moreover, he used techniques that aimed to lead PO to initiate or request actions that were intended or desired by himself. For example, LG proposed that he use hypnosis to help her overcome a problem with smoking. When she displayed some resistance to this, he asked PO to justify why he should help her give up smoking. In this way, the initial resistance of PO was turned to a request for LG to act in the way that he himself originally proposed.

Relatedly, he used communications throughout the interaction to get PO to assert one state of affairs by denying another. For example, by telling her that part of her problem was that she did not trust him, he led her to deny this. By denying that she did not trust him, PO was asserting in effect that she did trust him. LG emphasized the role of trust throughout the interaction, and linked the notion of trust to both hypnosis and sexual activity.

LG: I'd be able to teach someone to ballroom dance with hypnosis. Learn to relax, and be happy and at peace with yourself. If you're thinking that I'd use hypnosis to turn around and get into your pants or something. Well (a) I'm not interested, and (b) nah, that's just not on.

PO: Uh.

LG: Do you have a problem trusting me, sexually?

PO: No.

LG: Good, that's important.

PO: Why?

LG: It's similar to understanding hypnosis, hypnotherapy. It's important that you have no fears. And I have not and will never ever use hypnosis for ulterior motives.

By telling her that being hypnotized is trusting someone sexually, LG communicated that hypnosis is like sexual activity. Furthermore, by telling PO that he did not "want to get into [her] pants," he communicated that perhaps this was a possibility during hypnosis. The intent of such conflicting communications is generally to confuse and limit the choices available to the receiver of a message to the option that is desired by the sender of the message.

LG gave suggestions during hypnosis that ranged from indirect and permissive to direct and authoritative. Although some suggestions were aimed in a superficial way to help PO with a problem of smoking, the suggestions were essentially sexual in nature. For instance, during a suggestion for regression to the age of 9 years, he asked PO about her sexual experiences, as follows:

LG: Do you play around with boys now?

PO: Sometimes.

LG: What do you do when you play around with boys?

PO: Dance with them.

LG: How old are you when you started to dance with them?

PO: Eighteen.

LG: Do any of them make any advances to you sexually when you dance with them?

PO: No.

LG: Have you ever had a sexual experience with a man?

PO: No.

LG: Now and throughout your life, you will be happier if you want to make love to people. Have you ever been caressed before? Has anyone ever touched you?

PO: No.

LG: Would you like me to touch you?

PO: No.

LG: You wouldn't? Why not? It's just a natural thing, it's just a natural thing. Do you think sex is dirty?

PO: No.

LG: Do you think sex is dirty or to be enjoyed?

PO: It is not dirty.

LG: It is quite a natural thing to do, and so you go even deeper and deeper asleep.

He showed considerable skill in the administration of hypnotic suggestions and the establishment of fantasy experiences during hypnosis. For instance, during a suggestion of going for a swim in a hot jungle, LG suggested that other women were with her and they were removing their tops:

> Very, very hot, in the tropics of the jungle. You are perspiring all over. You are with a few other girls. All you want to do is cool down. You see a beautiful pool of water. All you want to do is to jump in and cool down. You unbutton your blouse and go into the water. All the other girls are doing exactly the same thing. All you want to do is jump in. You think to yourself, "Okay, I'll just take off my blouse and go in topless."

This highlights his skills in using imagery to establish a context for removing clothes and introducing the image of a number of girls sharing a common experience in an enjoyable way. LG apparently used this type of suggestion to legitimize the suggested fantasy experience of PO by incorporating others into it. After some further attempts at encouraging sexual involvement, their interaction ended suddenly when PO stopped LG from pulling her blouse out of her skirt. LG became angry with PO, then seemed to become nervous, and quickly left the motel room.

The sexualized aspects of the communications of LG are apparent throughout the entire interaction. From his initial comments about liking his coffee "hot, black, and sweet," to his reassurances that the subject could trust him sexually, to his inquiries during age regression about the subject's sexual experiences, to his suggestion of disrobing during the jungle fantasy, there is clear evidence of his attempts to manipulate the subject's orientation to sexual activity. Moreover, LG's statements about the nature of hypnosis and his use of hypnotic techniques indicates a close linking of hypnosis and sexual activity. During hypnosis, he used hypnotic deepening procedures before he administered suggestions that were sexually toned, and this continued to communicate the association of hypnosis and sexual activity that had already been implied. In summary, our analysis of the interaction indicated that he was experienced in the use of hypnotic techniques, and that his use of these techniques with the undercover police officer was oriented toward sexual activity.

LG was arrested and charged with sexually assaulting CK. He was committed for trial, and we both appeared as expert witnesses at the trial. The judge ruled that evidence relating to LG's interaction with the undercover police officer was not relevant to the charge, and that material was not dealt with in court. Under cross-examination, the procedures of the hypnosis session that we conducted with CK were evaluated in detail, and focus was placed on the scientific and clinical data concerning the impact of hypnosis on memory. In the trial, we had no opportunity to present plausible, alternative hypotheses about the events of the case. The outcome of the case turned almost entirely on the quality of the testimony of CK, rather than, for instance, on the disorganizing effects of past trauma on CK that might have endured through time.

Approximately 3 years after the incident, CK's testimony was emotional, internally inconsistent, and inconsistent with aspects of the statements that she had made to the police, and during the hypnosis session. The defense attorney was very well prepared for the trial, and she conducted a cross-examination that elicited statements from CK that raised serious doubts about the reliability of the testimony that she was offering. After CK testified, the judge advised the jury that it could acquit LG without hearing the defense case if it wished to do so. This advice conveyed the strong impression that the testimony of CK was not credible. The jury considered the matter and advised the judge that LG should be acquitted. CK was very distressed by this outcome, and the prosecutor asked us to arrange an immediate clinical referral for CK. We did that, but CK did not take up the referral.

SUMMARY COMMENT

The use of hypnosis to assist victims of alleged sexual assault to remember information is obviously problematic. Victims are likely to experience a mix of emotion that includes anger, fear, helplessness, and other emotions; they are likely to be experiencing a range of cognitive changes that include difficulties with attention and memory, and they may undergo appreciable changes in their self-image and their relationships with others.

The incident that they are reporting and/or trying to remember may have involved alleged assailants who were either strangers, acquaintances, or friends, and may have occurred in situations in which there were shifting perceptions, expectations, and actions by each of those involved. In cases of sexual assault, it may well be that there is little chance of independent physical evidence or independent witness statement confirming or disconfirming the evidence given by the victim and the accused. The cases considered here highlight many of the psychological and forensic complexities involved in sexual assault, and the addition of hypnosis does little to lessen those complexities.

When forgetting of significant events is present, hypnosis can be a useful clinical technique to assist people to recall and integrate events into their self-image and ongoing personal narrative. That recall and integration, however, may not be consistent with the use of other material in the forensic system. What people need to believe for themselves is not necessarily what the courts think is appropriate to believe. Sometimes there will be congruence, and sometimes not. In the cases discussed in this chapter, the courts came to the view that congruence did not exist. This outcome gives serious pause to the use of hypnosis to enhance the memory of anyone alleging sexual assault. However, it is worthy to note in the case of CK that the use of hypnosis appears to have been successful in accessing memories. The fit of memories with independent events (viz., undercover work by the police and their motel tapes) implied the validity of what was retrieved. What prevented LG from being convicted is perhaps not any problem with hypnosis, but rather the combination of the judge's exclusion of the undercover evidence coupled with CK's especially poor performance on the witness stand. Hypnosis may have done its job, but other events basically determined the legal outcome.

The cases evaluated in this chapter raise significant questions. The presence of independent evidence of abuse is hard to establish with sexual assault victims, and it is possible to argue that hypnosis should not be used with them. Following our experience with these cases, our position is that hypnosis should not be used on any victim if independent corroboration (see Chapter 3) is impossible.

CHAPTER 6

Stress and Faking
in Hypnosis

This chapter considers two cases that illustrate a range of the issues discussed in this book. They emphasize, especially, the matters of consistency of reporting, aspects affecting the welfare of the person being hypnotized, procedural issues relating to proper professional practice, motivational issues affecting the hypnotist and the person hypnotized, the legal impact of the forensic investigation, ethical issues, and matters indicating specific forensic relevance. In a number of important ways, they pick up themes that have emerged in the previous cases that we have discussed.

The first of these cases reports the use of hypnosis with a man who came forward as a witness of the apparent abduction of a young woman. There was some ambiguity, about the aspects that he witnessed, and hypnosis was used in an attempt to clarify that ambiguity as well as to assist the witness to remember particular details. The young woman has not been found, and the case remains unsolved. Because of the relevant scope of issues this case poses, we report it in some detail.

THE CASE OF SP

SP was a young woman in her early 20s who lived alone. She worked in a job that she enjoyed, had a close circle of friends, and maintained regular contact with her parents, who lived in the same city. She had recently become friendly with a young man and had told friends that she looked forward to that relationship developing in a positive way. One evening, SP and a female friend went shopping and subsequently returned to the friend's apartment, where they had coffee. On May 8, 1986, SP left her friend's apartment at approximately 10:45 P.M. with the intention of driving to her own apartment. It is believed that SP traveled her usual route to join a major arterial road, but her car ran out of fuel along that road, and it is believed that she walked to some public telephones. It is known from records of the telephone company and the statements of the recipients of the calls that SP made two telephone calls, one at 11:17 P.M. and the other at 12:03 A.M., to the home of her boyfriend. In the first call, she asked her boyfriend to come and help her; he reportedly left his home shortly afterward. In the second call, she spoke to the person who shared the apartment with her boyfriend, and he told SP that her boyfriend was "on his way." At approximately 12:30 A.M., SP was seen by passing drivers as she was walking from the public telephones to her car. There has been no reported sighting of SP since that time, except by the witness who participated in our hypnosis session.

This witness (DD) was one of many people who came forward in response to a public call for information about the disappearance of SP. DD was a married male in his early 30s, who lived with his family in a city about 200 kilometers from the one in which SP lived. The witness was unemployed and described himself as having a "drinking problem." He said that he drank beer virtually every night and also drank during the day when he had "nothing else to do." At the time of SP's disappearance, he was visiting the city in which she lived because of the serious illness of a relative. Almost 4 months later, he contacted the police in his own city and indicated that he might have information that would assist with the investigation. In his initial statement to police, he gave a complex account of what he had seen, heard, and done on the night of SP's disappearance. In it, he said that he borrowed a car from a friend, drank some beer, and then left to get more beer. He said that, on the way, he saw a girl outside a phone box talking to some men. He stopped his car up the road from this scene and urinated on the ground. As he did so, he noticed that a motor vehicle had stopped some distance back, where he had seen the girl walking. He returned to see if the girl was still there; she was not. Driving back along the road, he saw a purse lying on the ground. He stopped and noticed money and credit cards, and put the purse on the back of a car that was parked nearby. In the statement, he said that he was unable to say whether the girl he saw walking along the road matched the description of SP. He said that it was possible the girl was the same person, but he could not be sure.

This account strongly suggested that the witness may have seen the abduction of SP. Over the following 8 months, he was interviewed by police a number of times in relation to various aspects of his initial statement. These aspects had yielded either negative leads or were inconsistent with other information that the investigation had provided. This culminated in a formal record of interview of DD by the senior investigating officer. That lengthy interview yielded a number of additional inconsistencies.

The degree of inconsistency of DD's memory reports over time emerges as a major issue in this case. In his summary note on the formal interview, the senior investigating officer perhaps best captured the flavor of the police interactions with DD up to this stage in his comment that DD "is very irrational at times and contradicts himself." A major feature of the case is that this apparent contradiction changed after hypnosis had been introduced.

The Investigation

From its beginning, the investigation into SP's disappearance seemed to be hampered by a large number of complexities and difficulties. When she failed to arrive at work the following day, her employer contacted her parents, who visited her apartment, contacted some of her friends, and eventually found her car after retracing SP's movements on the previous night. Her parents then reported the disappearance of SP to the police, approximately 18 hours after she was last reported seen. However, they did not inform the police that they had moved the car from its original position in order to put it in a safer location. So the police search began approximately 100 meters from where the car had been left by SP. When the original location of the car had been established, SP's shoes, an earring, and her purse were found nearby. However, the value of this material and the search for other physical evidence was lessened by the fact that it had rained for approximately 48 hours after the last reported sighting of SP. When SP's parents contacted her boyfriend the day after her disappearance, he told them that he had not heard from

road, "DD noticed a girl . . . [and] a number of events occurred."
The hypnotist was also told that DD had provided a statement
to the police and had been interviewed about what he had seen.
Because of previous media reports, the hypnotist recorded his
general knowledge of the case. This essentially consisted of
remembering reports that "a young woman had disappeared"
when her "car had broken down for some reason."

The Hypnosis Session with DD

The interaction between the hypnotist and DD was lengthy and
complex and raised multiple issues of forensic relevance. The
hypnotist and DD were together for approximately 6 hours. The
only other person with whom they had contact during the time
they were together was the person who coordinated the session.
Here we summarize the overall session in terms of the (1) the
prehypnotic interview, (2) the first hypnosis session, (3) a second
hypnosis session, and (4) posthypnotic interview.

Prehypnotic Interview

The intent of the prehypnotic interview was for the hypnotist to
gather the details of the events that DD had been involved in on
the night in question. The hypnotist had minimal knowledge and
information about the events associated with SP's disappearance
and virtually no knowledge about DD's involvement in any
events on that night. Initially, the hypnotist focused on obtaining
relevant personal material about DD and his medical/psychol-
ogical history. Whenever appropriate, the hypnotist established
common personal experiences and made positive comments
about things that DD seemed proud of, such as his children. The
anxiety that DD displayed initially decreased during this period
of history taking and rapport building, and DD became increasingly cooperative and positive in his interactions with the hypnotist. Early on, the interaction seemed to be characterized by
DD's degree of "wanting to do the right thing"; and this was a
stance that he returned to throughout the session.

However, the discussion of DD's expectations of hypnosis
and what he wanted to achieve increased his anxiety. He displayed a range of misconceptions about hypnosis that he either
had or had been communicated to him by family members (e.g.,
his sister believed that "hypnosis is the work of the devil"). For

the most part, DD accepted the hypnotist's comments about the nature of hypnosis and integrated those comments into relevant personal experiences (e.g., his "drifting away when watching television"). DD expressed concern, however, as to whether he would be able to concentrate well enough for the hypnotist "to get him under." This concern about whether he would be able to be hypnotized deeply enough to achieve his aims is one that DD would return to during the hypnosis session. Interestingly, DD later took the position that the hypnotist could not get him out of hypnosis. This reversal of concern on his part may have had particular clinical relevance.

The prehypnotic discussion of the events the night of SP's disappearance was detailed and, for the most part, the hypnotist let DD narrate those events for as long as he wished. The hypnotist's questioning during this lengthy, nonsequential narrative was minimal and occurred mainly when the hypnotist became unsure about the nature of a detail that DD was giving (e.g., DD's reference to all the women he saw on the night as "this sheila" made it difficult to know which particular woman he was referring to at times). During this narrative, DD often made a distinction in his comments between what he remembered from the night itself and what he had since found out from the police. His overall memory appeared to involve the incorporation of information provided by the police and his visits with them to the scene of the various events. For instance, he told the hypnotist that only after driving around with the police did he "know" his driving and walking pattern that night. The reliability of his memory for these events and the integration of the subsequent information into his memory clearly have forensic relevance.

DD said that his major aim for the hypnosis session was "to get the number of the car" in which he saw the woman, whom he believed to be SP, struggling. There were other things that he indicated would be useful to clarify in his mind (e.g., the actions of a young man with a stick, with whom he interacted near the scene of SP's disappearance), but his major focus was the registration number. The frustration and emotion that he appeared to experience about the registration number was clearly evident; for instance, he began to cry when first asked to try to remember it.

First Hypnosis Session

Initially, the hypnotist explained the basic induction procedure to DD and asked him to close his eyes. The hypnotist instructed

DD to lift his right finger if he wanted to say something during the induction and also told DD that when he saw this, he would ask him what he wanted to say. DD took this instruction literally and continued to use the finger lift even after the induction procedure, until the hypnotist explicitly told him not to use it. During the induction procedure, DD displayed somatic symptoms of anxiety (e.g., rapid breathing, some shaking) and cognitive symptoms (e.g., various spontaneous comments about having "racing thoughts" in his head, having a "blank mind," and being unable to concentrate). DD frequently interrupted the induction procedure to say that he didn't think that he was going under hypnosis. In response to this repeated statement, the hypnotist explored with DD experiences that would meet his expectations that he was beginning to experience hypnosis, and DD offered the metaphor of "floating on a white cloud" as something that had worked previously in the context of a relaxation tape that a physician had given him to assist with his anxiety. Perhaps meaningfully, DD had not volunteered this information earlier when asked about any previous experiences similar to hypnosis. Rather, he offered the information only after the induction that the hypnotist had used had "failed," as it were. In addition to the "white cloud" procedure offered by DD, the hypnotist then used the Chevreul pendulum as an induction/deepening procedure. This quasi-hypnotic procedure seemed to impress DD and convince him that he was experiencing hypnosis. Use of ideomotor items (such as arm levitation), combined with deepening, allowed the hypnotist to conduct a modest assessment of hypnotizability.

The plethora of events covered during the first hypnosis session interweaved as the session developed. In terms of DD's behavior and experience, we summarize here because of their salience in his earlier reported viewing of the young woman struggling in the car and his attempts to remember the registration number of the car. The hypnotist and DD returned to the registration number a number of times. It provides the most compelling clinical material and the most challenging material for forensic interpretation that emerged from the case.

When the hypnotist approached this incident initially, DD displayed clear cognitive and emotional resistance to getting close to his memories of, and feelings about, the scene. This is not an uncommon problem in such cases. The strategy that the hypnotist used to overcome this problem was the use of a "hidden part" that could speak or write more easily than DD could; this procedure conveys cues for appropriate response, but is nevertheless useful for accessing material that is blocked from consciousness for some reason—it suggests a fantasy as a way of recalling a reality. Furthermore, the hypnotist established that this hidden part could engage in automatic writing. Clinical indications of conflict were strongly evident in the tremor of DD's hand when he tried to write "automatically." After some effort, DD accepted the metaphor of the hidden part and described it as his "inner self." He did not accept as readily the notion of automatic writing by this part.

The hypnotist gave explicit permission to DD to experience and express any feelings that he had about what was happening when it appeared that DD was experiencing significant conflict about the incident or his reporting of it. At a number of points, the hypnotist had to make decisions about the relative weight of forensic and clinical matters (for full discussion of this issue, see Chapters 7 and 8). This conflict for the hypnotist was perhaps best captured when DD began shouting "Ram it, ram it!" when talking about the young woman in the car. The interpretation that DD later put on this material was that, at the time, he had thought about using his vehicle to ram the car in which he saw the struggling woman. Prior to hypnosis, however, DD had never indicated that this was a thought that he had experienced at the time.

During the first hypnosis session, DD and/or his "hidden part" went over other incidents, but he kept returning to the scene of the struggling woman in the car and continued trying to remember the registration number. DD's emotional displays during this time were extreme and compelling. During them, he presented as a person who had been caught up in a situation in which he felt quite unable to act. Since that time, he appeared to have been paying psychological penance for failing to act. There was substantial evidence of repression for impulses and/or behaviors that DD appeared to find unacceptable. Although it is not possible to rule out simulation, his emotional displays did not appear to us to be contrived or strategic; rather, they appeared to have an involuntary, nonconscious quality that suggested the significance and primacy of powerful affective experience. DD's emotions were a key component of the session and were meaningful for him personally in the psychological sense of bringing him close to acknowledging the memory of a scene he wished to retrieve. But he was prevented from that acknowledgment because his cognitions were unable to incorporate the remembered material in any acceptable way.

After the display of such strong emotion, the hypnotist felt ethically constrained to terminate the first hypnosis session through the use of a standardized awakening procedure. Paradoxically, DD appeared to have been effectively dehypnotized, but still claimed that he was experiencing hypnosis. Following an explicit request from DD for more hypnosis and an indication by him that he thought he would be able to remember additional details, the hypnotist gave DD an undertaking that he would continue with a second hypnosis session after a short break.

Second Hypnosis Session

The second hypnosis session was strikingly different from the first. This could have been because of the hypnotist's plans, because of a shift in DD's agenda, or because of the combination of both these aspects. During the second session, DD or his "hidden part," tried to recall a number of incidents, and he made various additional attempts to recall the registration number. DD directed the hypnotist both verbally and nonverbally to do a number of things during this session. He clearly had an agenda in mind, and the hypnotist allowed DD to pursue that agenda in its broad outline. The emotions that DD displayed in this hypnosis session appeared to be less compelling and to have more of a voluntary, conscious quality. In contrast to the first hypnosis session, these emotions seemed to be secondary to the cognitions that DD was reporting. From a clinical perspective, such a scenario was probably necessary so that DD could leave the session more psychologically intact.

The awakening procedure that the hypnotist used paralleled the original induction procedure and was highly ritualized to provide DD with the impression that he was, in his words, "leaving straight." DD needed some expectations filled (e.g., canceling the "white cloud" metaphor) and he needed specific directions (e.g., about what he would remember afterward). The hypnotist indicated that after hypnosis, DD would remember the things that he "chose to remember." A very clear impression is that DD had substantial concerns about how to handle the emotional experiences that he had during the first hypnosis session, and the second session aimed in part to help him with that concern.

Posthypnotic Interview

The posthypnotic interview could have gone in a number of directions. The hypnotist chose to display minimal concern about DD's reported headache, stiffness, and feeling of nausea, and to focus instead on how things had gone from DD's perspective. DD clearly had mixed feelings about his experience of hypnosis as a whole. He indicated that he had thought it would be "easier," and that hypnosis would have "magically gotten at my memory" of the registration number. Nevertheless, DD said that he had enjoyed the session and got a lot out of it personally. There were some anomalous comments made by DD during this interview. For instance, he made a number of interesting side comments about the hypnotist and the senior investigating officer. He glanced sideways at the hypnotist at one stage and said, "You're cunning, that's for sure"; about the officer, he nodded toward the adjoining room and said, "He's a fair bloke." The hypnotist did not follow up these asides. Arguably, they were associated with the importance that DD placed on whether the hypnotist and the officer actually believed the memories he had reported. Consistent with the interpersonal strategy that the hypnotist had adopted from the beginning of the second hypnosis session, the hypnotist indicated that he "accepted" what DD had said to him when DD specifically asked him what he thought about his memories of the night in question.

During the posthypnotic interview, the hypnotist indicated to DD that he should consider talking with a mental health professional about his thoughts and feelings, and suggested that he perhaps not try so hard to remember what had happened. This was indicated clinically because of the interpretation we had formed that DD was punishing himself for something that had happened, or for some feeling he had about what had taken place. He said he was spending most of his time, both waking and sleeping, trying to remember the registration number.

Evaluation of the Hypnosis Session with DD

The use of hypnosis with DD provided little material of direct assistance to the investigation of SP's disappearance. It did not provide the registration number or a clear description of any individuals involved in the various events. Based on his comments in the police statement, in the recorded interview, and to the hypnotist, it was apparent that DD's memory of that night could not be said to be clear and detailed and based only on the events of that night. Rather, his memory seemed to have been shaped by what he witnessed, by what he felt about what he witnessed, by what he had felt subsequently, and by what he had been told and/or shown by the police afterward, or seen or heard in the media. DD claimed in the posthypnotic interview that he was 100% sure about his memory, but he also stated during that interview that on some things he was not sure whether they had happened or he had imagined them. Furthermore, DD seemed to have accepted the interpretations of some events that the police had offered in their numerous interactions with him. In this sense, the hypnotic procedures confirmed in a compelling way that DD's memory was very malleable.

The matter of the malleability of DD's memory raises the important issue of consistency of his reports. Reasons explaining DD's inconsistency have been discussed, but explanation inevitably relates also to how hypnosis might have influenced the nature of the memories that he reported. To demonstrate this point, statements given by DD at different times during our involvement with him were analyzed. They demonstrate massive changes in the style and consistency of his reporting.

Consistency and Style of Reporting

To some extent, we have already examined consistency across different reports by DD (first statement to the police, the recorded interview, and reports in the hypnotic setting). We turn now to focus closely on two formal statements made by DD: one before, and one after hypnosis.

DD gave two statements to the police, one in October 1986, and a second, after hypnosis, in June 1987. Comparison of the two statements is instructive. Statement 1 (before hypnosis) was 3 pages long. Statement 2 (after hypnosis) was 11 pages long. Extracts from similar sections, reporting on the same events are as follows:

> Statement 1: I then drove to the intersection of Wacol Station Road and Ipswich Road. I turned left into Ipswich Road with the intention of going to Darra Bowling Club to get some beer. After crossing a waterhole on a bend in Ipswich Road I saw a person walking on the gravel shoulder of the road in the direction of Brisbane. At first I thought that it was a male and as I

got level the person turned toward me and I noticed that it was a female. She had dark hair, thin build and dressed in jeans and a coat. The clothing was a dark color. I drove further up the road and saw a blue colored sedan parked in the driveway to the Migrant Centre. I stopped my car there and urinated on the ground. As I did so I noticed a motor vehicle had stopped on the inbound side of the road some distance back where I had seen the girl walking.

Statement 2: I then drove toward Ipswich Road and went to turn left but I had to stop to give way to traffic traveling Ipswich Road toward Wacol or Jindalee. All the traffic on my right passed by me except for one car which had his indicator on to turn right which would have taken him into Progress Road from Ipswich Road. I moved out into Ipswich Road and commenced traveling along it when I noticed that the vehicle that had been indicating to turn into Progress Road had not done so and was traveling about half a car length behind me in the right hand lane. I thought it was probably the police and slowed down and I noticed that this other vehicle slowed as well but I was able to get a quick look in his direction. I noticed that the windows of his vehicle were tinted but at this stage I cannot give an accurate description of what the driver looked like. I also recall that when this vehicle was stopped at the light at the intersection of Ipswich Road and Progress Road I looked at the number-plate, but, I cannot remember the number at present. I also looked at the driver at this time. As this vehicle slowed beside me I saw it was slowing so I sped off. I followed Ipswich Road over the little bridge and around a bit of a bend and was heading up the hill. Part of the way up this rise and at a point I now know to be about opposite the Army Barracks I saw a girl standing beside the driver's door of a car stopped on the left side of the road. The other vehicle I had referred to had by this time stopped on the grass section on his right hand-side between the inbound and outbound lanes. I stopped my vehicle beside this girl standing outside her car with the center pillar of my vehicle about level with the front parking lights of her car. I have since learned that this vehicle was a yellow-colored Datsun Bluebird, but this is because I have been told and not because I could remember it myself. As I was approaching this woman to stop I could see that she had dark hair about shoulder length, she was wearing a dark dress with short sleeves. I think it was one piece and went all the way to the neck. She had white step-in shoes and her dress came right down to her lower calf or just about ankle length. She was holding a purse and as I was just near her she made a movement as if to read her watch from my lights and then turned and appeared as if she was looking over the front of her vehicle and then to the rear of her vehicle. When I stopped my vehicle near this woman I leaned over to wind down the left hand window to speak to her but my seat belt stopped me reaching across. I sat back up straight and undid the belt and went to lean over again and as I did so my hand must have struck the light switch and the lights of the car went off. At about this time the woman started yelling. I don't know if she was yelling at me or what she was yelling, but I didn't want any trouble so I just drove off. . . . At the time I stopped my vehicle in the entrance to the Migrant Centre I saw a silvery blue car parked near the brick wall at the entrance. After the person with the piece of wood left I was having a piss and trying to make myself sick when I heard a noise coming from the direction of the yellow car where I had stopped.

Analysis of these two statements reveals dramatic changes over time. The two extracts are so inconsistent, one might seriously query whether they are reporting on the same events. Rather than viewing the second statement as an elaboration, it could be seen as a whole new start and a whole new story, and the detail suggests strong elements of "fantasy to please." The first statement was short and involved very little detail. In both style and content, there was no evidence of involvement with anybody. The witness took the stance purely of an uninvolved person. He saw the girl and then she disappeared, nothing more. Standing on its own, the statement is believable. It presents the position of someone who is a witness. Overall, however, one obtains the impression of the witness as someone who is willing to come forward and offer details of things seen on the night in question, but with no real involvement in the events being reported.

The second statement, which follows hypnosis, is rational; massive detail is set firmly in place and there are no glaring internal inconsistencies. The witness's account expresses much more confidence about what precisely happened when and where, and the account of the events is completely different. There are two aspects that are particularly striking, and they both relate to the style of the statement, which was altogether absent in the hypnotic setting. These two aspects relate to the amount of specific detail and the indications of strong motivation underlying the coherence of the report.

In the second statement, there are very specific details reported about conversations and dress. The extent of the detail is surprising, considering one could imagine it must have been difficult for someone recalling an incident that occurred over 12 months previously. The condition of the witness was also not ideal for the long-term retention of detail (e.g., DD had by his own admission continued to drink alcohol during the night in question). Furthermore, in contrast to earlier statements, there is the fact that everything appears now in a much more reasonable order. The hypnosis session contained descriptions that overlapped, referred to different incidents concurrently, and drew together seemingly irrelevant events. Report of memories in this second statement is much more precise and events were recalled with considerable confidence, raising the question of whether confidence itself was a consequential effect of hypnosis.

The second aspect refers to the influence of motivational factors. In the second statement, a motive is included for virtually all of the witness's actions, making his story appear more credible. The reason he drove, for example, was to buy some beer. In this statement, everything is well explained, and particular reasons are given for DD's behavior. As a result, the second statement appears to be more credible than the first. Whether the fact that it coheres more obviously is due to the cementing of details in the witness's mind as a consequence of hypnosis, or to the inadvertent influence of the person who typed the statement (itself a factor in the forensic setting, not to be ignored) is not entirely clear. It seems most plausible to conclude from the stark contrast between the two statements that a multitude of factors were associated with massive changes in reported memories and created greater conviction about what was reported. The criterion for reporting obviously shifted, releasing far more detail in recall and producing more rationale for actions. There were signs of florid elaboration of events, or substitution of new events, and also signs of closer observation of similar events. The evidence overall seems strongly weighted toward a contamination of memory and fantasy, evident probably before hypnosis was ever involved, and possibly reinforced by the presence of hypnosis that followed. This interpretation is further substantiated by the frequent swings in the story, which characterized DD's prehypnotic interviews. Hypnosis may have served more distinctly to help bolster the witness's "belief" in the story that he had formulated prior to hypnosis.

Changes in reported memories and greater self-confidence can occur for many reasons. Elaboration of memories, engagement in fantasy, and enhancement of confidence are all possible effects of hypnosis introduced in the forensic setting, but these effects are also true of memory in general. It is important to recognize that when hypnosis is used to facilitate recall, it may enhance or intensify already existing problems of emotional memory. Also, it is important to acknowledge that not everything that occurs following a hypnotic induction should be attributed to the effects of hypnosis; other influences and effects do not stop when hypnosis is introduced.

Role of Emotion

The use of hypnosis made it very clear that there were some events on the night in question that were overlaid by highly charged emotion in DD, and the reasons for this emotional overlay are relevant forensically. These matters are also of obvious clinical relevance in terms of DD's psychological well-being. The use of hypnosis highlighted that DD was an essentially cooperative individual who was willing to expose himself to a situation of considerable stress. The compelling nature of the emotion in the first hypnosis session, and to a lesser extent in the second hypnosis session, suggested that DD was not consciously attempting to deceive either himself or others. However, he did appear to be protecting himself from particular memories, consistent with deep concern apparently about what happened on the night. This protection is of direct clinical relevance and is also of direct forensic relevance in the sense that it prevented a clear picture from emerging in DD's mind and, of course, in the minds of the investigating authorities. What basically characterized the session was not what DD remembered, but the fact that DD wanted desperately to report something but did not.

Clinically, DD presented as an individual who was experiencing substantial intrapersonal conflict. Although he had become somewhat emotional about the night in his previous interactions with the police, the use of hypnosis provided the context and the mechanisms for him to display strong affective reactions and to come closer to the memories of that night than he had previously. The abreactive nature of his emotional displays probably emerged because of the convergence of a number of factors: the induction of hypnosis, the strategy of the hidden part (or "inner self," as DD called it), the rapport with the hypnotist, and the pressure of the overall context. Together, all these factors seemed to play a role in tapping the multiple layers of affect that were linked to his memories of the night in question. It is unlikely that further information could have been obtained from DD without placing undue stress upon him. The physical signs of distress in automatic writing suggested that he wanted to write something important but could not do so, no matter how hard he tried. Major conflict was evident, in particular, in relation to his many attempts to remember the registration number, which he claimed he had seen and scratched on the ground.

In a number of interesting ways, distinctive cognitive style features were evident in DD's response. At the stages of deepest involvement, DD responded only when his reporting was associated with the signal to respond that had been established or legitimized by the hypnotist. Elements of DD's response also suggested a strong degree of compulsivity, and this type of response was consistent with deep hypnotic involvement. Moreover, there were indications also that he was processing highly charged material, and struggling to remember material that was very conflicted for him. It was during one such time of high emotional display that DD talked angrily about the victim. At the time that DD was most clearly stressed by what was happening, he also expressed anger to both the assailant(s) and the victim.

The second hypnosis session produced material that was qualitatively different from what had preceded. Emotion was present in DD's responses, but he expressed it much less convincingly to the observer (e.g., a verbal stammer with slow, deliberate speaking emerged as a style of response that had not appeared before). DD seemed much more willing than he had been in the first hypnosis session to report information about what had happened. Here, also, a clinically interesting facet of the session was that DD directed the hypnotist to help him move away from the "hidden part" of his personality, and perhaps the conflict that was stressful to him, to the conscious part, in order to elaborate on his memories. This gave DD the appearance of being much more in control than he was in the first hypnosis session about the act of remembering, and of being strategically motivated for his own purposes. The material that he reported and elaborated, however, was unconvincing. Although there were no consistent, multiple indications of pretense in his performance, the nature of DD's affect and his behavior were very different qualitatively from what had occurred before.

In the second hypnosis session, there were indications that the rapport between DD and the hypnotist had shifted. The relationship no longer projected itself as positive and supportive, compared with the first hypnosis session. Nevertheless, this session was characterized by DD's willingness to report additional material and to express concern that his performance was good, acceptable, and convincing. In a final discussion just before he left, it is interesting to note that DD indicated that he thought that the hypnotist felt negatively toward him. Quality of rapport was obviously important to DD.

Our overwhelming impression gained from the use of hypnosis was that DD was experiencing deep conflict about what occurred on the night of SP's disappearance. Clinically, one possibility is that something major occurred, that DD saw something and was deeply upset by the experience. The level and intensity of this conflict seemed such that it is unlikely to be resolved, other than through intensive clinical intervention. There were no real indications of the precise nature of this conflict, except that it seemed that he had seen, experienced, or felt something that he could not, or did not want to bring to awareness at the time hypnosis was used. Of course, it is possible that DD saw nothing and that his conflict was over what he believed he should have seen, but did not. The feeling of guilt, together with the pressure of the investigating officers and the hypnotist's questions may have led DD to display conflict of the sort that was observed.

Reliability of Memory

In relation to the conflict that occurred in this case, we are conscious that the conflict may indicate confabulation, or may reflect our own conflict over what DD believed he should have seen. In terms of DD's memory reports, the data were nevertheless consistent with the hypothesis that DD's memory was highly unreliable. The inconsistency of reporting in the statements before and after hypnosis is consonant with memory unreliability, and this reflects the influence of both time and occasion of reporting. The degree of unreliability appeared striking. As to hypnosis itself, the apparent incongruity between the quality of reports in the first and second hypnosis sessions suggests that DD's memory reports had a substantial confabulatory overlay. Furthermore, if any real and potentially relevant memories existed, they may have been deeply repressed, and the path to those memories was likely to be through material that would have to be assimilated into DD's consciousness with care. The meaningfulness of these memories to any criminal investigation would have to be evaluated through careful clinical scrutiny. One of the most significant facts to emerge through the use of hypnosis was that DD could not remember the registration number of the car for the reason that other "memories" kept intruding whenever he made the effort to do so. For example:

> Help me, don't let it go . . . don't leave the car . . . get the number, help me . . . follow it (*breathing heavily*), follow the car (*throwing head about*) . . . I don't know what to do.

The utility of hypnosis, together with its impact on DD's memory reports, must be considered in the light of the style and content of DD's recall across the entire period of the investigation. We had access to information given by DD at five points: (1) the initial statement to the police; (2) the prehypnotic interview; (3) the hypnosis session; (4) the posthypnotic interview; and (5) the final statement to the police. The statements have been discussed. Accordingly, we turn now to consider the hypnotic material, with the aim of pointing to the major consistencies and inconsistencies in the content of the information given by DD at these different time periods. We further offer comment on the style and credibility of some of the information that he provided. Our aim essentially is to address the issue of the specific impact of hypnosis on DD's memory reports when those reports are considered within a broad time frame.

Prehypnotic Interview

DD qualified much of the material he reported during the prehypnotic interview with statements such as: "I don't know who he was at the time, I just figured it out lately"; "Don't want to tell nothing that's not right, I'm not right on this"; "I'm not even sure that this happened, you know being drunk and everything"; and "I didn't know nothing about nothing until [the police] showed me. I've got to convince them that what they've showed me I've already done before."

DD was obviously concerned with "doing the right thing," but he stressed time and time again that he was not sure of his memories, that some of his reports stemmed from things he had been told after the night in question rather than from actual memories, and how anxious he was to "get it straight" in his own mind. Nevertheless, DD reported substantial detail surrounding events that he claimed he could not remember previously (e.g., "I didn't know until he told me but somewhere in there, the truck came up, . . . the truck came up that had a house on it"). The mention here of his being told referred to the fact that the police had earlier informed him about the truck. This raises the possibility that DD's memory was contaminated by earlier interactions to a degree that he could no longer distinguish between what was an actual memory and what was not. Comments indicating that DD desperately wanted to comply with the requests of the police were made throughout this interview.

Hypnosis Session

From the perspective of his memory reports, DD provided relatively little detail in comparison to his reports during the prehypnotic interview. He focused with urgency on the registration number, but was distracted by images of SP struggling in the car. He talked a little about a young man with a stick, a little about a young woman in the car, and gave some description of the car, but otherwise this session provided no additional memory reports of substance that were not given outside of hypnosis at some time. This is an interesting fact considering how confident DD was after the hypnosis session, and it begs the question of how much his posthypnotic reports were influenced by all that preceded them. Memories were clearly inconsistent, but essentially DD believed that everything he had reported previously had now been validated, whether that material was discussed in hypnosis or not.

Posthypnotic Interview

Although there were obvious inconsistencies and contradictions in the material that DD reported, the most striking aspect of his reporting after hypnosis was his increased confidence in all of the material that he had ever reported to the police. This is seen in statements to the hypnotist such as: "Everything that I've known, I've proved it"; "I did see that number, I don't care what anybody says, I'm convinced of that 100 percent"; "Everything I've told you is right"; and "What I've told (the senior investigating officer) is true." In this interview, he only qualified his memory reports once by saying, "All I wanted to do was help, I panicked," but this qualification was overshadowed by his statements such as: "Everything I've told has been right. The bits I didn't know, I worked it out. Now I know." During this time, DD nevertheless looked to the hypnotist (H) for confirmation of his memory reports, as it were, as can be seen in the following exchange:

DD: Do you think I was talking the truth or what?

H: I don't know.

DD: Oh (*puts head in hands*).

H: I don't know anything more than what you've told me.

The final statement was taken about a week after the hypnosis session. Hypnosis may or may not have been responsible for the shift, but its coherence and detail contrast very sharply with all the reports that preceded it. As stated, the final statement as a whole had an unmistakable air of confidence and coherence about it that was missing from all previous statements and interviews. Its apparent lucidity, however, depends on whether one considers it is an elaboration of relevant detail, or a story relaying altogether new events.

Implications for Theory and Practice

The use of hypnosis with DD raised a number of issues of a theoretical and practical nature. We canvass them here and offer comment that aims not only to throw light on this case, but also to orient the reader to similar issues in other cases and in the area of investigative hypnosis as a whole. Forensically, it seems clear that an individual such as DD would offer the legal system very unreliable testimony, whether hypnosis were used or not. His memory reporting was erratic. Moreover, DD's memory was changeable and easily influenced by a number of sources. Consequently, it is probably the case that DD could easily be brought to think that events occurred when they did not.

The case also raises a number of other issues that are legal and/or ethical in nature. Ethically, it exposes the vulnerability of DD (as could be the case for other persons in the same circumstances) and highlights the need to protect the rights of individuals who are placed in strong, emotionally arousing situations. It could be argued that the session, if it had continued, might have created a scenario that interpreted or explained DD's internal struggle in a particular way. The question here is whether hypnosis should be used when the probability is high that this kind of situation will arise. The legal implications of providing an informed consent form (see Chapter 3) to meet the problem are complex, and one may seriously question whether such a form addresses the scope of this problem. These and other ethical issues are discussed in more detail in the next chapter.

This case, like others, raises significant issues in the theory and practice of forensic hypnosis and its complexity demands reassessment of its relevance within the forensic literature. In particular, such cases point to the need to consider far more closely the inherent variability that may exist in people's memory reports and the way hypnosis should be conceptualized in relation to it. Also, it seems clear that no guidelines can be fully adequate in managing the complexity of all clinical and ethical issues.

THE MIRANDA DOWNES CASE

We move now to our final major case that illustrates in its own distinctive way a range of complex forensic issues. Hypnosis was a key part of the trial, and the case was the most legally decisive in terms of hypnosis of those considered in this book. Hypnosis was also conducted in a setting that did not apply strict guidelines for its practice. In this case, the particular issue of focus was the genuineness of hypnosis, whether hypnosis was actually involved, and what indicators of genuineness were observable. We take up the general issue of faking in our analysis of forensic principles in Chapter 8. Analysis focuses on this issue here, however, because of its special legal importance in the case.

The case analyzed here also draws out some of the common issues that thread throughout our research. These include, in particular, the role of emotion, the consistency of reporting, and the unreliability of memory. All of these emerge as common forensic parameters, and ones that necessarily inform the development of proper guidelines for practice. The broad context for considering these forensic parameters ordinarily assumes hypnosis is genuinely present. This case demonstrates that the assumption that hypnosis is genuine is not always tenable. That issue is pertinent to other cases as well, but the salience of it here is distinctive.

Miranda Downes, was a 35-year-old scriptwriter who was on vacation in Queensland. She was murdered 24 kilometers north of Cairns on August 3, 1985, after having gone for a jog on the beach in the late afternoon. Her naked and battered body, lying face down at the water's edge on Buchans Point Beach, was found by police. A postmortem examination revealed that she had drowned, but she had injuries that suggested she had been struck earlier by a vehicle, raped, and then drowned in the sea. The body was found on the beach at 1:50 A.M. on August 4, but she had died some time earlier. Later on that day, Ernest Arthur Knibb, a 46-year-old unemployed male, whose psychological history was obscure, but who had had previous difficulties with the police, voluntarily told Cairns police that his vehicle had been on the beach the evening before. He said that he had heard a news broadcast in which mention was made of the deceased's body and of the fact that the police were concerned to talk with the driver of a four-wheel-drive vehicle that had been seen on the beach close to 6:00 P.M. He gave a statement to the police in which he said that he drove his four-wheel-drive vehicle on to the beach around that time on August 3. However, he denied seeing the deceased or being involved in her death. On August 11, he subsequently traveled to another town in Queensland, Maryborough, where he told police there that when he left Buchans Point Beach, he saw a blue four-wheel-drive vehicle on the beach. The police impounded his vehicle for several days for examination, and he was placed under surveillance for the period that he lived in Maryborough.

In January 1987, Knibb contacted the national current affairs television program *60 Minutes,* and he met and talked with a reporter for the program in February 1987. At Knibb's request, he underwent a hypnosis session with a psychologist arranged by the television program. Shortly after that session, he was arrested and charged with the murder of Miranda Downes. The trial was in September 1987, and he was convicted. Knibb lodged an appeal in May 1988, on the grounds that the verdict of guilty was "unsafe and unsatisfactory." The appeal was not upheld.

The case is extraordinary for the fact that a man, who declared himself innocent of the crime, related on national television how he would have gone about the murder if he had, in fact, been guilty. His appearance on the program also produced information that conflicted with what had been told to police, and this essentially led to his arrest. Specifically, he told police that he was on the beach for "a couple of minutes" on the evening that Miranda Downes was murdered, but the television program reported him as saying that he was there for half an hour, the latter being corroborated by independent witnesses who were in a car-park near the beach at the time.

Police told the court that injuries to Miranda Downes's shoulder were consistent with her having been struck by the right-hand rear-vision mirror on Knibb's four-wheel-drive car. They made a thorough examination of Knibb's vehicle on and subsequent to August 5. They gave special attention to the bracket that held the side mirror; they also took measurements of the height of the bracket and mirror above the ground. In evidence, the court was told that the mark on the shoulder of the deceased was consistent with having been caused by the projecting bracket and side mirror of the accused's vehicle. There was also clear evidence given to the jury that Knibb was driving his vehicle on the beach at the relevant time.

A number of witnesses identified Knibb and his vehicle as being on the beach. About 1 hour before Miranda Downes arrived there, an elderly couple pulled into the parking area in their bright red Mercedes sedan. They watched Knibb's vehicle drive through from the highway and onto the beach. Another witness was walking on the beach and was passed by a four-wheel-drive vehicle several times. On the last pass, the driver spoke to the witness, saying, "I'm not trying to run you down; I'm just giving my vehicle a go on the beach." This witness identified Knibb's vehicle as being similar to the one she saw. In hypnosis, Knibb reported seeing on the beach a mysterious figure who he thought was going to run him over, and a car with blazing headlights, which he thought was occupied by the killer. A key issue that emerged during the trial was the veracity of this report and the genuineness of Knibb's experience of hypnosis in the session that was recorded by the media. The interview on television was not the first contact Knibb had made with the media. He went to a newspaper to complain about police harassment after his vehicle was impounded. He also undertook a lie-detector test for the current affairs program, and was told he had failed that test. Furthermore, he was hypnotized by a local psychologist, and this became a focus at the trial.

Knibb appealed against his conviction through the Queensland Court of Criminal Appeal (*R. v. Knibb*, 1987) and the High Court of Australia (*Knibb v. The Queen*, 1988), which dismissed the appeal. Knibb complained in particular about the admission into evidence of the videorecording of hypnosis made for the television program. Moreover, he argued that evidence offered in the trial that he was not experiencing hypnosis should not have been allowed. Knibb failed to persuade the High Court to grant him leave to appeal against his murder conviction. Arguments that evidence in the videorecording was prejudicial to him, and objections made to questions answered by him while he was supposed to be under hypnosis were not sustained by the High Court. The prosecution had pressed for the admission of the hypnosis evidence, because it said Knibb was faking, and this was consistent with other indications that Knibb told significant lies with respect to his movements at the time in question on Buchans Point Beach.

In its judgment, the High Court of Australia (*Knibb v. The Queen*, 1988) ruled that the material introduced at trial did not unfairly prejudice Knibb. The High Court, furthermore, accepted expert evidence provided at the trial by us to the effect that the applicant was probably not under hypnosis at the time. It was also noted that the trial judge gave directions to the jury concerning the value of the questions and answers, and no objection was taken to the sufficiency of these directions at the time. "This being so, the case [was] not a suitable vehicle for the Court to grant special leave to appeal to consider the circumstances in which evidence can or should be received of statements made by a person whilst under hypnosis" (p. 95). Ernest Knibb is currently serving a life sentence for the murder of Miranda Downes.

The Hypnosis Session with Knibb

The hypnosis session was conducted by a practicing psychologist who was formally qualified with PhD degree and was a local resident. It was conducted in the presence of a television camera crew, and this probably influenced in part the behavior of both Knibb and the hypnotist. A full report of the session is published elsewhere by the hypnotist involved (Milne, 1992, 1994). In late January 1987, the hypnotist (Milne) received a phone call from the producer of *60 Minutes* and was told that he and his crew would shortly be visiting Cairns with a man who was suspected of murder. The lie-detector test had already been arranged, and the psychologist was requested to conduct a hypnosis session. The psychologist was cautious, but felt that hypnosis might free a blockage that could help in the case. The psychologist, who was unconnected to us, agreed to use hypnosis after explaining that, for evidential purposes, it was an unreliable procedure because subjects could willfully lie if it suited their purpose. On the other hand, he said that in a genuine case of traumatic amnesia, new leads might be uncovered that could be independently investigated for their veridicality.

Knibb came to the hypnosis session just after being told that he had failed the lie-detector test, and he was angry about that judgment. Prior to induction, he stated that he wanted to be hypnotized to clear up his recollections of the time spent on the beach and claimed that all he wanted was to arrive at the truth. The hypnosis session took about an hour, and Milne (1992) reported that Knibb engaged in "an incredible feat of word-spinning from a subject presumed to be hypnotized" (p. 72). Briefing and induction were not recorded, although some of the induction was repeated on camera when Knibb became restless.

A traditional hypnotic induction focusing on ideomotor suggestion was given with deep breathing and relaxation, followed by suggestions of heaviness and counting to deepen trance. Arm catalepsy appeared to be achieved successfully. This was followed by arm levitation, which also was passed successfully. The hypnotist reported it unusual on ideomotor signaling that Knibb's finger moved suddenly and was rigidly extended, the hypnotist noting that when subjects are hypnotized, the finger rises slowly and often not a lot. In this session, Knibb described in rather confusing detail everything he could recall while in the beach and car-park area at Buchans Point. In the hypnosis session, Knibb was asked to remain in hypnosis when the videorecording began and to repeat everything exactly as he had recalled it during the preliminary hypnotic session. Knibb became suspicious at this point that someone (presumably one of the police) was in the room and requested permission to open his eyes and "see if they are all out," thus implying to the hypnotist that he believed he was in a state of hypnosis.

Milne gave specific suggestions to Knibb for regression, and he was taken back to the time and scene of the crime. Knibb was taken back to the time when he drove his car off the highway, through the parking area, and onto the beach. In his account, Knibb said that he passed another person whom he passed several times in his vehicle while driving up and down the beach. Milne reported that Knibb saw two people jogging up the beach. One of these, a man, was viewed as an invention, "doubtless a potential murderer in the scenario he has prepared" (Milne, 1992, p. 74). After passing the witness who was jogging, he drove to the car-park on his way out of the beach area. Knibb reported a car there, with its lights on high beam. Specifically, he referred to a single male in the vehicle. He said at one stage that he was intending to go over to the vehicle and "ask them for a pump. I was going to go over and say, hey, listen, can you lend me a pump 'cause I . . . it's the old couple and . . ." When making these comments, Knibb became upset and confused, and after a long pause, during which he took a couple of deep breaths, he continued in a highly emotional way that drew the hypnotist into the interaction by the strength of the emotional outburst:

> There's something wrong out there. If I go out there he's going to kill me . . . If I try to run away he's gonna kill me . . . He knows I'm on to him . . . So I can't see in the car . . . Where'd that other jogger go? There was two joggers on the beach . . . I wonder if she's in there . . . he doesn't want me to see in that car . . . You're not the old couple, you're too fuckin' young. (Milne, 1992, p. 75)

Knibb here quickly proceeded to provide a rational logic, commenting that it was the old couple (rather than a solitary male), and that the old couple may have been in danger. Subsequently, the police were able to demonstrate that the only vehicle in the car-park at that time was the red Mercedes sedan owned by the elderly couple.

In his account of the hypnosis session, Milne asked whether Knibb was genuinely hypnotized, saying that "the major impression given was that he was overplaying a role, engaging in rationale debate" (p. 77). There was one period, however, when Milne felt certain that Knibb was in a genuine state of trance. This was during a scene at a rock "when he hallucinated the dead woman standing tall at the bonnet of his car; and then, 50 feet back again, the blonde-haired [woman] wearing Miranda's clothes" (p. 78).

While describing events in the car-park, and talking about the car with lights blazing and the elderly couple in a red Mercedes, there was a marked change in Knibb's demeanor. He changed to the present tense in his reporting, as if he were really in the situation, and reported seeing everything clearly and vividly. Although this indicated to the hypnotist that abreaction might be occurring in relation to recall of traumatic events, the hypnotist nevertheless noted a number of inconsistencies in reporting in which Knibb's words in hypnosis appeared to contradict his previous statements. The hypnotist's final judgment was that Knibb could have been genuinely experiencing hypnosis, but he was not certain. He concluded that his report should not be accepted as evidence unless it was confirmed by other evidence as a result of independent investigation.

Comment on this case is made by us in five categories: (1) genuineness of the accused's experience of hypnosis; (2) cue dependence of the accused's testimony; (3) hypnosis viewed as an access to truth; (4) motivation of the accused; and (5) emotional factors affecting memory reports. The case also has implications for the understanding of theoretical processes that underlie hypnosis and hypnotic experience.

Genuineness of the Experience of Hypnosis

There are several probabilistic clinical indicators that might be taken to highlight convincing performance in hypnosis:

1. Testimony given that one is deeply hypnotized, this testimony typically being accompanied by objective signs of successful hypnotic response to particular suggestions.
2. An appreciable reduction of rational thinking in which the subject no longer typically engages in frequent, unsolicited bouts of planful and logical thinking.
3. Dominance of unreal thinking, in the sense that the hypnotized person focuses on the frame of reference suggested by the hypnotist, rather than on the everyday frame of reference that exists outside the hypnotic setting.
4. Signs of high imaginative involvement in the events of the hypnotic session, such as the use of present tense in an age regression situation in which the subject is being "taken back" to the past.

Each of these indicators, none of which is definitive and all of which are relatively under-researched, will be discussed in turn and then drawn together to offer summary comment on the issue of faking. In the majority of these four respects, we consider that there were indications of atypical response by the accused that were contrary to the conclusion that he was hypnotized.

Testimony of Being Hypnotized

Testimony was offered early in the hypnotic session with Knibb when he reported that the hypnotist had him "under" ("You wouldn't have me under if I didn't trust you"). At this point in the set of hypnotic procedures, the videorecording presented what would, in our judgment, be regarded by an experienced professional as an unconvincing instance of hypnosis. For example, an assertion early in the session that he was hypnotized was offered by Knibb altogether uncritically, and his testimony about being hypnotized was unusual. He may later have been hypnotized (leaving aside the comments to follow), but assertions about hypnosis having been induced so early in the hypnotic session itself are suspect for a number of reasons. There were examples of behavior lacking in credibility, such as his preoccupation "in hypnosis" with matters external to hypnosis (e.g., wanting the hypnotist to stick tape over the door, and complaining about "slight indigestion"), and his overzealous responses in the very early stages of the hypnotic induction procedure.

The question of whether Knibb's behavior was genuine can also be evaluated in relation to Knibb's posthypnotic comment to the hypnotist that he could pretend to others that hypnosis was actually induced. There was apparent inconsistency in his claiming "hypnosis" and saying he could pretend, but this was not unlike, perhaps, his talking about how murder might be committed, while still claiming innocence of the crime. Knibb's testimony communicated a tolerance by him for simulation and a willingness to implicate the hypnotist in a request for a performance that was not genuine.

Reduction of Rational Thinking

There was clear evidence in the hypnosis session of unsolicited and unsuggested strategic and logical thinking. Knibb reported, for example, on a vehicle in the car-park, by stating categorically that "it's the old couple." Then he proceeded to argue conditionally why this could not be the case. Visually, it appeared as if Knibb had made a mistake and that his thinking was an attempt to strategically recover or correct that error. Such an impression aside, the progressive elaboration of the reasons why it could not be the old couple, and why it was an unknown man (the killer), was an indication of a qualitative style of thinking that seems atypical in hypnosis. At one level, Knibb communicated that he did not believe his own fantasies. At another level, however, he engaged in the same kind of strategic debate that characterized his testimony outside the hypnotic setting.

A further anomaly in his reporting arose from the fact that before the hypnosis session, Knibb had been informed that the elderly couple in the car-park had a red Mercedes. He admitted to this, but in the hypnosis session, he proceeded to report another car (which he had commented on at other times) that was attributed mistakenly to the couple. One might have expected that he would have recognized the earlier report and acknowledged the content of previous discussions at this point. His inconsistency in reporting was evident throughout the session and clearly tolerated by him.

Dominance of Unreal Thinking

An atypical pattern established by Knibb throughout the hypnosis session was his habit of "reflecting" on what he said to the hypnotist. Hypnotic subjects are generally aware of the everyday frame of reference that surrounds them (cf. Hilgard, 1977; Keegan, 1987; Laurence & Perry, 1981), but Knibb continually asserted and reasserted the reality of the situation in which he, as an accused person, had been placed. To us, this was not compatible with the behavior of someone engaged subjectively in the events of hypnosis as they are structured by the hypnotist. Examples of these processes of reflection were asides about people who he thought were sent by the police to trick him, reflections about his not having been on the beach in his four-wheel-drive vehicle before, asides about what he had been told previously about the people on the beach by others, and what other people had said to him before about the events of the murder. In fact, a stream of asides about his predicament and his current situation occurred throughout the hypnosis session. Dualistic thinking can and does take place in hypnosis among highly susceptible people, but it is the extent of such reflection and the consistency of it on Knibb's part that were diagnostic.

Signs of High Imaginative Involvement

There was clear evidence of Knibb's high emotional involvement in the session (e.g., the use of particularly strong language) and he used the present tense in passages describing emotional events recounted in the hypnotic age regression. However, Knibb's language demonstrated an emotional lability that was manifest outside hypnosis as well, and it seems important to note that his use of the present tense (viewed as a single indicator) could have been cued by the hypnotist in the way that the hypnotist prepared Knibb for an age regression performance, or made more probable by the presence of the TV crew during the session. The hypnotist, for example, used the present tense in his own description of what Knibb might experience in age regression.

The hypnotic performance record presented by Knibb was unconvincing in several major respects. There was no way of knowing for certain whether hypnosis was induced, but there were too many indications of atypical performance by Knibb to lead one to have any degree of confidence in any assertion that Knibb was genuinely hypnotized. There were also other indications that are consistent with this general conclusion, for example, Knibb's willingness to open his eyes at moments when subjects ordinarily would have been expected to keep them closed. The only evidence to support the conclusion that the performance was genuine was provided by behavior that can be said equally well to reflect the obvious cues for appropriate response given by the hypnotist.

Cue Dependence of the Memory Reports

There were multiple indications of the dependence of Knibb's behavior on cues arising from other sources. The use of the present tense in describing what happened at the beach on the day in question illustrated this point directly. Other aspects of his testimony, as well, indicated the influence of cued response. Knibb insisted, for example, that hypnosis had removed an emotional block, and he had remembered something that he had not known before. However, the suggestion of hypnosis releasing a block in memory had been used by him previously, and Knibb was exposed to that way of talking prior to the introduction of hypnosis.

Of course, an alternative way of describing hypnotic events used by Knibb is in terms of the subconscious allowing forgotten memories to emerge. The language of the subconscious had been established as legitimate by the hypnotist prior to these kinds of assertions being offered by Knibb. It is significant that the times when cues given were not taken up by Knibb occurred when elements of his testimony were basic to his "story," which was central to the block in memory supposedly released by hypnosis. For example, Knibb was told that the old couple had a red Mercedes, but he persisted with the story (in hypnosis) that the old couple had another kind of car, before he changed the story by "arguing" that he was mistaken and the car he saw was one that belonged not to the old couple, but to the killer. Overall, there was particularly strong evidence in this case of cue-dependent behavior. Knibb frequently offered testimony that was reported in a way consistent with the expectations communicated by the hypnotist about the appropriate language to use.

Hypnosis Viewed as an Access to Truth

From a variety of sources, Knibb was exposed to the viewpoint prior to hypnosis that the induction of hypnosis cannot guarantee access to truth. He persisted, however, in insisting that his report of another car with the lights on in the car-park was the truth of what hypnosis had revealed. As we argue in Chapter 8, there is no experimental evidence that hypnosis necessarily accesses truth. Evidence indicates that hypnosis can lead to an increased output in the amount of testimony that is offered, and more accurate and inaccurate facts may result. However, the truth of what is reproduced in hypnosis can in no way be inferred from the reports given in hypnosis alone. The evidence from this case demonstrated to us an accumulation of indications that Knibb was faking. On the basis of the material that we examined, we considered that there was a motivated, strategic attempt by Knibb to respond to cues available to him from a variety of sources.

Motivational Aspects of Memory Reporting

Knibb's motivation was perhaps the most puzzling aspect of this case and raises again the general issue of how best to cope with motivations in the forensic setting. Knibb's behavior was not superficially consistent with someone who was guilty. He actively sought out the authorities when he claimed he wished to avoid them; he acquainted them with his whereabouts and behavior, which invited suspicion; he told multiple untruths when offering testimony that he must have known would be checked and detected; and, he contradicted his own testimony throughout his reporting. If Knibb were guilty, then it could be the case that he wished to be caught. This explanation, however, is essentially unconvincing. It could also be that, if he were guilty, he wanted to keep in contact with the police to know how to compete with them, or he wished to convince others that he would hardly be seeking out the police unless he were really innocent. Neither of these last two explanations seems consistent with the extent of untruths that he told. In the case of all these inferences, the degree of supposition seems to us to be too strong.

Explanation of his behavior on psychological grounds seems to require some allegiance to a hypothesis of disturbance that encompasses pathological lying and a demonstrable lack of concern about being detected in telling untruths. This, of course, raises the matter of the relevance of close clinical scrutiny in correctly interpreting apparent inconsistencies in witnesses' or suspects' behavior.

Emotional Components of Memory Reporting

The emotions displayed by Knibb during the hypnosis session require special comment. On the one hand, the apparent emotions were probably in response to cues from the hypnotist (e.g., "What are you feeling now?"). On the other hand, emotions expressed at that time and in that way could be consistent in part with how a genuinely hypnotized subject might behave. Thus, consideration of the apparent emotions in isolation cannot address the issue of the nature of hypnotic response. Two other components need to be considered: (1) the consistency of the emotions that Knibb reported about himself as an individual; and (2) the extent to which Knibb engaged in purposeful, reflective analysis of the emotions themselves.

In a number of his reports, Knibb represented himself as an individual who has experienced substantial difficulties in his life, and developed the resources to handle a range of difficult and threatening situations. In a number of situations, Knibb had displayed himself as having the capacity and propensity to behave in a physically aggressive manner. The emotions that Knibb apparently experienced in the hypnosis session were inconsistent with the characteristics that Knibb either claimed to have experienced or displayed in the past. In essence, Knibb stated that the emotions he experienced blocked the recall of events from his memory, and hypnosis provided him with partial access to what really happened. It is not at all clear why, or how, looking at what happened in the car-park could have evoked an emotional reaction of such magnitude. Overall, there was a substantial incongruence between the emotional reactions that Knibb claimed to have had when faced with events in the car-park and the way in which he presented in situations of apparently greater threat in other circumstances. For example, he had previously coped with interactions involving undercover police. In almost every communication sequence with the hypnotist when Knibb was supposedly age regressed and purportedly remembering new events of emotional significance, Knibb commented on the event, highlighted its importance, and provided additional comments on how it related to other remembered events and events he did not yet remember. He clearly wanted to make sure that the observers understood his story.

Experience with hypnosis in both cases discussed in this chapter suggests to us that behavior in the hypnotic setting is normally motivated by the desire of the subject to respond in a socially appropriate and personally strategic way. In hypnosis, the effort is an active one in which the task of responding to hypnotic suggestions can be viewed as being akin to the process of problem solving in a context defined and regulated by rules set by the hypnotist, and which engages the hypnotist and hypnotic subjects in active interaction. In hypnosis, however, the process is not to be identified with conformity (see Spanos, 1982; Wagstaff, 1986), which seems readily apparent in the case of Knibb (but not DD), or passive obedience with what the hypnotist demands. Rather, it is the reflection of a motivated, cognitive effort by the hypnotic subject to respond to suggestions as they are understood within the context that is being defined by the hypnotist. The presence in Knibb's case of rational, purposeful thinking, which referred to external frames of reference and were frequently independent of the hypnotist, cued us to the lack of genuineness of Knibb's response. The most appropriate route to understand the nature of a hypnotic subject's commitment to his or her task is the style of the response, rather than the person's competency (e.g., how quickly the response occurred, or how much body movement took place). Style features of Knibb's record cued us again to the simulated character of his performance.

The indications from both cases informed us about the variability and inconsistency of memory reports. There is substantial evidence from both DD and Knibb that memory reports change over time to accommodate alterations in feelings toward, or information about, the events being reported. Unreliability in memory reporting characterized both cases and in the case of DD in particular, there was variability in both the content and the way in which memories were reported over time. In some cases, hypnosis will lead to an increase in the amount of material reported as memory, but this is not always so. Whereas some of the additional material may be accurate, other parts of it may be inaccurate. This is despite the fact that the person reporting may be substantially confident about the accuracy of what is being remembered, confidence being a special feature of DD's record. Finally, the Miranda Downes case demonstrates that the issue of whether a person is hypnotized is unquestionably a major one to work through in interpreting the meaning of memory-report data collected in the investigative setting.

Common key parameters emerged as significant in both these cases, which characterized other cases in this book as well (e.g., the cases discussed in Chapters 2 and 4). For example, emotional factors played a key part and the motivation of the person being hypnotized needed to be understood closely in each case before the data from the different sessions could be interpreted. Furthermore, in both cases, clinical interpretation was necessary to make sense of the complexities and anomalies that were present. Finally, in the Knibb case, the data allow us to infer probable indicators of genuine performance that can be generalized over other cases.

Indicators of Faking

Drawing together the threads of the previous discussion, it would seem helpful to focus summarily on the diagnostic indicators that might be used to detect the simulation of hypnosis. These indicators suggest themselves to us as generally relevant in forensic cases involving hypnosis. One would expect all of the following indicators to be accompanied in a simulating subject by the assertion or testimony that deep hypnosis is experienced. Such testimony would typically be accompanied by objective signs of hypnotic response to particular suggestions. It seems to us that faking can be conceptualized in terms of the following processes:

1. Appreciable indications of rational (vs. primary process) thinking in which the person supposedly in hypnosis engages in frequent, unsolicited bouts of strategic and logical thinking.

2. Dominance in hypnosis of the everyday frame of reference existing away from the hypnotic setting, rather than the frame of reference being established by the hypnotist.
3. Lack of high imaginative involvement in the suggested events of hypnosis.
4. Overplaying the role of the hypnotized subject.
5. Reliance on expectations established outside of hypnosis about appropriate ways of responding.
6. Overemphasis of behavior engaged in by the subject in hypnosis.
7. Demonstration of behavior that is generally atypical of people claiming to experience deep hypnosis.

Faked hypnosis is difficult to detect, especially in brief and relatively routine hypnotic manipulations. No single indicator is sufficient to prove that hypnosis is being faked, but when an accumulation of these indicators is present, it is very probable that the experience of hypnosis being reported is not genuine. Each of these indicators can be summarized briefly.

Occurrences of Rational Thinking

In hypnosis, one would not expect frequent occurrences of planful and logical thinking that are unsolicited and unsuggested. Such behavior might be illustrated by the progressive and repeated elaboration of the reasons behind particular experiences and actions. Strategic debate of the kind that expresses rational thinking frequently denotes a qualitative style of thinking that is not, in our opinion, typical of hypnosis. In putting forward this argument, we stress however, that the forensic setting itself may increase the probability that reality utterances will be given.

Dominance of Everyday Frame of Reference

In hypnosis the hypnotist routinely attempts to establish a suggested frame of reference that moves the hypnotized subject away from everyday reality. Hypnotic subjects are aware of the everyday frame of reference that surrounds them, but the genuinely hypnotized subject would not be expected to assert the nonsuggested frame of reference spontaneously and frequently during the hypnotic session. In this sense, the pattern of behavior that indicates faking is one in which the hypnotized subject frequently "reflects" on what he or she says to the hypnotist. It is the extent of such reflection and the consistency of it that are especially diagnostic of faking.

Lack of High Imaginative Involvement

Hypnosis is typically imaginatively involving for those who are able to experience it, and lack of such involvement may be an indication of poor or simulated involvement in the events of hypnosis. There are some patterns of hypnotic performance that tend to indicate less imaginative involvement than others, and these may indicate faking. Persons taken back to the past, for example, may be said to express less involvement in what is being suggested when they describe what happened long ago in the past, rather than the present tense, unless the use of present tense is cued by the hypnotist.

Overplaying the Role of the Hypnotized Subject

Deep hypnosis typically requires that persons radically alter their experience of reality. When such behavior is shown, but the behavior is heavily emphasized by the subject or zealously overplayed in the hypnotic setting, one would suspect that faking has occurred. An example of such a response would be overreacting with extreme surprise to a suggested response that has occurred. This was evident, for instance, in the case of the Hillside Strangler (for detailed analysis, see Orne et al., 1984).

Reliance on Expectations

When faking is suspected, one looks for strong evidence of cue-dependent behavior. This is behavior that is executed in hypnosis in a fashion that is consistent with expectations communicated outside of hypnosis in the waking state. Such cues might incorporate the actual pattern of behavior shown in hypnosis or the language used to describe it. Especially diagnostic is the carryover into hypnosis of expectations communicated outside of hypnosis that reflect statistically rare features of hypnotic response.

Atypical Hypnotic Behavior

Considering the extensive body of data that has now accumulated in the literature, there are a number of aspects of hypnotic performance that have established themselves as statistically infrequent. The cumulative occurrence of these is diagnostic of faking. In our experience, these may include talking freely while maintaining that one is in a stuporous state; spontaneously opening the eyes when the hypnotist has established an expectation that the eyes should remain closed; demonstrating unusual patterns of physical activity, such as reaching out in an unsolicited way to interact with an hallucinated person; and, repeatedly and rapidly executing suggested responses when radical departures from reality are involved. Overall, it seems evident (see Sheehan, 1973) that simulators are much more homogenous in their "hypnotic" performance and take fewer risks compared with susceptible subjects who are genuinely hypnotized and more heterogeneous in their response.

SUMMARY COMMENT

Both of these cases raise issues that are common to all of the cases analyzed in this book. Consistency and style of memory reporting, for example, were major issues in both cases. In the cases of DD and Knibb, style and consistency varied, demonstrating marked variability in reporting in different ways. Memory operated erratically in the case of DD, changing massively over time. In the case of Knibb, our knowledge of the operation of his memory was clouded by the fact that evidence showed that he was lying. Both cases highlighted the relevance of motivation and emotion. Stress was the predominant characteristic of the session with DD, and faking characterized the session with Knibb. The reported memories of both were unreliable, although the motivations underlying the variability were somewhat distinct. In both cases, the procedures followed appeared to adequately address the range of issues that was evident. Specifically, the rights of witnesses (e.g., in the case of DD) need better protection, and further assistance is required to draw an appropriate balance between clinical and forensic priorities. Furthermore, it seems sensible to argue that there would be utility in working to distinguish hypnosis from simulation. Such a distinction is not definitive, but the case involving Knibb points us toward being better able to assess the probable indicators of faking.

It has clearly been established in the literature that people can and do fake hypnosis, and faking hypnosis is frequently convincing enough that experts in the field experience great difficulty in detecting simulation. In our judgment, faking is indicated when there are multiple indications of the patterns of performance described previously. It is the accumulation of such indications that would confirm for us the hypothesis that a person is faking. The faking of hypnosis occurs when there is a motivated, strategic attempt to respond to cues about appropriate response that are available to the subject from a variety of sources, both inside and outside the hypnotic setting. The person who is faking hypnosis will intentionally use whatever cues he or she can detect and will seek to use them very convincingly. The same, of course, might be said of some highly hypnotized individuals, and it is the intentional use of cues that may well define what is diagnosed by us here as simulation. Intentionality is difficult to diagnose, but it is the aggregate pattern of behavior and reported experience that makes that diagnosis possible.

In Chapter 8, we explore further the distinction between lying in hypnosis and faking being hypnotized. We examine ethical issues in particular and will use the cases discussed here and previously to highlight major ethical issues and dilemmas.

CHAPTER 7

The Ethics of Hypnosis in the Forensic Setting

Than chapter highlights ethical issues in particular and uses the cases that we have discussed to emphasize their relevance. It also introduces the forensic details of cases involving lay hypnotists, which are seen to be relevant to this chapter because they raise particular issues relating to qualifications, experience, and expertise that reach out to address major ethical concerns. We also take the opportunity to discuss ethical issues that must be managed in one way or another and must be considered part of the comprehensive training of professionals who use hypnosis in the forensic setting.

In doing this, we address four major areas of concern: (1) technical accuracy versus humanity in professional practice; (2) difficulties in implementing guidelines for the practice of forensic hypnosis; (3) possible risks; and, (4) qualifications for practice. The risks discussed address the matters of access to stressful experiences, striking a balance between forensic and clinical priorities, dealing with hypotheses about processes, and coping with unsuggested effects.

In relation to the issue we have chosen to call technical accuracy versus humanity in professional practice, there are many manifestations of its relevance in the cases that we have examined. The issue poses definite dilemmas for the professional. We illustrate this by commenting on four cases involving hypnosis, as they raise the same issue in very different ways.

TECHNICAL ACCURACY VERSUS HUMANITY
IN PROFESSIONAL PRACTICE

The first case (Sheehan, Andreason, Doherty, & McCann, 1986) concerns alleged sexual abuse by a father of his 3-year-old daughter. In the course of hypnosis, which the father requested "because he wanted to know what he did," and the police requested because they were looking for evidence of abuse, he revealed incidents that very clearly pointed to his being an irresponsible father, but not necessarily an abuser. Following hypnosis, a key memory was reproduced, which was never before reported, involving recall of allegedly past events. Specifically, the father recalled a scene in which he was watching pornographic films while engaging in sexual self-stimulation. He watched this kind of film regularly in the home. This night, however, he noticed his daughter peeping at him from behind a curtain, and he felt guilty and embarrassed. The incident was one that needed to be checked factually, as it seemed relevant to the question of whether the daughter was stimulated to fantasize sexually or the father was abusing. Leaving aside the issue of whether the child had been socialized previously into a seductive pattern (see Faller, 1984), the memory recovered in the session was congruent with the notion that the problem lay in the child's fantasy rather than physical abuse by the father. The incident, however, was never checked because the factors were probably not regarded as relevant by the investigating authorities. No doubt, they were not seen as relating directly to the issue at stake.

Rather than bearing on the issue of understanding the alleged abuse of the daughter, the reported memory probably served to confirm the impression that this was the kind of person who might well do what was alleged and should be denied access to his daughter. The outcome of the case was that the father was denied legal access to the child, whereas previously access was permitted. The legal process operated in a technically precise and probably correct way but, arguably, in an inhumane manner. The dilemma experienced by the hypnotist was how much to press the legal process to pursue a route that might help the accused, but technically it was regarded by the police (who requested the hypnosis session) as having little direct bearing on the legality of the case. Inadvertently, the forensic session could well have served to consolidate impressions in others that subtly confirmed the guilt of the suspect.

Overall, three general questions are raised by this first case that relate to other cases. Should hypnosis be used in a setting where someone under suspicion of molesting wants to find out what he did? Should these exculpatory statements be given credence? And, finally, what confidence can we place in the fact that the memory of his daughter watching him suggests that the daughter fantasized what she said happened?

The second case comes from our discussion in Chapter 5 of the alleged sexual assault of CK by the taxi driver and lay hypnotist. CK's allegations were more clear-cut in that case, because there was physical evidence of intercourse having occurred. The woman in question claimed that she was not able to resist LG and he raped her. The man claimed that she was a willing participant and engaged in sex with him consensually. The hypnotist/taxi driver was acquitted of the charge. Formally, the judge advised the jury that it could acquit the defendant without hearing the defense case, the judge having obviously formed the view that the testimony of CK lacked credibility. The jury took the advice of the court and acquitted the defendant without hearing the defense case.

Arguably, the case might have been more appropriately prosecuted in terms of the occurrence of traumatic stress syndrome in which memories were confused because of the trauma that occurred. What the court saw was an inarticulate and uneducated young woman, confused and vague in her recall, who was not able to remember clearly what had happened 2 years previously. The hypnosis session discussed in detail in Chapter 5 was compelling, but the defense chose to place its emphasis on the clarity of memories 2 years later in an anxious and confused witness. It may have been technically correct to do so, but the experienced distress of the woman and events viewed humanely rather than technically might have alerted the prosecution to proceed in a different way.

The third case, well documented in the literature, is that of "Mr. Magic" (Laurence & Perry, 1988; Perry, 1979; Sheehan, 1977). Mr. Magic (Barry Palmer) was a New Zealand-born lay hypnotist who was accused in Australia of sexual assault of two women who had come to him so that he could treat their personal problems. Palmer claimed they were sexually willing, but they said they were not. He had a long history (eight convictions) for offenses that were primarily of a voyeuristic, sexual nature, and received a 1-year prison sentence in 1974 for making sexual advances toward different women within the hypnotic setting. He acquired the skills of a stage magician in New Zealand in the 1960s and became a self-styled hypnotherapist who set up practice in Sydney in the 1970s. Three women approached him in Sydney at a party in 1975, where he performed tricks and demonstrated different hypnotic phenomena. During the performance, he indicated he was available for consulting on tension problems.

Two of the women approached him for nail biting, and one for obesity. In the case of one of the women who consulted him for nail biting, for example, he treated her and his questioning quickly turned to sexual history, whereupon hypnosis was initiated. After some hypnotic items were administered, Palmer asked the woman to remove all her clothing, suggested that she was on a deserted beach, and led her to a bed where she lay down. He then stroked her breasts, placed his finger in her vagina, and was commencing intercourse when a knock on the door interrupted him. The woman stood up and asked for clothing to cover her. Palmer then attempted to kiss her, but she resisted. He then terminated hypnosis. Charges were brought 2 days later when the woman involved reportedly heard that another woman had brought charges against Palmer for similar behavior. In court, the woman maintained that she knew what was happening but could do nothing to prevent Palmer's overtures. Palmer had sexual intercourse with one of the other two women, who reported similarly that she was unable to prevent what occurred. Both women appeared to be susceptible to hypnosis. The outcome of the trial was that Palmer was found guilty of rape, attempted rape, and indecent assault, and sentenced to 14 years in prison. The judge commented that, in his opinion, the absence of physical force made the offenses (even) more serious. Because of some legal technicalities however, a mistrial was declared and Mr. Magic was released; he was arraigned later on a separate "Peeping Tom" charge.

The main issue at stake in this case was whether immoral or antisocial behavior is ever possible in hypnosis. Technically speaking, there is no argument that can be mounted to show definitely that the women engaged in behavior that could in no way be resisted (see also Gibson, 1991; Laurence & Perry, 1988). Laboratory evidence cannot be gathered that unequivocally answers the issue (see Chapter 9 for further discussion of this point of view), and data gathered in the natural setting are difficult to interpret because of the lack of systematic controls. Argument was made in court at the time that evidence failed to prove that antisocial behavior is possible in hypnosis, and this is a conclusion confirmed by the literature relating to whether hypnosis can be used to compel people to perform acts that are antisocial (dangerous, immoral, or criminal). Such a claim is technically correct, but it carries the implication that the women in question were perhaps "willing" to engage sexually with the hypnotist. That implication is potentially damaging to them personally. In engaging sexually with the women he had hypnotized, leaving aside the formal question of whether the women were compelled in some way to act against their will, clearly, Mr. Magic was massively unprofessional and irresponsible and took advantage of the women. The law, however, takes no stock of "being taken advantage of," whatever that term means; "advantage" is not a technical issue at stake.

Finally, the reverse side of the dilemma can be illustrated best by returning to the case of SP, discussed in Chapter 6. In this case, a possible witness of an abduction was hypnotized. During hypnosis, which was being watched by the police, the witness came to a key part of his memory in which he reported seeing the victim in a car being harassed. At that point, he became agitated and visibly upset, and recollections started to emerge in a clinically obtrusive way. Forensically speaking, it was unquestionably a relevant scene to pursue and explore further. The hypnotist, however, drew back. He became distinctly uncomfortable about proceeding further with the recall and thought the witness was about to reveal material that was personally stressful and self-damaging. There is no way of knowing what would have happened, but the consequences to the witness personally of proceeding further at this point were too great for the hypnotist to consider. If the only goal was to pursue forensic priorities, one might argue that the session should have proceeded further. It did not, and it was terminated; one can genuinely argue whether that was the correct course. Clinical priorities, for example, would suggest that the correct action was taken.

According to the guidelines set out in Chapter 3, before one conducts a forensic hypnosis session, a psychological evaluation and interview are administered. Obviously, at this time, a decision can be made about whether to proceed with hypnosis, and on this occasion the hypnotist can explain how the session will be carried out and what will be done if distress is experienced. Hypnosis, however, may lead to an aggravation of symptoms, and in such a case unexpected behavior can result. It is in such circumstances that the task of finding a balance between clinical and forensic priorities emerges in a particularly compelling way.

The ethical dilemma in all of these cases in which one or both of the authors were involved is that the forensic priorities or purposes of the investigative session placed the hypnotist at times in opposition to the interests of those being hypnotized and, paradoxically, at times, in defense of people who had behaved unprofessionally and irresponsibly. Evidence collected and given was delivered in a technically correct way, and such had to occur. The literature, for example, is not persuasive at all on the point that a hypnotized person will behave against his or her morals or behave antisocially under the influence of a hypnotist (for review, see Chapter 9), and expert argument appropriately conveyed that point of view in the Mr. Magic case. But the forensic priorities at stake were opposed to humane, commonsense considerations. It is also conceivable that such testimony may have the effect of retraumatizing the victim and possibly lending tacit encouragement to sexual predators with hypnotic skills who wish to prey at will among the vulnerable.

These cases all highlight a facet of the interaction between psychology and the law that needs to be discussed more openly. We need both to understand and appreciate how the legal system works, and professionals have no alternative but to relate to the law as objectively as they can. But in doing so, the law can find us, like itself, relating implicitly or even explicitly in an inhumane way toward others. It is an ethical dilemma of which we should be aware, and it needs to be worked through and resolved carefully.

DIFFICULTIES IN IMPLEMENTING GUIDELINES

The guidelines for forensic hypnosis that we recommend were applied as effectively as possible in the circumstances of the cases in which we were involved and have presented in this book. In these cases, for example, the entire session was videorecorded; no person other than the hypnotist and subject was present in the room at the time the subject was interviewed; a memorandum was prepared of "basic facts" of the case for presentation to the hypnotist; and the hypnotist was kept blind as to many details of the case. It is arguable, however, that a rape counselor should have been with the subject in the room in the case of AP (see Chapter 5), after the counselor had received some training or instruction on how to avoid direct or nonverbal suggestion (see Scheflin & Shapiro, 1989; and our guidelines in Chapter 3).

The various sessions raise a number of points for consideration in relation to the recommended guidelines that will be addressed further in Chapter 10. Here, they are discussed in relation to ethical principles. In each of the cases discussed, it was hard for the coordinator of the forensic session to formulate the correct amount of detail for the memorandum that was given to the hypnotist. In the SP case (see Chapter 6), for instance, it might have been more appropriate for the hypnotist to know that the subject had a record of "inconsistent reporting," a phenomenon that we have observed repeatedly throughout the cases we have analyzed. However, such information could have prejudiced the hypnotist as to the kind of memory material being investigated. Nevertheless, a knowledge of particular memories given in the past could clarify details given in the session in a potentially useful way.

All of the cases we have analyzed also raise the issue of the rights of the subject. With respect to these rights, a (false) confession could result in a subject who reports certain kinds of memories. One needs, therefore, to carefully consider procedures that protect the rights of people being hypnotized, while making it possible for useful information to be produced. The matter of rights also reaches beyond the session itself. For example, one needs to make sure, as far as possible, that material collected will not be misused by others. Guidelines are limited in what they can do and say about the rights of participants in forensic hypnosis and about what follows once the hypnosis session has concluded. Events beyond the session may be difficult to control, but the importance of the issue needs to be evaluated.

The guidelines are limited also in paying attention to the risks to some participants of pursuing particular lines of questioning. When high stress is involved (such as in the case of SP in Chapter 6, and AP in Chapter 5), a particular line of inquiry may produce forensically useful material, but be personally damaging or stressful to the subject. Relatedly, guidelines need to be procedurally oriented in ways that address the shifting status of the person who is being hypnotized. This shift in status during a session throws the hypnotist into a conflict as to whose interests to protect. Thus, not only is there a clinical versus forensic conflict issue, there is also an ethical issue about who precisely is the client and whose interests should be served; the conflict of client versus client should not be underestimated. At one point in a session, for example, the person being hypnotized may assume the status of a neutral witness, whereas at another point, that role can shift, posing also possible conflict of allegiance for the hypnotist. Procedures adopted at one stage may not be optimal at another. When one discusses ethical issues and principles, one is really concerned with possible risks to those involved. We turn now to consider a number of those risks, drawing again from the cases we have analyzed.

POSSIBLE RISKS

The issue of risks to persons from the introduction of hypnosis has been debated by others elsewhere (e.g., Coe, Kobayashi, & Howard, 1972, 1973; Coe & Ryken, 1979; Gibson, 1991; Hilgard, 1974), but the present cases cogently illustrate risks associated with the hypnotic retrieval of material where stress is present. A number of risks are necessarily associated also with the question of appropriate expertise.

Access to Stressful Experiences

In the case of SP, although DD was motivated and cooperative, he experienced substantial difficulty in accessing relevant memories and experiences. On a number of occasions, he seemed to want to draw the hypnotist away from relevant material, and hypnotists who have not been trained clinically and have no extensive experience with hypnosis may not be able to overcome this kind of barrier. In this case, the use of the "hidden part" procedure provided ways around the witness's resistance and allowed partial access at least to material that was of psychological importance.

Any access to stressful experiences requires sensitive, ethical care. Consider, for instance, the implications conveyed by the case involving CK and the taxi driver, LG, discussed in Chapter 5. Careful assessment was needed of the potential additional damage to a person traumatized through the use of hypnosis when its purpose was investigative, rather than clinical. For instance, the real depths of the women's traumatic reactions to a very stressful situation were not clear in this case. Investigative hypnosis is not geared essentially to providing therapy for any person; rather, it is aimed at isolating reports of events as they might have occurred.

The matter of accessing stressful experiences is linked to the choice of the person to be hypnotized. Normally, hypnosis is employed in the forensic setting with witnesses or victims of crime. Data tapping police attitudes to hypnosis (see McConkey & Sheehan, 1988a) showed that a majority of those surveyed were of the opinion that hypnosis should be employed with witnesses and victims. Only a small number of respondents believed that hypnosis should be used with defendants, and some experts in the field argue strongly that there are definite dangers in using hypnosis with people who are possibly guilty of crimes (e.g., Udolf, 1983). Ethically speaking, as indicated in our discussions of the Miranda Downes case, caution is needed when hypnosis is used in instances in which the person being hypnotized is under suspicion or is accused of the crime, and caution may additionally be advised when the person asks to be hypnotized. The parameter of relevance in such cases is obviously the nature of the motivation of the person being hypnotized, and the very real possibility exists that the person being hypnotized is lying about their experience (for a detailed analysis of this possibility and the diagnostic indicators for detecting faking, see Chapter 6).

The motivations of those possibly implicated in crimes are very different from the motivations of people who are not, and the degree of stress operating on the former can be much stronger. As one of us has pointed out elsewhere (Sheehan, 1988c):

> To handle the complexity of interpreting recall, where guilt, anxiety, and desire to prove one's innocence freely intermix, requires not only astute clinical judgment on the part of the hypnotist, but also that the hypnotist has a considerable degree of interpretive skill to enable the adaptation of procedures to the nature of the material that is being produced. (p. 106)

Finding a Balance of Forensic and Clinical Priorities

A major ethical issue in the practice of investigative hypnosis is finding the balance between forensic and clinical priorities. In each case that we have covered, we needed to strike a balance, recognizing that the pattern of risks varies according to the decision made. Particular cases demonstrate the dilemma. DD (see Chapter 6), for example, displayed substantial emotion and was stressed by memories of experiences that were emerging. The balance of forensic and clinical priorities was also an issue in the case of AP (see Chapter 5). AP was stressed by the memories retrieved in hypnosis, and with her level of distress, it was impossible at times not to be supportive and respond empathically in a relatively direct way to what she was reporting. In doing so, forensic principles were possibly compromised by the extent to which the hypnotist felt compelled to offer support and engage in more structured dialogue. The balance was also an issue in the case of BL (see Chapter 4), in which the wife of the man killed needed strong clinical support because of the trauma she experienced.

Ethical dilemmas associated with forging the balance between forensic and clinical priorities can also be seen in other ways. Consider, for instance, the actual use of hypnosis in the taxi driver case (Chapter 5), which investigated a matter that was itself linked to hypnosis. This issue is necessarily open to debate. On the one hand, it could be potentially traumatic to expose a possible rape victim (CK) to hypnosis when it was possibly this manipulation that injured her in the first place. On the other hand, used correctly and professionally, hypnosis had the potential to reveal aspects of memory that could help both the victim and the police in their investigations.

Assessment of the balance between forensic and clinical priorities also must take sensitive account of the benefits of using hypnosis in a situation in which corroboration is ordinarily not possible. Aspects that bear on the issue of corroboration and can be drawn from the cases discussed in this book are (1) the degree of consistency of the report given in hypnosis (and not given prior to hypnosis) with facts established independently by the investigating officers; (2) elements of the report consistent with facts established through events, such as an undercover operation (see Chapter 5 for further discussion of this aspect); and (3) elements of the report that have not been given previously, but fit harmoniously with clinical features of phenomena, such as trauma reactions. When corroboration is difficult, the weight of the case for the defense is thrown on the reports of those concerned. If it is assumed that someone who is hypnotized subsequently should not offer testimony, then use of hypnosis may be taking away an advantage that the victim needs to have.

Finally, in assessing the important matter of balance, the question should be asked whether a case truly has an investigative purpose. Major evidentiary concerns could throw the balance away from an investigative focus onto the evidentiary issues themselves. Furthermore, one might argue that the use of hypnosis in cases involving allegations of rape is unacceptably stressful in some situations. This could be so, for example, when the women involved might perceive that hypnosis is the kind of experience that reinforces the belief that rape is possible in hypnosis. It is necessary in all of the aforementioned instances to provide the means for professional clinical support to alleviate experienced stress or undue pressure created by hypnosis. When stress is present, it is essential that an experienced clinician provide both immediate and continuing care. Such care cannot be provided by the forensic hypnotist because of his or her quite different role responsibilities.

Overall, the balance of forensic and clinical priorities is a difficult one to judge, and such a judgment should not be undertaken by someone who does not have substantial knowledge of relevant clinical aspects and the interaction of those aspects with hypnosis in the forensic situation. The relatively untrained hypnotist may well proceed differently and achieve apparent short-term gains of a forensic nature but cause long-term clinical problems.

Formulating Hypotheses about Processes

In several of the cases analyzed in this book, even after sessions were completed, the nature of the conflict that the witness (or accused) was experiencing was not entirely clear. This was a major problem with DD and Knibb (Chapter 6) and occurred also with AP (Chapter 5). In such cases, one could be dealing with a subject's unstable personality, or handling a subject's anxiety reaction to a traumatic episode. Knowledge of the alternatives is critical in making decisions about what to do and what not to do in the hypnotic situation when subjects experience stress. In such cases, an adequate knowledge of hypnosis and its clinical uses and limitations is essential.

Coping with Unsuggested Effects

The notion of sequelae of hypnosis has been documented expertly by Hilgard (1974; see also Brentar & Lynn, 1989) and has emerged in current cases. DD, for example, reported "symptoms" of his involvement in hypnosis; he woke up with a headache; at another point in the session, he indicated he felt sick to his stomach; and at another stage, there were irregularities in his breathing. These were noted and monitored in the session and emerged in similar ways in the case of AP in Chapter 5. It must be concluded in cases in which stressful memories are being retrieved that with hypnotic subjects there is some probability that unsuggested effects or negative sequelae of hypnosis (see Hilgard, 1974, for discussion of sequelae in the clinical context) will occur. The hypnotist must anticipate the probability that those effects will persist and must adopt procedures to cope with those kinds of outcomes. Substantial professional experience is required to do this effectively. In all of the aforementioned risks, and there are others that could have been documented, the issue of qualifications and experience looms large. We turn now to consider this issue and to highlight it in relation to additional case material.

QUALIFICATIONS FOR PRACTICE

The issue of qualifications reaches deeply into the matter of ethical practice. Adequate professional expertise is necessary for the practice of hypnosis in the forensic setting, and this issue has been canvased in the cases considered in Chapter 2, where events were closely analyzed in relation to cases in which strong doubts were expressed about the ethics of what took place.

Professional issues associated with the investigative use of hypnosis have been debated heavily in the literature and have been discussed by us in detail elsewhere (see McConkey & Sheehan, 1988a). The main divergence in that debate has been about whether forensic hypnosis sessions should be run by psychologists and psychiatrists or by police officers. When hypnosis is being evaluated for use by police departments, a basic decision is whether the hypnosis session should be conducted by police officers trained in hypnosis, or by medical practitioners or psychologists who are trained in hypnosis, and have forensic knowledge as well. Our view is that investigative hypnosis should be conducted by mental health professionals who have proper familiarity with criminal investigation procedures. It should also be noted that, consistent with our emphasis on the importance of motivational and emotional factors in the forensic setting, the use of hypnosis to access memories in the forensic situation must at times be viewed in terms of the adoption of relevant clinical skills. As we argue in Chapter 10, the skills relevant to forensic investigations involving hypnosis reach beyond simple definition of formal qualifications. Appropriate investigation at different times requires standard professional skills, clinical acumen, and the skilled application of interrogative competency.

It is impossible to comment on the matter of qualifications without analyzing in some way the implications of using hypnosis when the hypnotist has no formal qualifications. Such implications are often dramatically illustrated by cases involving lay hypnotists, and some of these were presented in Chapter 2. We turn now to consider one further case and to make two essential points, one relating to ethics, and the other to common themes emerging across cases with respect to distortion of memory.

The Case of LH

This case went to trial in 1993. LH, a lay hypnotist, was accused of rape and sexual assault involving four people, three of whom were from the same family (two women and one boy). They all lived in the same town, were treated by LH for personal problems, and had multiple sessions with him. There was frequent contact among most of the victims about events in therapy with LH and their perceptions and feelings about what was happening to them.

The history of events suggests that the victims came to LH with a clear expectation that he would treat them for their problems. LH embedded hypnosis (thus clouding the issue of its use) within the context of neurolinguistic programming (NLP), and several NLP techniques were attempted, including "anchoring." During sessions with LH, the victims alleged that he touched them sexually and made suggestive approaches and multiple physical overtures. All of them reported feeling uncomfortable and confused, and made other allegations that included touching, fondling, and sexual interference; this includes the adolescent boy, who was a member of the same family as the two women. Physical contact was explained by LH in terms of what he believed would be therapeutic and good for his clients. The boy concerned reported being scared while the alleged acts were taking place, saying that he was too frightened to open his eyes and pretended at times that he could not hear the therapist. He said he was pretending so that he could endure what was happening in the session.

When the family sat around the table and talked about what was taking place in therapy with LH, they claimed they became anxious about what was occurring and saw common elements in the therapist's behavior toward each of them. They then contacted the police and charges were brought. All of the women had complex clinical histories and the family already had some history of sexual abuse and sexual exploitation by others. Evidence in the trial related to their unreliability of memory both in and out of hypnosis, and also to the issue of whether persons could fantasize that sexual contact had happened in hypnosis even though it may not have occurred in fact. Issues of particular relevance in the trial were (1) the level of the victims' hypnotizability; (2) the complex overlay of memories by experience and opportunities for distortion of memories among the claimants; and (3) the extent to which they were hypnotized.

Similar themes in this case appeared in other cases as well and included inconsistency of reporting across people, and discordant elements within the testimony of the same individuals. With respect to hypnosis, the thrust of the prosecution's case revolved around establishing the argument that memory outside of hypnosis was no different from what it was normally. The case for the defense was that memory was affected both in hypnosis and out of hypnosis, and the reports of the claimants were not reliable. However, precise statements about how much memory is distorted out of hypnosis are difficult to formulate. Sexually toned "gimmick" techniques used by LH may have colored their thinking and cognitions in hypnosis and so affected the claimants' later recall. The case also raised issues of the extent to which hypnosis is inherently distorting, the extent to which fantasy (distorted thinking) is reinforced by a treatment setting like NLP, and the influence of the level of suggestibility of the subjects concerned. The empirical issue of consequence was the degree to which claims of misconduct on the part of LH arose as an artifact from his attempts at hypnotic induction or from the influence of hypnosis itself.

There was no real disagreement in this case that the events occurred in a hypnotic setting. The claimants saw it that way and at times used language indicating that they had been tutored in ways of talking that admitted freely the validity of terms like "trance," "hypnosis," and "altered state." One of the women, for instance, reported in her statement to the police that "she was in an altered state, which is a state of deep relaxation where you are aware of what is happening, but you are not really in control of your body movements." However, there was disagreement in the trial about whether waking recall (which produced the claims of assault and rape) was uncontaminated. The most obviously influential parameter was the level of susceptibility of LH's clients. The female claimant who alleged the most abuse was also the most suggestible, and reports of "waking up" by the claimants were difficult to evaluate, especially when the influence of suggestion was problematic. The phenomenon of carryover of thoughts and ideation from the treatment setting to the waking state appeared to us as a salient one in the case and was the focus of questioning for the expert witnesses who offered their testimony. In the case, the matter of what were "the facts of hypnosis" was very difficult to judge.

The possible incorporation of hypnosis in a therapeutic context is instructive. In our view, there is no necessary link between NLP and hypnosis. NLP aims to enhance perception but may or may not enhance suggestibility. It is regarded as a controversial technique, and it does not have the status of behavior therapy, psychoanalysis, or other long-standing techniques, but it is used by some psychiatrists, psychologists, and other professionals. Typically, it uses sensation-enhancement techniques and focuses primarily on experience. Despite the absence of a necessary link between NLP and hypnosis, it is nevertheless our view that if a person were following the procedures of NLP, there could be created a situation in which a client might be put into a different mode of consciousness, legitimately labeled "hypnosis." It was just such a situation that appeared to us to apply in the case of LH. It can be argued, therefore, that LH was attempting to practice a technique that is easily sensationalized, and just as with hypnosis itself, there is no evidence to suggest that the technique of NLP is reliable in producing accurate recall. Like other cases discussed in this book, there was evidence in this case that aspects of a person's memory in hypnosis can easily become contaminated, and it is technically impossible to disentangle what has been said from what has occurred in fact. It seems probable to us that the memories reported by the claimants in this trial were distorted by what occurred, and what happened was overlaid with fantasy and previous recollections.

In an important sense, then, the issues highlighted by this case in terms of possible memory distortion and overlay of recollections by previous experiences are not distinctively different from those highlighted in other parts of this book, in which we have discussed cases when hypnosis has been conducted by qualified professionals. The important inference to draw, as far as memory processes are concerned, is that the nature and experience of a hypnotist probably has relatively little effect on how hypnosis per se exerts its effects. An experienced hypnotist, however, has probably learned from the mistakes that he or she made as a beginning hypnotist, and experience may well affect the distortion of memories being retrieved. Poor questioning can have a major distorting effect on memory retrieval (for review of the evidence, see Chapter 9). Qualifications and experience also matter in how they relate to the welfare of the people being hypnotized and the ethics of practice. That relationship, in our opinion, is especially significant.

All three women saw LH in relation to personal problems (e.g., depression, interpersonal difficulties). They alleged sexual contact, after first believing that such contact was part of the therapy that they had sought. The therapist, however, was in no way qualified to offer treatment or to use hypnosis. Hypnosis was also used inadvertently, perhaps, as an adjunct to another therapy technique. But that technique was one that can lend itself easily to misuse through inexpert use of sensation enhancement and focus on unusual experiences. The trial reports suggested strongly that hypnosis had been used, but it is not certain that it was used in the case of all of the persons involved, despite the claimants' ready grasp of appropriate language. The case also raised the relevance of the principle that hypnosis should never be used when the person being hypnotized is not told explicitly that hypnotic procedures are being administered, an issue highlighted elsewhere (Scheflin, 1994) as important, with the growing prevalence of what Scheflin has called "nonhypnosis hypnosis" (p. 31). One of the women, for instance, reported that LH "was talking to me in a very level type of voice, telling me that I was getting drowsy and I was going down a flight of stairs and that every step I took I would get deeper and deeper into a state of sleep." Another reported being given suggestions of numbness to the left side of the body as the therapist stroked her body from shoulder to knee. The women involved were left with memories that were obviously stressful, uncertain expectations about what had occurred, and had obviously experienced conflict that was not handled with clinical expertise.

We cannot endorse in any way the practice, inadvertent or otherwise, of hypnosis by unqualified persons. The principles of ethical practice outlined previously cannot be met in such circumstances. LH was acquitted of the charges, but the issues raised by this case and those analyzed in Chapter 2 highlight the salience of many of the principles we unequivocally espouse.

SUMMARY COMMENT

This chapter has addressed a sample of issues and principles that we consider important. Many of them deal with what Hess (1987) has called "ethical vulnerability," insofar as they deal with ethical dilemmas confronting practitioners involved in forensic hypnosis, and several of them have not been fully elaborated. It is possible, for example, to view the rights of participants as needing to extend from witness or victim to the hypnotist, and it is not clear how responsibility can extend beyond the investigative session, but it is our view that it should. Furthermore, each practitioner must individually face the dilemma posed at times by conflict between technical and humanitarian concerns. The law operates often in an inhumane way, and it is our view that ethical practice must always be caring.

There are no prescriptive guidelines that we can confidently offer for finding the correct balance of clinical and forensic priorities in individual cases. In specific instances, it is often a matter for professional judgment. That judgment, however, can and should be guided by the knowledge of relevant principles and the application of professional expertise. We argue that the nature of this balance is one of the most important aspects of the ethical practice of hypnosis. It is essential that relevant and skilled experience be brought to bear on the challenge of that task. It is also clear that no guidelines for forensic hypnosis can ever be fully adequate for recognizing the sensitive and complex issues involved. Ethical practice needs informed and conscientious decision making and cannot be achieved by a simple "cookbook" approach.

In many ways, the principles outlined in this chapter serve to assert the relevance and importance of as many psychologists as possible becoming active in attempts to protect consumers of psychological practices from "both unintentional and intentional unethical behavior" (American Psychological Association, 1988, p. 570). This means fostering awareness of evolving ethical principles and standards, and increasing sensitivity to the harm that can affect consumers when practitioners engage in substandard practices. Only when such awareness is enhanced can we limit the abusive exercise of power and the abrogation of the rights of clients.

CHAPTER 8

A Case Perspective on Hypnosis in the Forensic Setting

The forensic issues covered by the cases that we analyze in this book have been many and varied. In Chapter 2, the cases we discussed dealt with the issue of the appropriateness of introducing hypnosis and the question of the guidelines that should be adopted when hypnosis is used. Particularly important were the matters of the qualifications and expertise of the hypnotist, and the impact of the use of hypnosis on both witnesses and the investigation when no standard procedures were adopted.

In Chapter 5, we dealt with two cases of alleged sexual assault. There emerged the major theme of finding a proper balance between clinical and forensic priorities. This was related, in turn, to protecting the welfare of subjects while fostering the ethical involvement of individuals within the legal system. A second major theme emphasized in that chapter, and threaded through all of the cases that we have presented, was the consistency of memory reports and the potential unreliability of memory. We focused also on specific concerns about how to deal with the substantial personal and emotional impact of remembered events among the witnesses and victims of crime. An issue that came to the fore, which expresses the general theme of this book, was the matter of meeting the interests and needs of people by attempting to gain access to particular memories. This issue became especially compelling when hypnosis was used by un-qualified persons (see Chapters 2 and 7, in particular).

The issues that present themselves to us as especially impor-tant on the basis of the cases are (1) the impact on legal procedures; (2) the qualifications of the hypnotist; (3) the admis-sibility of hypnotic evidence; (4) the consistency of memory reports; (5) the possibility of lying; (6) the status of the person hypnotized and the role of emotion in hypnotic recall; and (7) the rights of participants. In addressing these issues, we leave aside areas such as psychological aspects relevant to the jury, for example, what influences jurors' decisions about the events to which they have been exposed; and the characteristics of people that render them vulnerable to confessions in interrogations. A related important matter of how to prepare for the challenging tasks of cross-examination and psychological assessment, and expert testimony under cross-examination can be seriously un-dermined by incomplete psychological assessment (Gudjonsson, 1994). These are not minor issues, but they are covered compre-hensively elsewhere (e.g., Deffenbacher & Loftus, 1982; Fitzger-ald & Ellsworth, 1983; Gudjonsson, 1992, 1994; Sherrod, 1985; Wells & Loftus, 1984). As in previous chapters, we draw on the case material to illustrate and help us understand the issues encountered in real-life forensic work.

THE IMPACT ON LEGAL PROCEDURES

The impact on legal procedures constitutes a special problem in investigative hypnosis. As argued elsewhere (Sheehan, 1986), the major impact that emerges from memory testing derives from the influence of information that witnesses are exposed to after original events have occurred. This information may be commu-nicated in the form of leading questions that potentially can distort facts or through information about events that is im-parted in a biased way by other procedures. Risks were clearly evident in the cases we analyzed in Chapter 2, when leading questions strongly cued particular replies. The problem, how-ever, reaches out far more widely than responses cued by specific questions. The impact on legal procedures refers broadly to the various influences of postevent information that include effects on both accuracy and confidence. In the case involving DD (Chapter 6), for example, strong evidence indicated that prior recall, across a range of situations, influenced subsequent reporting and resulted in extensive modification of events as they were recalled. Experimental evidence clearly demonstrates that postevent information can be assimilated into memory and reorganized memories can be accepted as real (Loftus, 1979; Pettinati, 1988), and the data from the cases in this book also bear on that conclusion.

The layperson's preconception about memory is that events seen can be retrieved in memory in an exact and literally correct way. It is argued by some who practice forensic hypnosis (e.g., Reiser, 1980) that hypnosis is a procedure that reliably achieves such a retrieval. Whether it does, however, must depend on the data in hand, and the evidence suggests that literal reproduction is not reliably achieved.

The major issue for attention in the experimental memory literature (for further comment, see Chapter 8) is what we call "the legitimacy of the memory gap." Is the failure to report memory of an event that we know has occurred a genuine loss, or simply an illustration of reduced motivation or ability to report? In attempting to answer this question, implicitly at least, we need to take into account the beliefs that observers, including the hypnotist, might have that something bad must have happened for someone not to talk about it. Beliefs of these kinds exert subtle influences on memory-report outcomes. In this respect, also, there are additional factors to consider, for example, why the investigating officers might be interested in using hypnosis. Predominantly, the motivation of those involved in the investigative exercise is to retrieve memories that are reportedly absent, but hypnosis is often used too confidently and uncritically within the forensic system because hypnotic suggestion is believed to be especially effective and because people also ask to be hypnotized. The case of AP (reviewed in Chapter 5), for instance, suggests that belief in the efficacy of hypnosis can flow from observation of the increased reporting that hypnosis produces, and beliefs of this kind can often override other perceptions. A worry of the investigating officers in the case of CK (see Chapter 5), for instance, was that they thought hypnosis would concretize her suspicions about what had happened. Despite this concern, however, they were interested in gaining access to her apparent memory gap.

With these motivations in mind, the importance of corroboration must be emphasized. Police often consider (see McConkey & Sheehan, 1988b) that some checking of events reported in hypnosis could and should be provided. Undercover officers in the case of CK, for example, were independently at work to try and determine the defendant's strategies involving the lay hypnotist (see Chapter 5). The case illustrated novel ways in which the investigating officers attempted to corroborate the testimony of CK and JD. We return to this matter later in our discussion of the rights of participants.

We have argued in this book for the adoption of explicit guidelines for the practice of hypnosis in the forensic setting. The absence of such guidelines poses massive problems of the kind that we noted in Chapter 2. As discussed in the subsequent cases, we followed guidelines as much as possible in an attempt to minimize the chances of distortion and reduce the probability that cues for distortion were introduced, or that the hypnotist and others would incorrectly interpret the nature of memory reports. The issue of the guidelines to employ and how closely to follow them may be associated with the qualifications of the hypnotist, and we turn now to consider that issue (see also Chapter 7).

QUALIFICATIONS OF THE HYPNOTIST

In a survey that we conducted on the use of hypnosis by police in Australia (McConkey & Sheehan, 1988b), the evidence suggests that the qualifications of hypnotists are viewed for the most part as relevant because of the recognition accorded to the importance of the possible clinical consequences of hypnosis. The same data, however, shows another dimension that has largely gone unnoticed in the controversy about qualifications is the interviewing competency of the investigator. There is especially strong endorsement in the survey of the notion that competence and/or training in relevant interviewing procedures is necessary within the forensic setting. This skill reaches out not only to address matters such as the procedures of questioning, but also broader issues, such as the way questions are framed and information is solicited from subjects to conform to legal requirements and standards. It is clear from our research, however, that often there are substantial departures from reasonable procedures being practiced in Australia and overseas.

The bodies that control the practice of hypnosis in Australia, for the most part, are Psychologists Registration Boards operating under different legal acts for each State (see McConkey & Sheehan, 1988a). The acts involved legislate the professional practice of psychology, but are not especially concerned with the issue of who is appropriately qualified to use hypnosis in criminal investigations. This raises directly the matter of the use of hypnosis by police officers (see Chapter 2) and the definition of skills that define appropriate professional practice in investigative hypnosis.

Strong argument has been made in the literature that forensic hypnosis sessions should be conducted by police officers (for full discussion of this issue, see McConkey & Sheehan, 1988a). A special feature of the argument is that investigative hypnosis is viewed as a speciality area that has virtually no overlap with other uses of hypnosis (e.g., Monaghan, 1981; Reiser, 1980, 1984). Reiser (1984) stated, for instance, that by the nature of their training, police officers should be viewed as "law enforcement behavioral science professionals" and are therefore appropriately qualified to practice hypnosis in the investigative setting. Monaghan argued against the employment of mental health professionals for the reason that therapeutic and investigative hypnosis have different goals and employ different procedures; because of this, criminal investigators were seen as the most appropriate persons to practice forensic hypnosis. The primary purpose of a hypnosis session was viewed as "gaining evidence in such a way [as] to protect the interview from defence challenges" (Monaghan, 1981, p. 76).

The core assumption in these positions is that investigative officers conduct forensic hypnosis effectively because the nature of their training accentuates skill in the use of interrogative procedures. In contrast, the Federal Bureau of Investigation (FBI) holds the view that psychiatrists and psychologists are the best qualified to use hypnosis in such settings, because the use of hypnosis by such professionals provides "a dimension of further protection for the witnesses or victims being questioned" (Ault, 1979, p. 450).

The major point of controversy in the debate about the use of police officers is the claim that they lack the skills to enable them to cope with complications in the hypnosis session. Following the contrary view, training in interrogation techniques is seen as distinct from the skills required when complications arise of the kind that we have discussed in a number of our cases. It is our view that training in interrogative competency does not address the clinical complexities, for example, of victims who, traumatized by physical abuse, are trying to retrieve memories that are personally threatening. As Kleinhauz and Beran (1985) argued:

Since the process of hypnotic recall to overcome amnesia following a criminal event may have psychological implications for the subject, and the psychological dynamics may require immediate professional intervention, the hypnotist participating in forensic investigations should be a psychiatrist or psychologist trained in hypnosis. (p. 324)

However, it seems clear to us that interviewing skill is necessary for the efficient and professional practice of forensic hypnosis. Its absence was a major problem in the cases that we reviewed in Chapter 2. The creation of pseudomemories (e.g., Barnier & McConkey, 1993; Labelle, Laurence, Nadon, & Perry, 1990; Laurence & Perry, 1988; Sheehan, Statham, & Jamieson, 1991a, 1991b; Weekes, Lynn, Green, & Brentar, 1992) and the contamination of existing memories can occur easily enough with all practicing professionals, and there is a definite need to view qualifications in investigative practice as involving both clinical and forensic skills. We have sympathy for Udolf's (1983) position that mental health professionals with experience in clinical hypnosis often do not have sufficient knowledge to act as forensic hypnotists, and that additional training in legal matters and techniques is necessary. The fully qualified professional, then, must be sophisticated legally and skilled in relevant interviewing techniques. This is especially important given that psychologists and psychiatrists have to relate to witnesses and victims in ways "that may affect their future testimony and its legal status" (Udolf, 1983, p. 164). The issue as a whole, however, is complex and probably reflects in part differences in perspective, as Gudjonsson (1992) asserts. Police interrogation manuals, such as Walkley's (1987) handbook for police in the United Kingdom, base techniques on experience reflecting practices that are sophisticated but coercive. Psychologists, on the other hand, tend to view their practices within a framework of thinking that has more to do with attitudes and compliance.

In the United States, there have been a substantial number of court decisions relating to hypnotically influenced testimony (for reviews, see Laurence & Perry, 1988, and Scheflin & Shapiro, 1989), and many depend heavily for their significance on the qualifications of expert witnesses. Decisions often have much to do with the relevance and importance of the expert witness who has experience in psychology or psychiatry and specific experience in hypnosis and its use in the forensic context.

In Australia, there is relatively little guidance through the court on what qualifications are important (e.g., Kirby, 1984; Odgers, 1988a, 1988b), although there are definite implications that forensic hypnosis is viewed as most appropriately falling within the field of qualified professionals (e.g., *R. v. Geesing*, 1984, 1985).

We suspect that this issue has not been resolved, because it seems that active lobbying is increasing in some jurisdictions for the right to have police specialists perform the hypnosis. There are no systematic data, it should be noted, on the differential consequences of police versus nonpolice personnel doing forensic hypnosis. In many ways, the focus on the role of police in forensic hypnosis has inadvertently drawn attention away from the major problem of investigative hypnosis being practiced by untrained lay hypnotists. For example, the case of BT (in Chapter 2) highlights the horrendous problems that can be introduced by the inexpert use of hypnosis when people who use hypnosis lack both forensic competency and clinical skill.

THE ADMISSIBILITY OF HYPNOTIC EVIDENCE

Prior to the late 1960s, hypnotic testimony was excluded generally from the courts because it was thought to be unreliable. As Scheflin and Shapiro (1989) note, the very first appellate case in the United States that involved a request for the admission of hypnotically refreshed testimony (*Harding v. State*, 1968) "started an avalanche of cases that continues to cascade through the courts" (p. 61). According to the judgment in this case, hypnotically refreshed testimony was admissible, but jurors had to make a decision as to whether they would believe the testimony or not. The law then became more conservative and the safeguards were developed and promulgated have been highly influential (see Chapter 3 for a summary of our guidelines and Chapter 10 for further discussion). Following the development and adoption of various safeguards, the thrust of the admissibility debate moved toward admitting evidence based on hypnotically refreshed testimony, providing that safeguards were satisfied. This was despite the fact that the person who was responsible for instituting a particularly influential set of such safeguards (see Orne, 1979) has argued forcibly that hypnosis reliably distorts memory of previously experienced events (e.g., see Dinges et al., 1992), and that safeguards ought not to be accepted as the criteria for determining admissibility of evidence. Not surprisingly, perhaps, the pendulum then swung back to emphasize total inadmissibility.

The position in the United Kingdom in recent years has been determined by the Home Office Circular that presents a relatively discouraging position with respect to forensic hypnosis (see McConkey & Sheehan, 1989). Moreover, the Home Office Circular noted that the Court of Appeal in the United Kingdom had not yet considered the status of evidence from someone who has been hypnotized. Notably, the Home Office did not seem to appreciate that hypnosis would be used in criminal investigations and had been lacking in providing guidelines for such use; the provision of such guidelines not only would allow the police a firm structure for their consideration and use of hypnosis, but also would give courts a meaningful basis for an evaluation of the impact of hypnosis on the subsequent testimony of a previously hypnotized witness. The guidelines that are missing from the Home Office Circular are missing also from most statements about forensic hypnosis, and that is one of the reasons why we have provided detailed guidelines in Chapter 3.

Guidelines developed by Orne (1979; Orne et al., 1984) have been influential in the United States, although the position in that country has been influenced by the U.S. Supreme Court judgment in the case of *Rock v. Arkansas* (1987); for detailed discussion of this judgment, see Orne, Dinges, and Orne (1990), Scheflin and Shapiro (1989), and Udolf (1990). This judgment determined that the constitutional rights of defendants to testify on their own behalf should take precedence over any State rules that relate to the exclusion of hypnotically refreshed testimony. The status of the U.S. Supreme Court's involvement has given an importance to the ruling that makes it especially influential. Essentially, the judgment was conflicted but neutral on the general matter of the admissibility of hypnotically refreshed testimony of witnesses. It recognized that the use of hypnosis for investigative purposes has no general agreement as far as law is concerned, and it supported the right of each State to pass judgment on the matter. This has now created a situation in which it is impossible to specify an agreed-on position in the United States with respect to the matter of the admissibility of hypnotic testimony (see also Scheflin, 1994).

The research literature and the courts exposed to its findings through the use of expert witnesses now recognize the limitations of verbal testimony and of hypnotically refreshed testimony, but not we would argue, the full complexity of issues that are at stake in cases in which hypnosis has been used. As Scheflin and Shapiro (1989) have pointed out, there are multiple broad approaches articulated by the courts. The legal system in Australia, like that in the United States, has become more familiar with hypnosis research and its findings as the use of hypnosis in the forensic setting in this country has increased. Like the United States, legislation in Australia is formulated within its separate States, and no position has yet developed that is heavily influential at the national level, although individual cases (e.g., *R. v. Haywood, Marshall, and Roughley,* 1994; *R. v. Jenkyns,* 1993) are providing some explicit directions (see also Chapter 1). For example, the position with respect to admissibility of hypnotic testimony has been stated by *R. v. Jenkyns* (1993), and that position supports one formulated in New Zealand (see *R. v. McFelin,* 1985). According to this judgment, "there is no inflexible rule that hypnotically induced testimony is inadmissible." The judge in *R. v. Jenkyns* recommended the guidelines put forward in *R. v. McFelin,* which were adapted from the requirements of the California Evidence Code (for this code, amended through 1988, see Scheflin & Shapiro, 1989, pp. 103–107). This code limits hypnotically induced evidence to matters that a witness has recalled and reported prior to hypnosis. Furthermore, the substance of that original recollection must be recorded by audiotape or videotape; the hypnosis must be conducted in accordance with set procedures, such as informed consent; and hypnosis must be performed by an experienced person. It recognizes the kinds of risks in forensic hypnosis that we have outlined in Chapter 7, and pays attention to the probable confabulation of memories in hypnosis and the likely enhancement of confidence that occurs in relation to previously expressed memories. Also important, it acknowledges that the person who is hypnotized ought to know, in fact, that hypnosis is being attempted.

Special note should be taken of the fact that in *R. v. Haywood, Marshall, and Roughley* (1994) the prosecution was considered to be obliged to satisfy the judge that it was safe to admit material that had been elicited during hypnosis in particular circumstances. An important emphasis of this judgment is that the prosecution must demonstrate that the procedures adopted had no adverse or negative effects upon the reliability of the evidence obtained in hypnosis, and that in determining whether hypnotically refreshed evidence should be admitted,

the truth is known to be stronger than the motive to be hypnotized, and in which preservation of the self is more important
than allegiance to the hypnotist. Evidence should address these
questions but, to date, has not.

As we have argued elsewhere (see Sheehan & McConkey,
1988), when faking is indicated, planning to tell lies must also
play some part. Planned lies enhance plausibility and believabil-
ity, and the process of planning itself can effectively hide nonverbal deception cues (Littlepage & Pineault, 1984), and distortions, both intentional and unintentional, can complicate greatly
the process of assessment of malingering (Rogers, 1988). Just as
clinicians cannot assume that psychiatric patients will not distort
their clinical presentation, so too it is evident that deception may
be evident in the forensic hypnosis setting for a variety of
compelling reasons.

THE STATUS OF THE PERSON HYPNOTIZED
AND THE ROLE OF EMOTION IN RECALL

Although this issue is one that we addressed in Chapter 7, it
merits additional emphasis here because of the critical role that
emotions play in determining the nature of reported events.
Emotional and motivational factors influence not only the status
of the person who is reporting, but interpretation of the veracity
of the events being recalled. The nature of the strategies that the
hypnotist uses in conducting a session and determining a balance
between clinical and forensic priorities would seem to be critical.

The status of DD (Chapter 6) potentially shifted, for example, in the SP case as clinical priorities came to be accepted as
more important in coping with the needs of the witness. The
status of AP (Chapter 5) also shifted when it was found out that
reported memories were consonant with her earlier reported
dreams. In the latter case, the forensic priorities of the case led
to negative consequences for the person involved (e.g., a suicide
attempt), raising serious questions about the humanity of the
legal system and demanding some recasting of the concept of
"care" within the forensic system. One might indeed ask the
serious forensic question whether hypnosis should ever have
been employed, if knowledge of AP's dream had been available
in the first instance. Equally, one can seriously question whether
hypnosis should have been used if all of the reasons why DS was
present (Chapter 4) had been known by the hypnotist.

In relation to the cases we have reviewed, one of the major issues affecting the status of witnesses is clearly the effect of hypnosis on judgments by others about criminal liability. Some of the cases we have reviewed in this book have dealt with witnesses of crimes who were themselves not directly involved in the events in question, whereas others were more explicitly concerned with people involved in the events being investigated. The reasons for wanting hypnosis to be used are inevitably more complex in the case of the latter, and it is argued for this reason that police departments may prohibit the use of hypnosis on known suspects in criminal cases (Ault, 1979; Udolf, 1983). On the other hand, police do use hypnotic techniques, which may be incorporated into interrogation procedures but not labeled "hypnotic."

In Chapter 7, we reported on the use of hypnosis in an investigation of alleged sexual abuse (see also Sheehan et al., 1986), and there was considerable difficulty in interpreting the memories reported in that case. One of the major risks involved was that hypnotic events can be easily taken by others to confirm or justify impressions of the guilt or innocence of the person being hypnotized. And preconceptions about hypnosis can be especially risky when the person being hypnotized stands "poised" to be blamed. Equally, it is virtually impossible to cope with the situation when the presence of suspicion is not understood fully by the hypnotist or the other participants in the setting.

THE RIGHTS OF PARTICIPANTS

The rights of participants are the final forensic issue that we address, and they were discussed earlier as well (Chapter 7) and signaled as important in our guidelines (Chapter 3), because they relate to matters of serious ethical concern. Also, the issue is not unrelated to the matter of the choice of the person to be hypnotized. Conduct of a session can abrogate rights more readily when the person being hypnotized is emotionally vulnerable and, for this reason also, the rights of persons under suspicion of a crime are a special problem.

The civil rights of participants have been discussed in some detail in well-known cases in the USA such as *Rock v. Arkansas* (1987; see also Udolf, 1990). Our emphasis, however, has been more on subtle indications of the need to protect participants' rights, for example, the case of DD (Chapter 6), who appeared to us to be at the point of reporting memories in hypnosis that were clinically very stressful and potentially damaging. The issue of rights is additionally important given the possibility that a person, who cannot be charged for what has happened on the basis of what is remembered in hypnosis, may still be charged with another crime if the authorities investigating it are influenced by "other things" that are reported in hypnosis (Sheehan, 1988c).

The aforementioned are all essentially clear reasons why firm guidelines should be practiced in hypnosis and every opportunity taken to corroborate material. However, as the cases we discussed have illustrated, corroboration is not always possible. Indeed, in many of the cases involved in this book, events could not have been proved at all as they were reported. For this reason, the protection of participants' rights can be a special problem. Procedures are needed that address the rights of those who are hypnotized in this way; corroboration should be sought whenever possible, and attempts should be made whenever possible to reduce the possibilities of distortion. Finally, it is not just the hypnotized witness or defendant who has rights. As the case of DS (discussed in Chapter 4) illustrated, the hypnotist also has rights, and they need to be respected by the forensic system.

SUMMARY COMMENT

Among other things, this chapter deals with the difficulties of formulating accurately the forensic meaning and value of shifting memory reports. All the cases in which we have used guidelines highlight the inherent inconsistency of memory reports, and a central task for us was to find a balance between clinical and forensic priorities, particularly when emotionally traumatic events were recalled. In all of the cases we have discussed, our focus inevitably has been on issues that arise when one is trying to conduct or evaluate attempts to enhance memory in hypnosis. For this reason, a heavy emphasis has been placed on matters that highlight memory processes and their features. Although memory reports are frequently to be mistrusted, practitioners must nevertheless relate ethically and professionally to them, while at the same time satisfying the obligations of their investigative role.

The overriding challenge with respect to the majority of the issues we have considered is the essential task of forging a balance between investigative and clinical priorities, a theme that we have stressed throughout this book. Our essential position is that the utility of hypnosis in the forensic setting is limited, but the introduction of hypnosis can be useful. The well-being of the person being hypnotized, however, should be the major dimension for ethical practice, and professionals must always assess their actions against that dimension.

CHAPTER 9

A Laboratory View of Issues in Forensic Hypnosis

Many of the effects of hypnosis on memory, including memory enhancement and distortion, and confident reporting in hypnosis have been documented elsewhere (see Krass et al., 1988; Laurence & Perry, 1988; McConkey, 1992; Orne et al., 1984; Pettinati, 1988; Relinger, 1984; Smith, 1983; Wagstaff, 1984, 1989). This chapter examines the experimental literature from the perspective of issues highlighted in the cases that we have analyzed. Not surprisingly, those issues that we take up overlap with those that have been reviewed elsewhere. Our conclusions, however, are not necessarily the same following exposure to the cases that we have discussed. A number of significant issues are not addressed in this chapter, because they are not especially relevant to the cases. These include the use of hypnosis to inhibit or interfere with memory (e.g., Evans, 1988), historical issues dealing with early relevant research in the field (e.g., Hull, 1933; Prince, 1914), and the community's perceptions of the reliability of hypnosis (for review, see McConkey, 1992).

Here we focus on enhancement and distortion of memory in hypnosis, and memories retrieved when strong emotion is related to their expression. We also think it appropriate, given the nature of our cases, to consider some of the major findings on coercion in hypnosis. The review heavily emphasizes laboratory findings, and for the most part, coverage is of research findings in the last two decades.

The main laboratory findings reach out to address both the processes responsible for the operation of memory in hypnosis and the nature of the interplay between memory and emotion in determining memory retrieval. The interaction between mood and memory (e.g., Friswell & McConkey, 1989), for example, seems an especially relevant issue, considering the extent to which emotional factors influenced outcomes in the cases that we have presented. In doing so, however, we chose not to discuss the role of hypnosis in therapeutic settings, because coverage of that lies elsewhere (e.g., Frankel, 1988). Other issues also are relevant, such as the normal social psychological processes that define deception, and they are evaluated closely elsewhere (e.g., Littlepage & Pineault, 1984; Zuckerman, Koestner, Colella, & Alton, 1984).

The chapters in this book have highlighted the primary importance of the consistency of hypnotized people's memory reports. The matter of the reliability of memory is critically relevant to findings in the general experimental literature on memory, and to experimental data on the relationship between memory and hypnosis, in particular.

THE NATURE OF MEMORY
AND ITS RELATIONSHIP TO HYPNOSIS

Memory is a complex and labile phenomenon, and its inherent plasticity is clearly acknowledged in the literature (Annon, 1988; McGuire, 1986; Welden & Malpass, 1981). It is influenced strongly by preexisting representations (Echabe & Rovira, 1989; Read & Rosson, 1982), and postevent information and misinformation can also lead to distortion of memory in both adults and children (Bowers & Bekerian, 1984; Ceci, Ross, & Toglia, 1987). As far as the forensic utility of hypnosis is concerned, the key issue is the introduction of postevent information with its ensuing implications for memory distortion.

Basically, we view memory as illustrating the processes of construction and reconstruction at work, and that view essentially reflects the outline we gave of its nature in Chapter 1, in which the reconstruction of memory was tied to forensic implications. Many different arguments have been formulated to take account of the role of hypnosis in memory, however, and they each have different implications for understanding the nature of memory and its variability in the forensic setting.

Following one view, hypnosis is said to revive traces of the original perception and to facilitate vivid access to original stimulus material (e.g., Reiser, 1980). If this view is correct, then the forensic implications are substantial. It follows, for instance, that recall should be vivid and accurate in hypnosis and that hypnosis will guarantee access to true recollections. This view is tied normally in the hypnotic literature to a "videorecorder model" of memory, which suggests that hypnotic suggestion operates effectively to access events in a veridical manner. This is especially relevant in the situation of hypnotic age regression, in which the susceptible subject is typically coaxed to use his or her imaginative skills and is highly motivated to respond. The regression situation, however, is also one that lends itself to misuse (see Perry, Laurence, D'Eon, & Tallant, 1988), and use of regression procedures does not imply the reinstitution of specific events (Nash, 1987; Nash, Drake, Wiley, Khalsa, & Lynn, 1986).

A second view highlights very contrasting forensic implications. According to this account, which is promulgated in many psychological and legal debates about the utility of hypnosis (e.g., Orne et al., 1984), memories retrieved in hypnosis are likely to be inaccurate, because they are constructed products of hypnotized subjects' imaginative capacities at work (for discussion, see Alba & Hasher, 1983). This view recognizes the fantasy-oriented character of the hypnotic setting that facilitates unreal reporting and predicts substantial distortion in hypnosis. It begs the question, however, whether misinformation that is accepted is merely reported by the subject or actually involves an alteration in the original memories. A key theoretical issue for this view is whether original memories can be retrieved once misinformation has been accepted and error reported. Evidence outside the hypnosis setting suggests that radical alteration of actual memory does not occur (see Smith, 1983, and Welden & Malpass, 1981).

The view that hypnosis is characterized by significant distortion is not inconsistent with the widely held notion that hypnosis operates to produce a laxer criterion in the subject's level of overall response. Criterion shifts occur when there is greater motivation on the subject's part, as in hypnosis, to report memories that normally would not reach the critical threshold used by subjects for their memory reporting. A shift in threshold results in a greater likelihood of reports being correct and also an increased probability of their being false. According to this view, which is argued especially cogently by Klatzky and Erdelyi (1985), genuine memory enhancement can only really be argued if the increase in correct recall occurs under conditions in which it is known that there is no variation in report criteria. For a stringent test of the hypothesis that memory performance in hypnosis will be greater than that out of hypnosis, special methodological procedures are needed in the laboratory to prevent response criterion shifts influencing the data. Forced-choice recall is one of those, because it requires subjects to respond by reporting a fixed number of responses on each recall attempt. Also, this procedure prevents a criterion shift by requiring subjects to give the same output on all tests of memory.

These last two views have very different forensic implications from the first view. They do not predict memory enhancement overall, but hypothesize significant overall memory distortion. They do not necessarily imply that hypnosis is inherently distorting, but they recognize the special nature of the hypnotic setting (with its motivational and exhorting features) and acknowledge the particular relevance of distorting processes such as confabulation. An important point of view to keep in mind when assessing these two accounts is that hypnosis might lead reliably to an increase in memory distortion, but this may not be more than what would result from the administration of other techniques that motivate recall. We now turn to look more specifically at the evidence to support the two general positions—memory enhancement, and memory distortion in hypnosis.

The phenomenon in which repeated testing of memory is predicted to lead to appreciably more accurate recall or recognition of events seen previously is known as "hypermnesia." Reviews exist elsewhere regarding its occurrence both in normal waking memory (e.g., Payne, 1987) and in the hypnotic setting (e.g., McConkey, 1992; Relinger, 1984). The methodology of repeated testing that leads to hypermnesia has also been used in many different studies (e.g., Dywan & Bowers, 1983; McConkey & Kinoshita, 1988; Nogrady, McConkey, & Perry, 1985).

A major assumption of the videorecorder model of memory is that memory is enhanced in hypnosis, but the experimental evidence on this question indicates inconsistent support for the enhancement model. There is some evidence that material can be recalled more accurately (e.g., McConkey & Kinoshita, 1988; Nogrady et al., 1985; Stager & Lundy, 1985), but the generality of memory enhancement required by this model of memory is not sustained by the evidence.

More increased memory recall has been found for meaningful material than for material that is not meaningful (e.g., DePiano & Salzberg, 1981; Dhanens & Lundy, 1975), but work by Shields and Knox (1986) suggests that it is the level of processing that matters, rather than the meaning as such. Shields and Knox asked subjects inside and outside hypnosis to perform shallow and deep processing of a series of words. The subjects were given suggestions for memory enhancement and tested for both recall and recognition of the material. Data showed that hypnotic procedures increased recognition and recall of the material that was processed by susceptible subjects at the deep but not the shallow level. The predicted enhancement effect was not associated with any increase in inaccurate memory, and this finding was consistent with that of Stager and Lundy (1985). Other studies have not confirmed the hypermnesia effect (e.g., Lytle & Lundy, 1988; McKelvie & Pullara, 1988), however. Lytle and Lundy, for example, failed to replicate the earlier work of Stager and Lundy and notably indicated an increase in inaccurate recall.

Overall, results suggest that when hypermnesia occurs, the process at work is likely to be a shift in response criterion. The research of Crawford and Allen (1983) has suggested additionally that when memory enhancement occurs in hypnosis, it is related to the level of hypnotizability of subjects, rather than the presence or absence of hypnotic instruction. Furthermore, evidence from extensive programs of work conducted by the authors in their separate laboratories (for review, see next paragraph) indicates no support at all for the hypothesis that memory is generally enhanced in hypnosis. This position is consonant also with Kihlstrom's (1985) and Wagstaff's (1989) conclusions that no general effect of enhancement of memory can be observed in the experimental literature.

We have noted that special methodological controls can be used to prevent criterion response shifts, and it is thus relevant to review a number of studies that have used them. Generally, when appropriate controls have been adopted, results have failed to support memory enhancement. Three major studies are by Dywan and Bowers (1983), Dinges et al. (1992), and Whitehouse, Dinges, E. Orne, and M. Orne (1988). In the study by

Whitehouse et al., for example, in which forced-choice techniques of recall were used to test for memory, there was no significant difference in accuracy of memory between hypnotic and waking subjects. These researchers concluded that "hypnosis yields information that otherwise would be withheld from the memory report . . . the process is one of facilitation of report tendency rather than an enhanced accessibility to stored memories" (p. 294). The process of facilitation whereby subjects report material that might not otherwise be reported is consistent also with other findings (e.g., Grabowski, Roese, & Thomas, 1991).

When investigating the relationship between hypnosis and memory, any appeal to the relevant evidence must also focus on whether hypnotically refreshed recall is more or less distorted than waking memory. We turn, therefore, to look at the evidence on the relationship between distortion of memory and hypnosis. The data are reviewed in a paradigm-specific way, because effects vary according to the procedures that are employed.

HYPNOSIS AND MEMORY DISTORTION

The Application of Loftus-Type Procedures

Loftus and her associates (for reviews, see Loftus, 1979, 1993a) have experimented over a long period of time with procedures associated with substantial distortion of memory. Her work has generally not been related to hypnosis, but the procedures are distinctive enough and sufficiently relevant to work in hypnosis that we review them as a special category of experimental data.

It is important to emphasize that the pattern of effects obtained from application of her procedures are associated with false information being injected into the test situation in a particular way. The research typically uses a methodology for the injection of misinformation that conveys incorrect information subtly in questions posed to subjects when memory is tested. Routinely, items that pose questions, or make statements about the stimulus material that subjects have seen previously, provide information to subjects that is false and misleading. Such methods are ideally suited to investigating the strength of the relationship between hypnosis and reduced resistance to false information. If false information is incorporated reliably into waking memory through the subtle injection of false cues about events seen previously (e.g., Loftus, Miller, & Burns, 1978), then it becomes an important question, and one with major forensic implications: whether specific distortion effects for the same procedures will be especially evident in hypnosis.

Loftus's procedures have been adapted for use in our laboratories. Typically, a slide series of a robbery was shown before hypnosis; false information was presented prior to induction in some studies but following induction in others; the program used standard waking–hypnosis comparison groups and also applied Orne's (1959, 1972) real-simulating methodology to isolate cues for memory performance inherent in the overall test situation.

In an extensive program of work on memory performance across a range of different comparison conditions and memory controls, we (for review, see Sheehan, 1988a) have shown that the presence of different controls (e.g., time of injection of false information), modes of memory testing (e.g., free recall and recognition), and comparison conditions (e.g., state instruction, real-simulating instruction, and level of suggestibility) do not appreciably result in memory enhancement. Rather, the data are characterized by memory distortion. Memory performance was quite inconsistent (Sheehan & Tilden, 1986), and especially so when false information was injected after, rather than before, hypnosis was introduced and effects involved level of hypnotizability. When Loftus-type procedures were adopted for study of memory distortion in the hypnotic setting, it was subjects' level of susceptibility to hypnosis that appeared to be the major defining parameter, rather than hypnotic instruction. The only evidence of hypnotically related memory enhancement in the total program of work using Loftus-type procedures (involving six independent studies) was the single presence of an effect for high versus low suggestible persons, when object detail in free recall was observed to be higher for more susceptible subjects. However, in this instance, there was also greater intrusion of errors, and this is consistent with the hypothesis of the occurrence of a shift in threshold. Overall, the data were congruent with the notion that hypnosis produced a laxer criterion that affected the output of responses, both correct and incorrect.

Summarizing the findings of this illustrative program of work, we note a number of points (see also Sheehan, 1988a). In four of the six independent experiments conducted, and when distortion was evident, high suggestible subjects who received hypnotic instruction displayed a significantly greater error effect than did low suggestible subjects. Furthermore, recall subjects who were hypnotized showed more distortion than did simulating subjects (who were not hypnotizable and were told to act as if they were good hypnotic subjects). The most consistent effect across all studies in the program was that high hypnotizability in the hypnotic setting was related appreciably to distortion. Data indicated that the hypnotic setting itself also conveyed cues for distortion, but that memory distortion was likely to be shown by those who were more suggestible than others.

The same importance of level of susceptibility to hypnosis has been observed by Barnier and McConkey (1993) in their independent work. Using Loftus-type procedures and exposing subjects to a purse-snatching incident, false information was injected subtly in the memory testing procedures. Data indicated that hypnotizability, and not hypnosis, was associated with false memory reports, and more high than low susceptible subjects reported memories that were incorrect. This work also showed that the factor of hypnotic instruction still operated influentially when memory assessment was conducted by an independent experimenter under standard conditions of testing.

In all of these studies, and where comparison with waking subjects has been used, there is no support for the position that hypnosis is appreciably more distorting than the waking state, but hypnosis (compared with waking) does appear to lead reliably to greater confidence in the memories that are reported. Through all of the paradigms of research that we consider, confidence emerges as increasingly important (see also Krass et al., 1988, and Sheehan, 1988a). However, when false information was injected into the laboratory situation, the pattern of effects varied depending on how that injection was done. The direction in which they changed is instructive, and we turn now to examine briefly the pattern of effects found when false information was conveyed differently by direct suggestion and through the creation of pseudomemories.

Pseudomemory and Hypnosis

Whereas Loftus-type procedures convey false information in relatively subtle and unobtrusive ways (Loftus, 1979; Loftus et al., 1978), pseudomemories introduced in the hypnotic setting by the hypnotist typically convey false accounts of past events in a directly misleading way. It is a procedure that explicitly suggests a false account of past events that subjects have witnessed.

leading questions with high versus low cue structure and for high versus low susceptible subjects. Data showed main effects for cue structure and level of subjects' susceptibility, but there was no support for the involvement of hypnosis; and no support for the prediction that high susceptible persons responding under hypnotic instruction would be most influenced by highly cued material. Across two sessions, as predicted, high susceptible subjects accepted more false suggestions in the questions asked, and especially from more highly structured questions, than did low susceptible subjects. The paradoxical effect was the finding that high versus low cue structure demonstrated a lower, rather than higher, rate of acceptance of false information.

This was investigated further in later work (Linton & Sheehan, 1994) which suggested that the key to the paradox lay in the fact that confidence was additionally related to both the parameters of susceptibility level and cue structure. Data indicated that high susceptible subjects were more confident on low versus high leading questions. Results strongly suggested that the impact of confidence was pervasive enough to override the possible effect of level of hypnotizability in determining the degree of distortion associated with differences in cue structure. Subjects were simply not confident about the answers they gave to high structure, false information questions; this implied that cognitive processing of high cued, misleading items was more difficult for them than the processing of low cued items and the pattern of distortion effects was thereby affected.

This work serves to highlight the general significance and importance of the confidence variable. Confidence has emerged as relevant in multiple studies, including those using quite different paradigms. Any research that has produced support for memory enhancement in hypnosis has also shown that although hypnotic procedures may add occasionally to improvement, this effect seems to be at the cost of greater error and increased confidence being associated with the material that is incorrect. Wagstaff (1982), for instance, found that when he presented subjects with photographs of faces and 1 week later tested subjects for recall, hypnotic subjects made more incorrect identifications than waking subjects but were more confident they were accurate. Also, Dinges et al. (1992) concluded that "it is clear that introducing hypnosis to refresh memory not only fails to increase accurate memory reports but also significantly augments the likelihood that pseudomemories will be reported with some confidence" (p. 1146).

Finally, although many results attest the relevance of possible shifts in response criteria occurring in hypnosis, they also focus on the major part that confidence plays in shaping memory outcomes. Whereas not all studies have shown strong effects for confidence (e.g., see Mingay, 1986; Putnam, 1979; Yuille & McEwan, 1985; Zelig & Beidleman, 1981), there is nevertheless sufficient consistency as far as this variable is concerned (for review, see Krass et al., 1988, and McConkey, 1992) to argue that the conviction of subjects should be regarded as a major relevant parameter. Overall, the data on memory distortion and response to leading questions inform us that broad-based suggestibility effects are replicable, and effects for high susceptible subjects are generally congruent with those observed in other aspects of interrogative questioning (see Gudjonsson, 1984, 1987, 1992, for a detailed report of research on interrogative suggestibility). Most of the studies we have analyzed here ignored the relevance of emotion to determining the nature of subjects' memory reports. We turn now to consider more closely the literature in that respect.

HYPNOSIS, MEMORY, AND EMOTION

The influence of emotion on memory, of memory on emotion, and the impact that hypnosis may have on both emotion and memory have attracted a substantial amount of attention in recent years (e.g., Blaney, 1986; Christianson, 1992a, 1992b, 1992c; Friswell & McConkey, 1989).

Part of the discussion concerning emotion and memory focuses on the notion that emotional stress leads to an impairment in memory. Whether that impairment is labeled forgetting, repression, or dissociation is a matter of some theoretical preference. Consistent with the general notion that material associated with traumatic emotional events is remembered less accurately than material associated with neutral events, Kassin, Ellsworth, and Smith (1989) reported that 79% of experts on eyewitness testimony agreed with the statement that high levels of stress impair the accuracy of eyewitness memory, and 71% said that this statement would be sufficiently reliable to offer in court. As Christianson (1992a) pointed out, following a review of relevant literature, however, there are conflicting empirical findings on this matter. In his work, Christianson differentiated between two classes of to-be-remembered information: (1) memory for emotionally loaded, detailed information of an emotionally arousing event; (2) memory for information surrounding an emotional event (neutral-detail information occurring within an emotional scenario). He argued that emotional events are remembered differently from neutral or ordinary events, but cautioned that there is no simple relationship between intense emotion and memory. Following his argument, it is not necessarily the case that the more negative the emotion or stress, the poorer the memory; or, conversely, the more intense the emotion, the more detailed, accurate, and persistent the memory. In fact, and in contrast to notions of repression, Christianson argued persuasively that very negative emotional events are relatively well retained, both in terms of the emotional event itself and the central, critical detail of the emotion-eliciting event. Certain critical, detailed information of emotionally arousing events and some circumstantial information are less susceptible to forgetting, compared with detail information in neutral counterparts over time. Memory for information associated with negative emotional events (i.e., information preceding or succeeding such events) or peripheral information within an emotional scenario seems to be less accurately retained, especially when tested after short retention intervals. This detrimental memory effect may recede with strong retrieval support if delayed testing is used, or after repeated memory testing. Christianson's (1992b) analysis challenges any unidimensional view of a simple relationship between emotion and memory, and it underscores our position that memory for stressful emotional events needs to be understood in terms of complex interactions between type of events, type of detail information, time of test, and nature of the retrieval conditions.

This is consistent also with the position of Yuille and Tollestrup (1992) that the influence of emotion on eyewitness memory depends on the particular event, the specific response of the witness, and the variety of factors that subsequently affect the storage and retrieval of memory. Yuille and Tollestrup usefully highlighted that the overall impact of the event on the witnesses, and their ongoing lives, may have a greater effect on memory than the specific emotion that was experienced at the time of the event. Specific emotions, however, do have an influence even when the overall impact of the event may be low. For instance, Loftus and Burns (1982) reported that the presence of an upsetting segment in a film led to a reduced recall of detailed information. Also, Christianson and Nilsson (1984)

found that there was poorer recall for descriptive words presented together with mutilated faces than for those presented
together with neutral faces. Overall, the range of experimental
and clinical studies on emotion and memory indicates that there
is no simple relationship between emotion and memory. Emotionally charged memories are not necessarily remembered inac-
curately or accurately, or indeed remembered at all.

In this context, and consistent with the material that we
presented in Chapter 2 and the guidelines in Chapter 3, we
comment selectively now on the debate in the literature concerning repressed memories of traumatic childhood events. Cases of
memories returning after decades, often while a person is in
therapy, have become highly publicized in recent years.

Recovering Memories of Abuse

Cases have now been reported of individuals who have entered
therapy with no specific recollection of incest or molestation
and, during the course of therapy, have uncovered detailed
recollections of repeated sexual abuse by family members. Apparently encouraged during therapy, some of these people have
come to believe that the recovered memories are veridical, and
in a number of the cases they have taken legal action on the basis
of these memories, which have sometimes been recovered
through hypnosis. The theoretical, therapeutic, judicial, and
social controversy surrounding the recovery of repressed and/or
dissociated memories has broken into full-scale debate in the
scientific, professional, and mass-market literature (e.g., Bass &
Davis, 1994; Berliner & Williams, 1994; Bloom, 1994; Byrd,
1994; Ceci & Loftus, 1994; Cohler, 1994; Frankel, 1994; Garry
& Loftus, 1994; Gleaves, 1994; Gold, Hughes, & Hohnecker,
1994; Goldstein, 1992; Herman, 1992; Kihlstrom, 1994; Lindsay & Read, 1994; Loftus, 1993b, 1994; Loftus & Ketcham,
1994; MacLean, 1993; Morton, 1994; Mulhern, 1994; Nash,
1994; Neisser, 1993; Ofshe, 1992; Ofshe & Singer, 1994; Ofshe
& Watters, 1994; Olio, 1994; Pendergrast, 1994; Peterson,
1994; Pezdek, 1994; Read & Lindsay, 1994; Sales, Shuman, &
O'Connor, 1994; Spanos, C. Burgess, & M. Burgess, 1994;
Spence, 1994; Spiegel & Scheflin, 1994; Terr, 1994; Wright,
1994; Yapko, 1994). The memories that are being recovered
include childhood abuse of many kinds: physical, verbal, sexual,

and emotional. Overlapping "memory recovery" and "abuse" movements have emerged, as have strong reactions to them both.

Serious questions have been raised about the validity of recovered memories (Loftus & Ketcham, 1994; Ofshe & Watters, 1994), although the position that robust repression does not exist is difficult, in fact, to sustain (e.g., see Spiegel & Scheflin, 1994). Major issues to address include the validity of repression as a psychological mechanism and the role of the therapist in encouraging memories of childhood abuse. We commented on these in our guidelines in Chapter 3, and note here that there is a need for much more research on the role of hypnosis in the recovery of these memories, and the forensic implications of such recovered memories. It is important to note that the material presented in this book allows inferences to be made about the factors that may influence the long-delayed recall of personal events and that may have legal consequences.

There is substantial evidence that people can be very confident about the accuracy of their memory of events long ago, even when those memories are inaccurate. Emotion does not insulate memory from error. Analyses of the experience of flashbulb memories (see Winograd & Neisser, 1993), for instance, indicates that such memories of emotionally charged events are widely inaccurate. Despite this, one of the defining features of flashbulb memories is the confidence with which they are held (Weaver, 1993). The level of confidence is somewhat similar to the level of belief that some people who recover memories of childhood sexual abuse have in always feeling that something bad happened to them during childhood (Lindsay & Read, 1994). As Lindsay and Read pointed out, distortions of memory and memories of events that did not happen occur in the laboratory and in everyday life. Moreover, memories of distant events, and particularly memories of early childhood, appear to be particularly susceptible to distortion and error.

Repression is a cornerstone of psychoanalytic theory, and it has had wide influence, even though the concept of "repression" itself has continued to be seriously challenged (Loftus, 1993b, 1994; Loftus & Ketcham, 1994). Although "functional" and "psychogenic" amnesias following a single horrible traumatic experience have been reported, they are relatively rare (Loftus, 1993b; Lindsay & Read, 1994; Neisser, 1993). Many victims of trauma do not repress events in this way, but remember them clearly and often report uncontrollable, intrusive memories.

Neisser argued that total repression of an overt and repeated set of dramatic experiences has not been documented convincingly. The debate over amnesia for childhood sexual abuse is clearly not resolved, although it is generally acknowledged that the precise rate of incidence of such amnesia is not at all known, and that the confabulation of abuse may occur. This does not mean that the forgetting of childhood sexual abuse, whether through repression, dissociation, or normal forgetting, never occurs; rather, it means that caution must be used in assuming any particular incidence rate on the one hand, and in accepting or rejecting the recovered memory of an individual on the other hand (Lindsay & Read, 1994; Nash, 1994).

Generally in therapy, the veracity of memories is not at issue, because it is the personal meaning rather than the objective reality of the material that is clinically important (Spence, 1982, 1994). However, given that recovered memories are being used at times as the basis for criminal and civil law suits, it is reasonable to look closely at their validity (Spiegel & Scheflin, 1994). Precisely because guidelines are needed to assist the courts in the determinations that they make, we offered guidelines (Chapter 3).

Loftus (1993b; Loftus & Ketcham, 1994), Ofshe and Watters (1994), Pendergrast (1994), and Yapko (1994) suggested that many individuals enter therapy without memories of abuse but acquire memories during therapy, and they have documented cases in which therapists have persuaded clients that they must have experienced childhood sexual abuse, because their lives show the possible symptoms. During treatment by such therapists, all memories, feelings, and behavior are reinterpreted within the model of sexual abuse. Not surprisingly, the end result can be a client who confidently asserts memories of abuse that he or she believes have been repressed for many years. Some indication of the possible issues involved in such cases can be drawn from the case of BT (discussed in Chapter 2).

When hypnosis is used for the recovery of memories, specific guidelines should be followed. Intentionally, we broadened our guidelines to comment in particular on procedures that attempt to recover memory. However, much of the literature concerning the possible confabulatory impact of hypnotic procedures can apply equally to related visualization and imaginative techniques. Although, in general, memories elicited in the clinic do not need to be tested for objective accuracy, when they are the basis for legal proceedings, they need to be put to the same stringent tests as have been outlined in this and other chapters.

As Loftus (1993b) argued, although child sexual abuse may be tragically common, the emerging culture of unearthing traumatic, repressed memories may be creating as many problems as it is claimed to be solving. Bloom (1994) reminds us of the basic and most important tenet of therapy: "First, do no harm." Moreover, if false memories of abuse are suggested inadvertently and accepted uncritically, then society will be less believing of genuine cases of abuse. Indeed, a portion of the shame of the debate over recovered memory is that it may throw into question the reports of people who are genuine victims.

We now turn in this chapter to address the issue of hypnosis and coercion. It is a theme relevant to several of the cases that we have discussed.

HYPNOSIS AND COERCION

Coercive uses of hypnosis have included claims of its use as a tool of seduction (Gibson, 1992; Hoencamp, 1990; Kline, 1972; Perry, 1979; Venn, 1988), in criminal activities (Gibson, 1991; Laurence & Perry, 1988), and in the creation of antisocial or self-injurious behavior (Kline, 1972). On the one hand, actual cases of clinicians using hypnosis to seduce patients or of crimes being committed "under the influence" of hypnosis have been reported since the 18th century (see Laurence & Perry, 1988). On the other hand, experimental work that has attempted to examine the possible coercive impact of hypnosis has yielded little support for its coercive power.

There have been various reports and accusations of hypnosis being used as a tool to entice people to engage in various behavior, and we saw evidence of attempts to do that in some of the cases in this book. Recently, Gibson (1992) reported a case of a man charged with using hypnosis for rape and other sexual offenses, and Hoencamp (1990) reported the case of a lay hypnotist who was accused of abusing nine women in the context of a therapeutic relationship. Kline (1972) presented clinical material relating to the treatment of several patients who had been using hypnosis to coerce other individuals into immoral behavior. Perry (1979; see also Laurence & Perry, 1988) analyzed the Mr. Magic case involving the alleged use of hypnosis to facilitate sexual contact with two women. Finally, Venn (1988) reported the use of hypnosis by a military officer to attempt homosexual relations with young men.

The research issue in question here is whether hypnotic techniques can be used to coerce individuals into participating in behavior to which they normally would not consent. Early experiments by Lyon (1954), Rowland (1939), and Young (1952) attempted to get hypnotized subjects to perform acts that appeared very dangerous, such as picking up a dangerous snake and throwing acid at another person. Although it seemed that subjects could be coerced to perform such behavior, these studies were poorly controlled. Orne and Evans (1965) included hypnotized, simulating, and nonhypnotized subjects and found that they all performed the apparently dangerous tasks when told to do so. These results strongly suggested that the compliance previously reported was not necessarily a function of hypnosis. Later experiments (Coe, Kobayashi, & Howard, 1972, 1973; Levitt, Aronoff, Morgan, Overley, & Parrish, 1975) focused on inducing subjects to carry out acts that violated general standards of morality, and they provided similar results; both hypnotized and nonhypnotized subjects were willing to perform these acts (Barber, 1961; Brenman, 1942; Coe et al., 1972; Gibson, 1991; Laurence & Perry, 1988; Levitt et al., 1975; O'Brien & Rabuck, 1976; Orne, 1972; Orne & Evans, 1965; Rowland, 1939; Sheehan, 1977; Wagstaff, 1991; Watkins, 1972; Wells, 1941). Experimental evidence suggests that the hypnotized person, even when genuinely hallucinating, is perfectly well aware of what he or she is doing, and of the consequences (Gibson, 1991), and this was particularly true in the experiments outlined previously. Comments made by subjects in many of the studies indicated that they were aware that no matter how harmful or antisocial the behavior or consequences appeared to be, they felt confident that the experimenter would not let any real harm come to them. Although there is no proof that hypnosis cannot be used to coerce antisocial behavior, no experiment has really tested this adequately, nor perhaps can an experiment do so ethically (see Gibson, 1991; Laurence & Perry, 1988; Orne & Evans, 1965). Importantly, subjects usually know that they are in an experiment. Although it may look dangerous, experimental subjects know that the experimenter would have taken precautions to protect them; therefore, an adequate test may never be attainable in a laboratory setting. Hypnosis may facilitate antisocial or coercive conduct (as evidence from a number of clinical cases would suggest), but it is impossible to prove this case. Specifically, more research needs to be done on the concept of voluntariness and its relevance to the current debate. The empirical evidence—limited perhaps—leads us to the inevitable conclusion that an individual will not behave in a way that contravenes his or her morality, but this assumption cannot be said to generalize to settings in which the motivations involved are conflicted and hypnosis is used in conjunction with other persuasive techniques (Gibson, 1991; Laurence & Perry, 1988).

Hoencamp (1990) recognized the special interactive nature of hypnosis with treatment factors in the therapeutic setting. He identified various mechanisms that may lead to coercion. These included the nature of the therapeutic relationship; the expectations the patient brings to therapy and how the therapist deals with them; expectations about hypnosis; the experience of non-volition; hypnosis as an "alibi" for uncharacteristic behavior; the lack of critical judgment about the therapy; and the possibility for changes in perception to restructure behavior in ways that are acceptable. Hoencamp (1990, 1994) concluded that hypnosis itself is not necessarily the sole causal factor in cases of coercion. If the relationship between hypnotist (therapist) and client is defined in a way that provides a sexual rationale, whether hypnosis is involved or not, an avenue for abuse may be opened. Hypnosis may, in certain cases, enhance the subjective experience of nonvolition and the vulnerability for abuse. Equally, however, other factors present in the relationship can result in coercive power. As Perry (1979) stated, "In all of the cases cited to support the view that hypnosis may be used to coerce at least some people, there is no analysis of the motivations of the people coerced. Hence, the degree to which hypnosis is either a necessary or a sufficient condition for coercion remains problematic" (p. 207). Finally, we wish to comment on the implication in our cases that a distinction needs to be drawn in the literature between coercion that reflects an abuse of trust to coerce a person to have sex, and the abuse of trust in which outcomes are the antisocial effects of acquiescence. Our cases suggest that this distinction is valid, and it needs to be researched. Clearly, those who have sex with a hypnotist are not engaged in an antisocial act, although they are engaged in behavior that they perhaps would not engage in normally.

SUMMARY COMMENT

The laboratory findings that we have reviewed in this chapter in relation to multiple sets of procedures and different methodologies can be linked to the forensic relevance of the phenomena we have analyzed in this book. Overall, the evidence does not support the view that hypnosis either particularly enhances or pervasively distorts memory accuracy. The data support the position that whereas significant distortion may be evident in hypnosis (for both accuracy and confidence), accurate reports can indeed be produced in hypnosis and may convey information not reported previously.

There is no experimental support for any broad assumption that memories will be more accurate in hypnosis than in the waking state. Hypermnesia can and does occur, but it is likely to be accompanied by a shift in response criterion and relevant parameters to include the level of processing, the absence of methodological controls to prevent criterion shifts, and the presence of conviction on the subject's part about what is being reported. The issue of memory distortion is less clear-cut.

Across the studies that we have reviewed, the evidence is most consistent with the view that distortion can readily occur in memory reports, whether a person is hypnotized, and whether he or she is suggestible. This confirms our repeated observation in the cases we have studied that memory itself is highly variable in its consistency. Although there is no evidence for uniform memory distortion, some variables nevertheless play a more significant part than others in influencing the extent of distortion that will be observed, and one especially important variable is the level of susceptibility to hypnosis. So important is the relevance of individual differences for us, that it is plausible to argue that objective testing of suggestibility or hypnotizability might be best done even before a decision to use hypnosis is made.

The question naturally arises in review of experimental findings as to which processes mediate effects that are observed. Effects may be similar inside and outside the hypnotic setting, but very different processes may be responsible for what occurs in hypnosis.

As Lynn et al. (1989), Spanos and McLean (1986), and Weekes et al. (1992) argued, what may be distinctive about hypnotic subjects' reactions is not the memory reports themselves but the increased probability that "events are weaved around the suggested memory" (Weekes et al., 1992, p. 359). Such a process is consistent with other evidence (see Sheehan & McConkey, 1982) that hypnotic subjects actively construct experiences that are suggested to them through idiosyncratic processing of the information that is communicated. Also important, subjects who reverse their testimony in hypnosis evidence specific cognitive styles at work (Laurence et al., 1986). Imagery has been researched specifically in relation to hypermnesia (Dywan, 1988) and is probably an important component of style that generally affects the display of memory distortion. Preference for imagic cognitive style has emerged, for example, in the literature on memory creation in hypnosis (see Labelle et al., 1990). In this research, hypnotic susceptibility and preference for imagic cognitive style better predicted pseudomemory creation than did any of the main effects alone. The interaction of susceptibility with the imagery-based cognitive style reinforces again the complexity of variables involved in the study of false memory effects. There is clearly a range of parameters related to memory distortion in hypnosis, and not all of the relevant factors produce uniform effects. We have observed that level of susceptibility is related more positively to the phenomenon of memory distortion than other parameters, but evidence would suggest that it works most effectively in combination with other factors, such as imaging style.

One possible hypothesis for explaining effects among highly susceptible subjects is that subject differences in style of information processing mediate effects. It may well be the case also that subjects who are susceptible to hypnosis attempt to acquire a global understanding of events and pay relatively little attention to precise details, such as individual words. These kinds of processing features can be consolidated in hypnosis. Relevant to this notion, Crawford and Allen (1983) argued persuasively that hypnotic subjects use a holistic strategy rather than one that attends to precise detail.

The weight of evidence overall in support of contextual influences is such that the major question to answer in relation to the issue of the consistency of subjects' memory reports is whether social variables play an exclusive part in determining memory effects, or whether they are a strong determinant. There are firm data sets suggesting that report biases operate in the hypnotic setting (e.g., see Spanos, Gwynn, Comer, Baltruweit, & de Groh, 1989; Wagstaff, 1981). Other data, however, suggest that the bias hypothesis is limited in its explanatory power. This limitation is evident, for example, in research on the breaching of pseudomemory. Work on this problem (e.g., McCann & Sheehan, 1987) has demonstrated that when pressures such as contextual constraints are placed heavily on subjects to change their response, a small number of highly susceptible subjects under hypnotic instruction appear unable to conform to the pressure on them to remember. The motivations of these subjects have to be defined separately from simple compliance or obedience. Tentatively, we suggest that not all memory-distortion effects in hypnosis can be explained in terms of the influence of contextual variables; those memories that are retrieved under pressure, or as constraints vary, are not likely to reflect genuine memory impairment. Whatever is the correct hypothesis that explains these effects, multiple factors of influence clearly determine performance effects in the hypnotic memory test setting and argument must ultimately come to endorse the influence of the interaction between trait and situational influences. Moreover, mood and emotion are important interactive components of this mix, evidence being most consistent with the adoption of a multidimensional model of the relationship between emotion and memory. Parameters that shape the influence of emotionally stressful events on memory are complex, but the pattern of effects seems meaningful, nevertheless. Clearly, there are many important questions that lie unanswered in the experimental literature. One may approach memory distortion in hypnosis and the interaction between mood and memory in altogether different ways than have been surveyed here, or experimented with to date.

Using the methodology of Council, Kirsch, and Haffner (1986), for example, one might usefully study the impact of hypnosis on subjects' expectancies as a major mediating factor in the production of memory distortion. This is an important approach to the issues, given that genuine memory outcomes should be teased apart from subjects' goal-directed attempts to perform reliably. Also, more work needs to be done on analyzing the impact of leading questions when the influence of subjects' confidence is controlled; in this way, distortion effects independent of cue structure can better be determined.

In addition, study of the importance of emotions and their influence on memory suggests to us the value of conducting more systematic work on how emotions actually operate in real-life settings. There are limits to the inferences we can draw from within the laboratory (and in the field), and special efforts are needed to understand better the impact of trauma on memory and the impact of created memory and beliefs about trauma. We need especially, perhaps, to isolate the range of parameters determining recollections of abuse. Looking at the influence of specific emotions seems fruitful, also; when emotions involve

that witnesses give may be distorted by other information. Experimental data tell us that hypnotizability is the most influential of the independent variables operating on memory performance in the hypnotic setting to produce distortion. The introduction of hypnosis can be influential and distorting in its consequences, but the data suggest that this will be so mostly when hypnosis occurs in a situation in which false information is communicated to persons who are susceptible. Susceptibility to hypnosis is most influential in distorting memory when it is in combination with other factors, but it appears to us that susceptibility alone constitutes a forensic problem. In summary, memory itself is malleable and memory reports vary in their consistency across occasions of testing; hypnosis can enhance memory distortion appreciably; and many factors are responsible for how much distortion will be manifest, including especially the hypnotizability of the witness.

A FORENSIC POSITION

Our position on the utility of hypnosis in the forensic setting is one of "admissibility with safeguards," these being provided by the guidelines we have developed. Utility exists, but it is limited. Hypnosis should not be used in an attempt to establish the validity of witness reports. By itself, it offers no guarantee of the truth value of what the witness says. To argue for the truth value of what is said in hypnosis, the data would have to be entirely conclusive that memory is reliable in hypnosis, but it is not. Nor does it seem likely to ever be, because memory is so often unreliable out of hypnosis. There is no way of knowing whether the memory reports produced in hypnosis are accurate, unless reports are checked independently of the hypnosis session and corroborated. Corroboration in many of our cases, however, was difficult, if not impossible.

Looking back to the cases reported in this book, and recognizing the strong influence of contextual factors highlighted in our review of the evidence in Chapter 9, it is not at all clear that the use of hypnosis itself is responsible for the substantial increases in distortion seen in a number of the cases we have analyzed. By virtue of the use of hypnosis, or for other contextual reasons, one has to conclude that there are boundaries to the utility of hypnosis, and especially so in the absence of independent corroboration.

It is important to underscore what is communicated elsewhere in the memory literature (e.g., Laurence & Perry, 1988; Pettinati, 1988). The witnesses' confidence in their reports during and following hypnosis should be viewed both as a probable effect of hypnosis and a concomitant of the context in which hypnosis takes place. The subjective conviction of witnesses offers no reliable indication of objective veracity of what is being reported. In fact, its presence can mislead. The importance of witnesses' convictions is confirmed by the experimental data, and the evidence tells us that confidence can override the influence of other parameters to exert its effect. The subjective conviction of hypnotized witnesses could easily lead to a too-ready acceptance of the information given, and that should be guarded against when hypnosis is used in the forensic setting.

From the data we reviewed in Chapter 9, it also appears that the influence of hypnosis will be greater when misleading information is conveyed explicitly and directly. A problem arises, therefore, from the obviousness with which false information is at times communicated, and that was very evident to us in Chapter 2. In these circumstances, it is not just accuracy that is at issue, it is our interpretation that forensic events can be affected greatly and mistakenly by the hypnotized witness's conviction that there is truth in what he or she says. This is a particular problem in cases of recovered memories of childhood sexual abuse. Subjective belief can be enhanced spuriously both during and after hypnosis, and this can have major effects on the perceptions of investigating authorities and ultimately on jurors' perceptions of guilt (see Greene, Wilson, & Loftus, 1989; Spanos, Gwynn, & Terrade, 1989; Wilson, Greene, & Loftus, 1986). Case and experimental data considered together suggest that the most substantial risk to using hypnosis lies perhaps not so much in the tendency to misreport, although that is substantial, as in the tendency for hypnotized persons to be overconfident in their reporting. This confidence effect is pervasive enough in itself that it offers sufficient grounds for limiting the use of hypnosis in the forensic setting. Confidence can create a witness who may resist the normal impact of cross-examination.

Finally, it has to be said that the extent of inconsistency in reports from one occasion to another must reflect, at least in part, the inherent variability of memory. The major problem for the professional in the forensic system then, is perhaps not the skill with which questions are posed as much as knowing where and when verbal reports can be accepted. Forensically speaking, the issue of acceptance for us is tied necessarily to the process of confirming whether those reports can be independently corroborated.

QUALIFICATIONS OF THE HYPNOTIST

The expertise of the hypnotist represents, in our opinion, a core issue in any discussion of forensic hypnosis. In Chapter 1, we reviewed findings on the practice of hypnosis by police in Australia, and they indicated that police who replied to the survey recognized the problems posed by inexpertness and were supportive of the position that hypnotists in the forensic setting should be appropriately qualified. In their judgment, and we would concur, multiple skills are needed for the tasks of the investigative hypnotist. Psychological expertise, clinical skills, and interviewing competency are all essential requirements for practicing the investigative role when hypnosis is involved. Forensic skill is not sufficient without the clinical expertise required to know that risks to the welfare of witnesses may be at stake. Equally, soliciting information that can be useful is not possible without the ability to probe skillfully in a relevant way, but not so directively that misleading information will be accepted and incorporated into memory. Finally, there is a broad context of skill and experience, obviously relevant to the psychologically or psychiatrically trained person, which should be respected. This alone is not sufficient to maintain a proper professional role, but it does provide relevant background and experience that helps to establish the conditions for ethical and professional practice.

MAJOR FORENSIC ISSUES

Throughout this book we have attempted to draw out the forensic implications of each of our cases, and we have integrated these in Chapter 8. It is important, however, to single out in this concluding chapter those implications that appear to be central. These involve finding an appropriate balance between clinical and forensic priorities; determining the amount of credence that can be given to memory reports; recognizing the essential variability of memory; respecting the need for the hypnotist to be properly qualified; and guaranteeing ethical practice. Other less central but still important issues are the responsibility the hypnotist has in determining or guiding the consequences of giving memory reports, and the assurance of adequate follow-up after a forensic session has been completed.

It is not possible to prescribe the conditions that will establish a correct balance between clinical and forensic priorities. With the cases in which we were involved, there was always some uncertainty about whether the right balance was struck. This uncertainty aside, guidelines should nevertheless recognize this issue more and alert practitioners to its primary significance. To do this requires expertise that reflects qualifications in essential skills. Clinical skills protect the welfare of the witness. Psychological skills sensitize practitioners to issues such as the inherent malleability of memory, and the unreliability of reported recollections. Not all verbal reports, in or out of hypnosis, can be trusted, and it is necessary for the practitioner to be informed about those data distinguishing reports that can be trusted from those that cannot. Finally, practice must promote and facilitate the proper conduct of a forensic session, and ethical practice will necessarily be augmented by professional allegiance to and respect for a well-formulated code of professional conduct.

UNDERSTANDING MEMORY AND HYPNOSIS

The research that we have conducted has led us to think more analytically about the nature of memory and hypnosis. As far as memory is concerned, we are persuaded that it is more variable than we had previously thought. The kind of inconsistency shown by DD (Chapter 6), for instance, is compelling. It seems clear to us that distortion is probable enough in the normal waking state, and it is very difficult to know just how much hypnosis or the hypnotic setting increases or enhances that same tendency. With the case and experimental data in mind, we would argue that hypnosis obviously plays a part; however, it seems vividly apparent to us that many memory reports cannot be trusted unquestionably out of hypnosis. Without doubt, hypnosis together with other opportunities for distortion, can profoundly affect the consistency of a witness' reports and render them unreliable. Also, memory clearly operates constructively and reconstructively. There is no literal representation of past events recorded in memory. Events are integrated and reintegrated in ways that may produce a confident mix of recollections, but only some of the recollections are likely to mirror events that actually occurred.

As far as hypnosis is concerned, our study of the investigative context has highlighted further for us just how socially complex is the setting in which hypnosis typically takes place (see also Sheehan & McConkey, 1982). Many social features of its setting can themselves be expected to facilitate memory distortion (see Chapter 9 for review), but their sundry influence makes it difficult indeed to attribute cause and effect to the presence or absence of hypnosis. Hypnosis creates a myriad of effects, and significant changes in memory reporting can occur in the hypnotic setting. This is an essential point for the investigative practitioner to know; however, any quest for understanding the nature of hypnosis requires us to explore in a more probing way what effects reflect contextual features and what effects are associated distinctively with hypnosis. To do this, practitioner and researcher alike must go to the experimental data. It seems clear, therefore, that practitioners and scientists must always stay in close interaction with each other. This plea has special relevance perhaps to the field of investigative hypnosis, where conflict, heated argument, and, at times, misplaced elitism can operate to discredit both groups. Science is placed to inform what the practitioner does, and practice will alert the scientist to important issues that need to be explained. For instance, the compelling data from the laboratory literature alerted us plainly to the significance of the natural traits (viz., hypnotizability) of the witness that are tied closely to the degree of memory distortion that may be shown.

REFLECTIONS

Looking back on the cases and their complexity, it is impossible not to reflect on the frustrations associated with our study of forensic hypnosis. There are a number of frustrations that stand out for us in the research we have conducted. One is the difficulty of coping with the enormous complexity of events that define real-life issues and questions in the forensic setting. It is tempting to focus on trying to detect when hypnotic testimony is genuine and when not, but the plethora of needs and emotions that lie behind events being remembered and the witness's role in them makes that goal enormously hard to achieve. It is far easier—but incorrect—to be an armchair detective in ignorance of the complexity of individuals and their own kinds of social interactions. In the case of CK, for example, we were perplexed by the fact that when CK needed a taxi to take her home, she allowed the same taxi driver to take her to her apartment who had allegedly used hypnosis previously to take advantage of her friend. CK's life circumstances were such that she obviously saw nothing unusual in that, but to us it was hard to understand, given her anxieties and the driver's alleged behavior. Our cases have indicated that judgments about trust are simply not possible to understand without knowing the full impact of the witness's feelings, circumstances, and motivations. Essentially, the investigative hypnotist has to interpret the data he or she collects, and that interpretation will be affected critically by knowledge of the relevance or otherwise of a variety of events. The investigative hypnotist does not know the truth, and should not be tempted to construct it. Apparent simplicity, more often than not, clouds considerable complexity.

We were enormously impressed with the professionalism of many of the police officers and lawyers with whom we interacted in our cases. There were, however, frustrations at times in some interactions. In some instances, the police were not as responsive as they said they would be (e.g., a scheduled session time was not respected [see Chapter 1] and pertinent information was not given to us [see Chapter 4]). The police role, understandably, is often one of saying what needs to be said and doing what needs to be done, but problems can arise when that tendency interferes with the tasks that need to be completed. On another front, the legal profession sometimes conveyed a limited appreciation of psychological expertise and seemed to assume too readily at times that experts were there solely to service the needs of the attorney, rather than to convey specific knowledge to the forensic system. These frustrations are obviously not unique to our experience or to forensic hypnosis, but they highlighted for us some of the difficulties that can be experienced when stepping into the messiness of forensic situations.

With the cases behind us, our position is that hypnosis is useful, but it is dispiriting to realize that the most conclusive instance in our analyses of investigative hypnosis was a case in which the court accepted expert testimony that hypnosis was *not* involved (Chapter 6). Yet, that outcome yielded important consequences in a trial, was informed by knowledge in the field that was accepted legally, and was clearly forensically significant. The law seeks to move with certainty and directness, but judgment about the genuineness of hypnosis is necessarily problematical. Nevertheless, in the case of Miranda Downes (see Chapter 6), the evidence was collected, analyzed, communicated, and accepted, and then specific legal decisions flowed as far as the High Court of Australia. One must also look aside at times from the technicality of the law. We need to consider not just matters affecting the welfare of witnesses, but also how we should relate to conclusions about the admissibility of evidence that are formally nullified by the law, but which otherwise seem reasonable, plausible, and sensible when hypnosis has been involved. For these reasons, it is relevant to strongly endorse the need for stringent ethical and legal guidelines that can be applied in the formal conduct of investigative hypnosis sessions. The spirit of our research and this book is to endorse movement of that kind entirely, and we need to appreciate the connections between appropriate procedures for forensic practice and the relevance of particular current concerns about issues such as recovered memories.

It is important to us that experimental evidence is available to help interpret the meaning of the case data that are collected. It is frustrating, however, that the level of complexity that defines the laboratory setting is often so distant from the defining features of actual forensic situations. Professional judgments and inferences are required to fill that gap, and there is always the possibility of filling it incorrectly or prematurely. Professional practices and criminal cases, however, do not allow one to wait until the next experiment is done, and the attempt to bridge the gap between existing experimental data and demanding professional practice has to be made. It is laboratory data, for instance, that tell us to be cautious about interpreting the confidence of the witness, and determine how we regard changed recollections in hypnosis when they can be modified so much out of hypnosis. What seems certain in the forensic setting may not actually be so. This speaks again, of course, to the value of professional practice moving hand in hand with scientific, systematic inquiry. As the body of scientific data grows, the inferences that are necessary to fill this critical gap will narrow and also become less subjective.

Systematic research in the forensic setting seems likely to move us much closer to the position in which the professional is better and more usefully informed in the judgments that he or she has to make. It may be that we will never know fully the causes of events about which we puzzle, but the data collected should guide practice to make involvement in the forensic system worthwhile and meaningful. Above all, our aim is that our work contributes to lifting the standard of care. The agonies and complexities of practice today hopefully lead to being better informed and to providing better care for others in the future.

References

Aboud. L. (1985). Hypnosis used to restore memory of witness: Regina v. Speechley. *Law Society Journal, 23*, 80.

Alba, J. W., & Hasher, L. (1983). Is memory schematic? *Psychological Bulletin, 93*, 203–231.

Altman, B., & MacLeod, G. (1982). Hypnotism: Its utilization in criminal law. *New York State Bar Journal, 54*, 377–386.

American Psychological Association. (1988). Trends in ethics cases, common pitfalls, and published resources. *American Psychologist, 43*, 564–572.

Anderton, C. H. (1986). The forensic use of hypnosis. In F. A. DePiano & H. C. Salzberg (Eds.), *Clinical applications of hypnosis* (pp. 197–223). Norwood, NJ: Ablex.

Annon, J. S. (1988). Detection of deception and search for truth: A proposed model with particular reference to the witness, the victim, and the defendant. *Forensic Reports, 1*, 303–360.

Ault, R. L., Jr. (1979). FBI guidelines for use of hypnosis. *International Journal of Clinical and Experimental Hypnosis, 27*, 449–451.

Australian Psychological Society. (1995). Guidelines relating to the reporting of recovered memories. *Bulletin of the Australian Psychological Society, 17*, 20–21.

Barber, J. (1994, August). Dangers of hypnosis: Sex, pseudo-*memories, and other complications.* Keynote address presented at the 13th International Congress of Hypnosis, Melbourne, Victoria, Australia.

Barber, T. X. (1961). Antisocial and criminal acts induced by "hypnosis": A review of experimental and clinical findings. *Archives of General Psychiatry, 5*, 311–312.

Barnier, A. J., & McConkey, K. M. (1993). Reports of real and false memories: The relevance of hypnosis, hypnotizability, and context of memory test. *Journal of Abnormal Psychology, 3*, 521–527.

Bass, E., & Davis, L. (1994). *The courage to heal: A guide for women survivors of child sexual abuse* (3rd ed.). New York: Harper Perennial.

Berliner, L., & Williams, L. M. (1994). Memories of child sexual abuse: A response. *Applied Cognitive Psychology, 8,* 379–387.

Blaney, P. H. (1986). Affect and memory: A review. *Psychological Bulletin, 99,* 229–246.

Blau, T. H. (1984). *The psychologist as expert witness.* New York: Wiley.

Bloom, P. B. (1994). Clinical guidelines in using hypnosis in uncovering memories of sexual abuse: A master class commentary. *International Journal of Clinical and Experimental Hypnosis, 42,* 173–178.

Bowers, J. M., & Bekerian, D. A. (1984). When will postevent information distort eyewitness testimony? *Journal of Applied Psychology, 69,* 466–472.

Brenman, M. (1942). Experiments in the hypnotic production of anti-social and self-injurious behavior. *Psychiatry, 5,* 49–61.

Brentar, J., & Lynn, S. J. (1989). "Negative" effects and hypnosis: A critical examination. *British Journal of Experimental and Clinical Hypnosis, 6,* 75–84.

Brodsky, S. L. (1991). *Testifying in court: Guidelines and maxims for the expert witness.* Washington, DC: American Psychological Association.

Burrows, G. D. (1981). Forensic aspects of hypnosis. *Australian Journal of Forensic Sciences, 13,* 120–125.

Byrd, K. R. (1994). The narrative reconstructions of incest survivors. *American Psychologist, 49,* 439–440.

Ceci, S. J., & Loftus, E. F. (1994). Memory work: A royal road to false memories. *Applied Cognitive Psychology, 8,* 351–364.

Ceci, S. J., Ross, D. F., & Toglia, M. P. (1987). Suggestibility of children's memory: Psycholegal implications. *Journal of Experimental Psychology: General, 116,* 38–49.

Christianson, S.-A. (1992a). Emotional stress and eyewitness memory: A critical review. *Psychological Bulletin, 112,* 284–309.

Christianson, S.-A. (1992b). Remembering emotional events: Potential mechanisms. In S.-A. Christianson (Ed.), *The handbook of emotion and memory: Research and theory* (pp. 307–340). Hillsdale, NJ: Erlbaum.

Christianson, S.-A. (Ed.). (1992c). *The handbook of emotion and memory: Research and theory.* Hillsdale, NJ: Erlbaum.

Christianson, S.-A., & Nilsson, L.-G. (1984). Functional amnesia as induced by a psychological trauma. *Memory and Cognition, 12,* 142–155.

Coe, W. C., Kobayashi, K., & Howard, M. L. (1972). An approach toward isolating factors that influence antisocial conduct in hypnosis. *International Journal of Clinical and Experimental Hypnosis, 20,* 118–131.

Coe, W. C., Kobayashi, K., & Howard, M. L. (1973). Experimental and ethical problems of evaluating the influence of hypnosis in antisocial conduct. *Journal of Abnormal Psychology, 82,* 476–482.

Coe, W. C., & Ryken, K. (1979). Hypnosis and risks to human subjects. *American Psychologist, 34,* 673–681.

Cohler, B. J. (1994). Memory recovery and the use of the past: A commentary on Lindsay and Read from psychoanalytic perspectives. *Applied Cognitive Psychology, 8,* 365–378.

Council, J. R., Kirsch, I., & Haffner, L. P. (1986). Expectancy versus absorption in the prediction of hypnotic responding. *Journal of Personality and Social Psychology, 50,* 182–189.

Council on Scientific Affairs, American Medical Association. (1985). Scientific status of refreshing recollection by the use of hypnosis. *Journal of the American Medical Association, 253,* 1918–1923.

Crawford, H. J., & Allen, S. N. (1983). Enhanced visual memory during hypnosis as mediated by hypnotic responsiveness and cognitive strategies. *Journal of Experimental Psychology: General, 112,* 662–685.

Deffenbacher, K., & Loftus, E. F. (1982). Do jurors share a common understanding concerning eyewitness behavior? *Law and Human Behavior, 6,* 15–30.

DePiano, F. A., & Salzberg, H. C. (1981). Hypnosis as an aid to recall of meaningful information presented under three types of arousal. *International Journal of Clinical and Experimental Hypnosis, 29,* 383–400.

Dhanens, T. P., & Lundy, R. M. (1975). Hypnotic and waking suggestions and recall. *International Journal of Clinical and Experimental Hypnosis, 23,* 68–79.

Diamond, B. L. (1980). Inherent problems in the use of pretrial hypnosis on a prospective witness. *California Law Review, 68,* 313–349.

Dinges, D. F., Whitehouse, W. G., Orne, E. C., Powell, J. W., & Orne, M. T. (1992). Evaluating hypnotic memory enhancement (hypermnesia and reminiscence) using multitrial forced recall. *Journal of Experimental Psychology: Learning, Memory, and Cognition, 18,* 1139–1147.

Dywan, J. (1988). The imagery factor in hypnotic hypermnesia. *International Journal of Clinical and Experimental Hypnosis, 36,* 312–326.

Dywan, J., & Bowers, K. S. (1983). The use of hypnosis to enhance recall. *Science, 222,* 184–185.

Echabe, A. E., & Rovira, D. P. (1989). Social representations and memory: The case of AIDS. *European Journal of Social Psychology, 19,* 543–551.

Evans, F. J. (1988). Posthypnotic amnesia: Dissociation of context and content. In H. M. Pettinati (Ed.), *Hypnosis and memory* (pp. 157–192). New York: Guilford Press.

Evans, B. J., & Stanley, R. O. (Eds.). (1994). *Hypnosis and the law: Principles and practice*. Melbourne: Australian Society of Hypnosis.

Faller, K. C. (1984). Is the child victim of sexual abuse telling the truth? *Child Abuse and Neglect, 8*, 473–481.

Fitch, W. L., Russell, R. C., & Wallace, J. (1987). Legal ethics and the use of mental health experts in criminal cases. *Behavioral Sciences and the Law, 5*, 105–118.

Fitzgerald, R., & Ellsworth, P. C. (1983). Due process vs. crime control: Death qualifications and jury attitudes. *Law and Human Behavior, 8*, 31–51.

Frankel, F. H. (1988). The clinical use of hypnosis in aiding recall. In H. M. Pettinati (Ed.), *Hypnosis and memory* (pp. 247–264). New York: Guilford Press.

Frankel, F. H. (1994). The concept of flashbacks in historical perspective. *International Journal of Clinical and Experimental Hypnosis, 42*, 321–326.

Frazier, P. A., & Borgida, E. (1985). Rape trauma syndrome evidence in court. *American Psychologist, 40*, 984–993.

Frazier, P. A., & Borgida, E. (1988). Juror common understanding and the admissibility of rape trauma syndrome evidence in court. *Law and Human Behavior, 12*, 101–122.

Frazier, P. A., & Borgida, E. (1992). Rape trauma syndrome: A review of case law and psychological research. *Law and Human Behavior, 16*, 293–311.

Freckelton, I. R. (1987). *The trial of the expert: A study of expert evidence and forensic experts*. Melbourne: Oxford University Press.

Friedman, W. J. (1993). Memory for the time of past events. *Psychological Bulletin, 113*, 44–46.

Friswell, R., & McConkey, K. M. (1989). Hypnotically induced mood. *Cognition and Emotion, 3*, 1–26.

Garry, M., & Loftus, E. F. (1994). Pseudomemories without hypnosis. *International Journal of Clinical and Experimental Hypnosis, 42*, 363–378.

Gibson, H. B. (1991). Can hypnosis compel people to commit harmful, immoral and criminal acts? A review of the literature. *Contemporary Hypnosis, 8*, 129–140.

Gibson, H. B. (1992). A recent British case of a man charged with using hypnosis for rape and other sexual offences. *Contemporary Hypnosis, 9*, 139–148.

Gleaves, D. H. (1994). On "The reality of repressed memories." *American Psychologist, 49*, 440–441.

Gold, S. N., Hughes, D., & Hihnecker, L. (1994). Degrees of repression of sexual abuse memories. *American Psychologist, 49*, 441–442.

Goldstein, E. (1992). *Confabulations: Creating false memories—Destroying families*. Boca Raton, FL: SIRS Books.

Grabowski, K. L., Roese, N. J., & Thomas, M. R. (1991). The role of expectancy in hypnotic hypermnesia: A brief communication. *International Journal of Clinical and Experimental Hypnosis, 34,* 193–197.

Grant, G. (1977). Hypnosis in criminal investigation. *Australian Journal of Clinical Hypnosis, 5,* 65–72.

Greene, E. (1986). Forensic hypnosis to lift amnesia: The jury is still out. *Behavioral Sciences and the Law, 4,* 65–72.

Greene, E., Wilson, L., & Loftus, E. F. (1989). Impact of hypnotic testimony on the jury. *Law and Human Behavior, 13,* 61–78.

Griffiths, G. L. (1982). Pros and cons of investigative hypnosis. *Police Journal (SA), 63,* 14–20.

Gudjonsson, G. H. (1984). A new scale of interrogative suggestibility. *Personality and Individual Differences, 5,* 303–314.

Gudjonsson, G. H. (1987). Historical background to suggestibility: How interrogative suggestibility differs from other types of suggestibility. *Personality and Individual Differences, 8,* 347–355.

Gudjonsson, G. H. (1992). *The psychology of interrogations, confessions and testimony.* London: Wiley.

Gudjonsson, G. H. (1994). Confessions made to the expert witness: Some professional issues. *Journal of Forensic Psychiatry, 5,* 237–247.

Harding v. State. (1968). 5 Md. App. 230, 246 A.2d 302.

Hembrooke, H. (1994, October). *"Use your imagination!": Children, fantasy and suggestibility.* Paper presented at Second International Symposium on Suggestion and Suggestibility, Rome, Italy.

Herman, J. L. (1992). *Trauma and recovery.* New York: Basic Books.

Hess, A. K. (1987). The ethics of forensic psychology. In I. B. Weiner & A. K. Hess (Eds.), *Handbook of forensic psychology* (pp. 653–680). New York: Wiley.

Hilgard, E. R. (1965). *Hypnotic susceptibility.* New York: Harcourt, Brace & World.

Hilgard, E. R. (1977). *Divided consciousness: Multiple controls in human thought and action.* New York: Wiley.

Hilgard, J. R. (1974). Sequelae to hypnosis. *International Journal of Clinical and Experimental Hypnosis, 22,* 281–298.

Hoencamp, E. (1990). Sexual abuse and the abuse of hypnosis in the therapeutic relationship. *International Journal of Clinical and Experimental Hypnosis, 38,* 283–297.

Hoencamp, E. (1994, August). *Truth in and outside the therapy room: Some theoretical and practical considerations.* Keynote address presented at the 13th International Congress of Hypnosis, Melbourne, Victoria, Australia.

Hull, C. L. (1933). *Hypnosis and suggestibility: An experimental approach.* New York: Appleton-Century-Crofts.

International Society of Hypnosis. (1979). Resolution. *International Journal of Clinical and Experimental Hypnosis, 27,* 453.

suggestion: Pseudomemory in hypnotizable and simulating subjects. *Journal of Abnormal Psychology, 98,* 137–144.

MacLean, H. N. (1993). *Once upon a time: A true story of memory, murder, and the law.* New York: HarperCollins.

MacLeod, J. I. (1988). Just keep feeling very relaxed: While you tell us about finding the body. *Australian Journal of Clinical and Experimental Hypnosis, 16,* 83–89.

McCann, T. E., & Sheehan, P. W. (1987). The breaching of pseudomemory under hypnotic instruction: Implications for original memory retrieval. *British Journal of Experimental and Clinical Hypnosis, 4,* 101–108.

McCann, T., & Sheehan, P. W. (1988). Hypnotically induced pseudomemories: Sampling their conditions among hypnotizable subjects. *Journal of Personality and Social Psychology, 54,* 339–346.

McConkey, K. M. (1984). Clinical hypnosis: Differential impact on volitional and nonvolitional disorders. *Canadian Psychology, 25,* 79–83.

McConkey, K. M. (1988). A view from the laboratory on the forensic use of hypnosis. *Australian Journal of Clinical and Experimental Hypnosis, 16,* 71–81.

McConkey, K. M. (1989). Confidence in hypnotic hypermnesia. In A. F. Bennett & K. M. McConkey (Eds.), *Cognition in individual and social contexts* (pp. 489–496). Amsterdam: Elsevier/North-Holland.

McConkey, K. M. (1992). The effects of hypnotic procedures on remembering: The experimental findings and their implications for forensic hypnosis. In E. Fromm & M. R. Nash (Eds.), *Contemporary hypnosis research* (pp. 405–426). New York: Guilford Press.

McConkey, K. M. (1995). Hypnosis, memory, and the ethics of uncertainty. *Australian Psychologist, 30,* 1–10.

McConkey, K. M., & Jupp, J. J. (1985). Opinions about the forensic use of hypnosis. *Australian Psychologist, 20,* 283–291.

McConkey, K. M., & Kinoshita, S. (1986). Creating memories and reports. *British Journal of Experimental and Clinical Hypnosis, 3,* 162–166.

McConkey, K. M., & Kinoshita, S. (1988). The influence of hypnosis on memory after one day and one week. *Journal of Abnormal Psychology, 97,* 48–53.

McConkey, K. M., Labelle, L., Bibb, B. C., & Bryant, R. A. (1990). Hypnosis and suggested pseudomemory: The relevance of test context. *Australian Journal of Psychology, 42,* 197–205.

McConkey, K. M., & Roche, S. M. (1989). Knowledge of eyewitness testimony. *Australian Psychologist, 24,* 377–384.

McConkey, K. M., Roche, S. M., & Sheehan, P. W. (1989a). Television reports of forensic hypnosis: What's on the news? *Australian Journal of Social Issues, 24,* 44–53.

McConkey, K. M., Roche, S. M., & Sheehan, P. W. (1989b). Reports of forensic hypnosis: A critical analysis. *Australian Psychologist, 24,* 249–272.

McConkey, K. M., & Sheehan, P. W. (1988a). Forensic hypnosis: Current legislation and its relevance to practice. *Australian Psychologist, 23,* 323–334.

McConkey, K. M., & Sheehan, P. W. (1988b). Hypnosis and criminal investigation: An analysis of policy and practice of police in Australia. *Criminal Law Journal, 12,* 63–85.

McConkey, K. M., & Sheehan, P. W. (1989). The Home Office Circular and Australian data on forensic hypnosis. *British Journal of Experimental and Clinical Hypnosis, 6,* 109–112.

McGuire, W. J. (1986). The vicissitudes of attitudes and similar representational constructs in twentieth century psychology. *European Journal of Social Psychology, 16,* 89–130.

McKelvie, S. J., & Pullara, M. (1988). Effects of hypnosis and level of processing on repeated recall of line drawings. *Journal of General Psychology, 115,* 315–329.

Miller, R. D., & Stava, L. J. (1988). Hypnosis and dissimulation. In R. Rogers (Ed.), *Clinical assessment of malingering and deception* (pp. 234–249). New York: Guilford Press.

Milne, G. (1992). Investigative hypnosis in clinic and court. *Australian Journal of Clinical and Experimental Hypnosis, 20,* 63–78.

Milne, G. (1994). *Hypnosis and the art of self-therapy.* Port Melbourne: Lothian Books.

Mingay, D. J. (1986). Hypnosis and memory for incidentally learned scenes. *British Journal of Experimental and Clinical Hypnosis, 3,* 173–183.

Mingay, D. J. (1987). The effect of hypnosis on eyewitness memory: Reconciling forensic claims and research findings. *Applied Psychology: An International Review, 36,* 163–183.

Monaghan, F. J. (1981). Warning—Doctors may be dangerous to the health of your investigation. *Police Chief, 48,* 73–76.

Morton, J. (1994). Cognitive perspectives on memory recovery. *Applied Cognitive Psychology, 8,* 389–398.

Mulhern, S. (1994). Satanism, ritual abuse, and mulitple personality disorder: A sociohistorical perspective. *International Journal of Clinical and Experimental Hypnosis, 42,* 265–288.

Nash, M. R. (1987). What, if anything, is regressed about hypnotic age regression? A review of the empirical literature. *Psychological Bulletin, 102,* 42–52.

Nash, M. R. (1994). Memory distortion and sexual trauma: The problem of false negatives and false positives. *International Journal of Clinical and Experimental Hypnosis, 42,* 346–362.

Nash, M. R., Drake, S. D., Wiley, S., Khalsa, S., & Lynn, S. J. (1986). Accuracy of recall by hypnotically age regressed subjects. *Journal of Abnormal Psychology, 95,* 298–300.

Neisser, U. (1993, April). *Memory with a grain of salt*. Paper presented at the False Memory Syndrome Foundation Conference (Memory and Reality: Emerging Crisis), Valley Forge, PA.

Nogrady, H., McConkey, K. M., & Perry, C. (1985). Enhancing visual memory: Trying hypnosis, trying imagination, and trying again. *Journal of Abnormal Psychology, 94*, 195–204.

O'Brien, R. M., & Rabuck, S. J. (1976). Experimentally produced self-repugnant behavior as a function of hypnosis and waking suggestion: A pilot study. *American Journal of Clinical Hypnosis, 18*, 272–276.

Odgers, S. J. (1988a). Trial by trance: Hypnosis, witnesses and the development of new rules of evidence. *Australian Bar Review, 4*, 18–50.

Odgers, S. J. (1988b). Evidence law and previously hypnotized witnesses. *Australian Journal of Clinical and Experimental Hypnosis, 16*, 91–102.

Ofshe, R. J. (1992). Inadvertent hypnosis during interrogation: False confession due to dissociative state; mis-identified multiple personality and the satanic cult hypothesis. *International Journal of Clinical and Experimental Hypnosis, 40*, 125–156.

Ofshe, R. J., & Singer, M. T. (1994). Recovered-memory therapy and robust repression: Influence and pseudomemories. *International Journal of Clinical and Experimental Hypnosis, 42*, 391–410.

Ofshe, R. J., & Watters, E. (1994). *Making monsters: False memories, psychotherapy, and sexual hysteria*. New York: Scribner's.

Olio, K. (1994). Truth in memory. *American Psychologist, 49*, 442–443.

Orne, M. T. (1959). The nature of hypnosis: Artifact and essence. *Journal of Abnormal and Social Psychology, 58*, 277–299.

Orne, M. T. (1972). Can a hypnotized subject be compelled to carry out otherwise unacceptable behavior? A discussion. *International Journal of Clinical and Experimental Hypnosis, 20*, 101–117.

Orne, M. T. (1979). The use and misuse of hypnosis in court. *International Journal of Clinical and Experimental Hypnosis, 27*, 311–341.

Orne, M. T., Dinges, D. F., & Orne, E. C. (1990). Rock v. Arkansas: Hypnosis, the defendant's privilege. *International Journal of Clinical and Experimental Hypnosis, 38*, 250–265.

Orne, M. T., & Evans, F. J. (1965). Social control in the psychological experiment: Antisocial behavior and hypnosis. *Journal of Personality and Social Psychology, 1*, 189–200.

Orne, M. T., Soskis, D. A., Dinges, D. F., & Orne, E. C. (1984). Hypnotically induced testimony. In G. L. Wells & E. F. Loftus (Eds.), *Eyewitness testimony: Psychological perspectives* (pp. 171–213). New York: Cambridge University Press.

Orne, M. T., Whitehouse, W. G., Dinges, D. F., & Orne, E. C. (1988). Reconstructing memory through hypnosis: Forensic and clinical implications. In H. M. Pettinati (Ed.), *Hypnosis and memory* (pp. 21–63). New York: Guilford Press.

Payne, D. G. (1987). Hypermnesia and reminiscence in recall: A historical and empirical review. *Psychological Bulletin, 101*, 5–27.

Pendergrast, M. H. (1994). *Victims of memory: Incest accusations and shattered lives.* Hinesburg, VT: Upper Access Books.

Perry, C. W. (1979). Hypnotic coercion and compliance to it: A review of evidence presented in a legal case. *International Journal of Clinical and Experimental Hypnosis, 27,* 187–218.

Perry, C. W., & Laurence, J.-R. (1983). The enhancement of memory by hypnosis in the legal investigative situation. *Canadian Psychology, 24,* 155–167.

Perry, C. W., Laurence, J.-R., D'Eon, J., & Tallant, B. (1988). Hypnotic age regression techniques in the elicitation of memories: Applied uses and abuses. In H. M. Pettinati (Ed.), *Hypnosis and memory* (pp. 128–154). New York: Guilford Press.

Peterson, R. G. (1994). Comment on Loftus. *American Psychologist, 49,* 443.

Pettinati, H. M. (Ed.). (1988). *Hypnosis and memory.* New York: Guilford Press.

Pezdek, K. (1994). The illusion of illusory memory. *Applied Cognitive Psychology, 8,* 339–350.

Pinizzotto, A. J. (1989). Memory and hypnosis: Implications for the use of forensic hypnosis. *Professional Psychology: Research and Practice, 20,* 322–328.

Prince, M. (1914). *The unconscious.* New York: Macmillan.

Purnell, H. F. (1981). The law and hypnosis. *Australian Journal of Forensic Sciences, 13,* 126–130.

Putnam, W. H. (1979). Hypnosis and distortions in eyewitness memory. *International Journal of Clinical and Experimental Hypnosis, 28,* 437–448.

R. v. Geesing, 15 A. Crim. R. 297 (1984), hearing on the admissibility of evidence; 38 SASR 226 (1985), appeal from trial verdict upheld and conviction quashed.

R. v. Haywood, Marshall, and Roughley, No. A37/1994 Supreme Court of Tasmania (May 27, 1994), unreported.

R. v. Horsfall, 51 SASR 489 (1989).

R. v. Jenkyns, No. 070013/89 Supreme Court of New South Wales (October 20, 1994), unreported.

R. v. McFelin, NZLR 750 (1985).

R. v. Knibb, C. A. No. 299 Court of Criminal Appeal, Queensland (1987), unreported; leave to appeal granted, appeal dismissed.

R. v. Speechley, No. 8215/1327 District Court of New South Wales (August 23, 1982), unreported, defendant committed for trial; Supreme Court of New South Wales (October 12, 1984), unreported, trial hearing, accused acquitted.

Read, J. D., & Lindsay, D. S. (1994). Moving toward a middle ground on the false memory debate: Reply. *Applied Cognitive Psychology,* 8, 407–435.

Read, S. J., & Rosson, M. B. (1982). Rewriting history: The biasing effects of attitudes on memory. *Social Cognition, 1,* 240–255.

Register, P. A., & Kihlstrom, J. F. (1988). Hypnosis and interrogative suggestibility. *Personality and Individual Differences, 9,* 549–558.

Reiser, M. (1980). *Handbook of investigative hypnosis.* Los Angeles: LEHI.

Reiser, M. (1984). Police use of investigative hypnosis: Scientism, ethics and power games. *American Journal of Forensic Psychology, 2,* 115–143.

Relinger, H. (1984). Hypnotic hypermnesia: A critical review. *American Journal of Clinical Hypnosis, 26,* 212–225.

Rock v. Arkansas. (1987). 107 S. Ct. 2704, 97 L.Ed.2d 37.

Rogers, R. (1987). Ethical dilemmas in forensic evaluations. *Behavioral Sciences and the Law, 5,* 149–160.

Rogers, R. (Ed.). (1988). *Clinical assessment of malingering and deception.* New York: Guilford Press.

Rowland, L. W. (1939). Will hypnotized persons try to harm themselves or others? *Journal of Abnormal and Social Psychology, 34,* 114–117.

Sales, B. D., Shuman, D. W., & O'Connor, M. (1994). In a dim light: Admissibility of child sexual abuse memories. *Applied Cognitive Psychology, 8,* 399–406.

Sanders, G. S., & Simmons, W. L. (1983). Use of hypnosis to enhance eyewitness accuracy: Does it work? *Journal of Applied Psychology, 68,* 70–77.

Scheflin, A. W. (1994). Forensic hypnosis: Unanswered questions. *Australian Journal of Clinical and Experimental Hypnosis, 22,* 25–37.

Scheflin, A. W., & Shapiro, J. L. (1989). *Trance on trial.* New York: Guilford Press.

Sheehan, P. W. (1971). Countering preconceptions about hypnosis: An objective index of involvement with the hypnotist. *Journal of Abnormal Psychology Monograph, 78,* 299–322.

Sheehan, P. W. (1973). Analysis of the heterogeneity of "faking" and "simulating" performance in the hypnotic setting. *International Journal of Clinical and Experimental Hypnosis, 21,* 213–225.

Sheehan, P. W. (1977). Antisocial behavior under hypnosis: Some theoretical and professional issues. *Australian Journal of Clinical Hypnosis, 5,* 79–85.

Sheehan, P. W. (1980). Factors influencing rapport in hypnosis. *Journal of Abnormal Psychology, 89,* 263–281.

Sheehan, P. W. (1986, August). *Hypnosis, memory, and legal practice.* Paper presented at the Annual Conference of the Australian Psychological Society, Townsville, Australia.

Sheehan, P. W. (1988a). Confidence, memory and hypnosis. In H. M.

Pettinati (Ed.), *Hypnosis and memory* (pp. 323–334). New York: Guilford Press.

Sheehan, P. W. (1988b). Memory distortion in hypnosis. *International Journal of Clinical and Experimental Hypnosis, 36,* 296–311.

Sheehan, P. W. (1988c). Issues in the forensic application of hypnosis. *Australian Journal of Clinical and Experimental Hypnosis, 16,* 103–111.

Sheehan, P. W. (1992, July). *Pseudomemory in hypnosis: Parameters, estimates of its incidence, and speculations about process.* Paper presented at the International Congress of Psychosomatic Medicine and Hypnosis, Jerusalem, Israel.

Sheehan, P. W., Andreasen, A., Doherty, P., & McCann, T. (1986). A case of the application of guidelines for investigative hypnosis. *Australian Journal of Clinical and Experimental Hypnosis, 14,* 85–97.

Sheehan, P. W., Garnett, M., & Robertson, R. (1993). The effects of cue level, hypnotizability, and state instruction on responses to leading questions. *International Journal of Clinical and Experimental Hypnosis, 41,* 287–304.

Sheehan, P. W., & McConkey, K. M. (1982). *Hypnosis and experience: The exploration of phenomena and process.* Hillsdale, NJ: Erlbaum.

Sheehan, P. W., & McConkey, K. M. (1988). Lying in hypnosis: A conceptual analysis of the possibilities. *Australian Journal of Clinical and Experimental Hypnosis, 16,* 1–9.

Sheehan, P. W., & McConkey, K. M. (1993). Forensic hypnosis: The application of ethical guidelines. In J. W. Rhue, S. J., Lynn, & I. Kirsch (Eds.), *Handbook of clinical hypnosis* (pp. 719–738). Washington, DC: American Psychological Association.

Sheehan, P. W., Statham, D., & Jamieson, G. A. (1991a). Pseudomemory effects over time in the hypnotic setting. *Journal of Abnormal Psychology, 100,* 39–44.

Sheehan, P. W., Statham, D., & Jamieson, G. A. (1991b). Pseudomemory effects and their relationship to level of susceptibility to hypnosis and state instruction. *Journal of Personality and Social Psychology, 60,* 130–137.

Sheehan, P. W., Statham, D., Jamieson, G. A., & Ferguson, S. R. (1991). Ambiguity in suggestion and the occurrence of pseudomemory in the hypnotic setting. *Australian Journal of Clinical and Experimental Hypnosis, 19,* 1–18.

Sheehan, P. W., & Tilden, J. (1986). The consistency of occurrences of memory distortion following hypnotic induction. *International Journal of Clinical and Experimental Hypnosis, 34,* 122–137.

Sherrod, D. (1985). Trial delay as a source of bias in jury decision making. *Law and Human Behavior, 9,* 101–108.

Shields, I. W., & Knox, V. J. (1986). Level of processing as a determinant of hypnotic hypermnesia. *Journal of Abnormal Psychology,* *95,* 350–357.

Slovenko, R. (1987). The lawyer and the forensic expert: Boundaries of ethical practice. *Behavioral Sciences and the Law, 5,* 119–148.

Smith, M. C. (1983). Hypnotic memory enhancement of witnesses: Does it work? *Psychological Bulletin, 94,* 387–407.

Spanos, N. P. (1982). Hypnotic behavior: A cognitive and social psychological perspective. *Research Communications in Psychology, Psychiatry, and Behavior, 7,* 199–213.

Spanos, N. P., Burgess, C. A., & Burgess, M. F. (1994). Past-life identities, UFO abductions, and satanic ritual abuse: The social construction of memories. *International Journal of Clinical and Experimental Hypnosis, 42,* 433–446.

Spanos, N. P., Gwynn, M. I., Comer, S. L., Baltruweit, W. J., & de Groh, M. (1989). Are hypnotically induced pseudomemories resistant to cross-examination? *Law and Human Behavior, 13,* 271–289.

Spanos, N. P., Gwynn, M. I., & Terrade, K. (1989). Effects on mock jurors of experts favorable and unfavorable toward hypnotically elicited eyewitness testimony. *Journal of Applied Psychology, 74,* 922–926.

Spanos, N. P., & McLean, J. (1986). Hypnotically created pseudo-memories: Memory distortions or reporting biases? *British Journal of Experimental and Clinical Hypnosis, 3,* 155–159.

Spence, D. P. (1982). *Narrative truth and historical truth: Meaning and interpretation in psychoanalysis.* New York: Norton.

Spence, D. P. (1994). Narrative truth and putative child abuse. *International Journal of Clinical and Experimental Hypnosis, 42,* 289–303.

Spiegel, D., & Scheflin, A. W. (1994). Dissociated or fabricated? Psychiatric aspects of repressed memory in civil and criminal cases. *International Journal of Clinical and Experimental Hypnosis, 42,* 411–432.

Spiegel, D., & Spiegel, H. (1984). Uses of hypnosis in evaluating malingering and deception. *Behavioral Sciences and the Law, 2,* 51–66.

Spiegel, D., & Spiegel, H. (1987). Forensic uses of hypnosis. In I. B. Weiner & A. K. Hess (Eds.), *Handbook of forensic psychology* (pp. 490–507). New York: Wiley.

Stager, G. L., & Lundy, R. M. (1985). Hypnosis and the learning and recall of visually presented material. *International Journal of Clinical and Experimental Hypnosis, 33,* 27–39.

Terr, L. (1994). *Unchained memories: True stories of traumatic memories, lost and found.* New York: Basic Books.

Udolf, R. (1983). *Forensic hypnosis: Psychological and legal aspects.* Lexington, MA: Heath.

Udolf, R. (1987). *Handbook of hypnosis for professionals* (2nd ed.). New York: Van Nostrand Reinhold.

Udolf, R. (1990). Rock v. Arkansas: A critique. *International Journal of Clinical and Experimental Hypnosis, 38,* 239–249.

Van Vliet v. Griffith. (1978). 19 SASR 195.

Venn, J. (1988). Misuse of hypnosis in sexual contexts: Two case reports. *International Journal of Clinical and Experimental Hypnosis, 36,* 12–18.

Wagstaff, G. F. (1981). *Hypnosis as compliance and belief.* New York: St. Martin's Press.

Wagstaff, G. F. (1982). Hypnosis and recognition of a face. *Perceptual and Motor Skills, 55,* 816–818.

Wagstaff, G. F. (1984). The enhancement of witness memory by "hypnosis": A review and methodological critique of the experimental literature. *British Journal of Experimental and Clinical Hypnosis, 2,* 3–12.

Wagstaff, G. F. (1986). Hypnosis as compliance and belief: A sociocognitive view. In P. L. Naish (Ed.), *What is hypnosis?* (pp. 59–84). Philadelphia, PA: Open University Press.

Wagstaff, G. F. (1989). Forensic aspects of hypnosis. In N. P. Spanos & J. F. Chaves (Eds.), *Hypnosis: The cognitive–behavioral perspective* (pp. 340–357). Buffalo, NY: Prometheus Books.

Wagstaff, G. F. (1991). Hypnosis and harmful and antisocial acts: Some theoretical and empirical issues. *Contemporary Hypnosis, 8,* 141–146.

Walker, W.-L. (1988). Problems in hypnotically elicited evidence. *Australian Journal of Clinical and Experimental Hypnosis, 16,* 113–120.

Walkley, J. (1987). *Police interrogation. A handbook for investigators.* London: Police Review Publication.

Watkins, C. R. (1982). Crime prevention. *Australian Police Journal, 26,* 257–277.

Watkins, J. G. (1972). Antisocial behavior under hypnosis: Possible or impossible? *International Journal of Clinical and Experimental Hypnosis, 20,* 96–100.

Weaver, C. A. (1993). Do you need a "flash" to form a flashbulb memory? *Journal of Experimental Psychology: General, 122,* 39–46.

Weekes, J. R., Lynn, S. J., Green, J. P., & Brentar, J. T. (1992). Pseudomemory in hypnotized and task-motivated subjects. *Journal of Abnormal Psychology, 101,* 356–360.

Weiner, I. B., & Hess, A. K. (Eds.). (1987). *Handbook of forensic psychology.* New York: Wiley.

Welden, D. E., & Malpass, R. S. (1981). Effects of attitudinal, cognitive, and situational variables on recall of biased communications. *Journal of Personality and Social Psychology, 40,* 39–52.

Wells, G. L., & Loftus, E. F. (Eds.). (1984). *Eyewitness testimony: Psychological perspectives.* New York: Cambridge University Press.

Wells, W. R. (1941). Experiments in the hypnotic production of crime. *Journal of Psychology, 11,* 63–102.

Wentworth v. Rogers, No. 5. Court of Appeal New South Wales (October 3, 1986), unreported.

Whitehouse, W. G., Dinges, D. F., Orne, E. C., & Orne, M. T. (1988). Hypnotic hypermnesia: Enhanced memory accessibility or report bias? *Journal of Abnormal Psychology, 97,* 289–295.

Wilson, L., Greene, E., & Loftus, E. F. (1986). Beliefs about forensic hypnosis. *International Journal of Clinical and Experimental Hypnosis, 34,* 110–121.

Winograd, E., & Neisser, U. (Eds.). (1993). *Affect and recall: Studies of "flashbulb" memories.* New York: Cambridge University Press.

Wright, L. (1994). *Remembering Satan.* New York: Knopf.

Yapko, M. (1994). *Suggestions of abuse: True and false memories of childhood sexual trauma.* New York: Simon & Schuster.

Young, P. C. (1952). Anti-social uses of hypnosis. In L. M. LeCron (Ed.), *Experimental hypnosis* (pp. 376–409). New York: Macmillan.

Yuille, J. C., & McEwan, N. H. (1985). Use of hypnosis as an aid to eyewitness memory. *Journal of Applied Psychology, 70,* 389–400.

Yuille, J. C., & Tollestrup, P. A. (1992). A model of diverse effects of emotion on eyewitness memory. In S.-A. Christianson (Ed.), *The handbook of emotion and memory: Research and theory* (pp. 201–215). Hillsdale, NJ: Erlbaum.

Zelig, M., & Beidleman, W. B. (1981). The investigative use of hypnosis: A word of caution. *International Journal of Clinical and Experimental Hypnosis, 29,* 401–412.

Zuckerman, M., Koestner, R., Colella, M., & Alton, A. O. (1984). Anchoring in the detection of deception and leakage. *Journal of Personality and Social Psychology, 47,* 301–311.

Index